Adventuring in the Alps

THE SIERRA CLUB
ADVENTURE TRAVEL GUIDES

Adventuring Along the Gulf of Mexico, The Sierra Club Travel Guide to the Gulf Coast of the United States and Mexico from the Florida Keys to Yucatán, by Donald G. Schueler

Adventuring in Alaska, The Ultimate Travel Guide to the Great Land, Completely revised and updated, by Peggy Wayburn

Adventuring in the Alps, The Sierra Club Travel Guide to the Alpine Regions of France, Switzerland, Germany, Austria, Liechtenstein, Italy, and Yugoslavia, by William E. Reifsnyder and Marylou Reifsnyder

Adventuring in the Andes, The Sierra Club Travel Guide to Ecuador, Peru, Bolivia, the Amazon Basin, and the Galapagos Islands, by Charles Frazier with Donald Secreast

Adventuring in the California Desert, The Sierra Club Travel Guide to the Great Basin, Mojave, and Colorado Desert Regions of California, by Lynne Foster

Adventuring in the Pacific, The Sierra Club Travel Guide to the Islands of Polynesia, Melanesia, and Micronesia, by Susanna Margolis

Adventuring in the Rockies, The Sierra Club Travel Guide to the Rocky Mountain Regions of the United States and Canada, by Jeremy Schmidt

Adventuring in the San Francisco Bay Area, The Sierra Club Travel Guide to San Francisco, Marin, Sonoma, Napa, Solano, Contra Costa, Alameda, Santa Clara, San Mateo Counties and the Bay Islands, by Peggy Wayburn

Trekking in Nepal, West Tibet, and Bhutan, by Hugh Swift

Trekking in Pakistan and India, by Hugh Swift

Walking Europe from Top to Bottom, The Sierra Club Travel Guide to the Grande Randonnée Cinq (GR-5) through Holland, Belgium, Luxembourg, Switzerland and France, by Susanna Margolis and Ginger Harmon

William E. Reifsnyder
and Marylou Reifsnyder

Adventuring in the Alps

*The Sierra Club Travel Guide
to the Alpine Regions of
France, Switzerland, Germany, Austria,
Liechtenstein, Italy, and Yugoslavia*

Sierra Club Books   San Francisco

The Sierra Club, founded in 1892 by John Muir, has devoted itself to the study and protection of the earth's scenic and ecological resources—mountains, wetlands, woodlands, wild shores and rivers, deserts and plains. The publishing program of the Sierra Club offers books to the public as a nonprofit educational service in the hope that they may enlarge the public's understanding of the Club's basic concerns. The point of view expressed in each book, however, does not necessarily represent that of the Club. The Sierra Club has some sixty chapters coast to coast, in Canada, Hawaii, and Alaska. For information about how you may participate in its programs to preserve wilderness and the quality of life, please address inquiries to Sierra Club, 730 Polk Street, San Francisco, CA 94109.

Copyright ©1986 by William E. Reifsnyder and Marylou Reifsnyder

Library of Congress Cataloging in Publication Data

Reifsnyder, William E.
    Adventuring in the Alps.

    Bibliography: p. 269
    Includes index.
        1. Hiking—Alps Region—Guide-books.   2. Alps Region—
Description and travel—Guide-books.   I. Reifsnyder,
Marylou.   II. Title.
GV199.44.A4R45   1986   914.94'7   85-18471
ISBN 0-87156-754-7

Cover design by Bonnie Smetts
Book design by Rodelinde Albrecht
Illustrations by the authors
Printed in the United States of America
10 9 8 7 6 5 4 3 2

Contents

Acknowledgments

We have spent many happy days wandering through the Alps. Countless hutmasters, innkeepers, hikers, officials of the various national tourist offices, clerks in local tourist offices, and many others have contributed information and guidance; we are grateful for their help.

A few persons deserve special mention. Dr. Albert Baumgartner has been especially helpful in suggesting worthwhile walks in the Munich area. Earl Steinbicker gave permission to use material from his brochures *Great Trips/Europe*. Fred Gooding graciously provided information on the Julian Alps in Yugoslavia. Helmut Klee, director of the Swiss National Tourist Office in New York, drew our attention to the spectacular and unspoiled mountains of the Ticino in southern Switzerland.

And special thanks go to Andrew and Betty Peluso, whose hospitality in inviting us to use their home in Heidelberg as a haven during interludes in our walking tours transcended filial responsibilities many times over.

Principal cities and best hikes in the Alps

Introduction

Europe is a continent of walkers. Trails connected villages in centuries past; some of these became cart tracks and eventually roads. Many others remain today as paths through the forest, over the hills, joining towns and villages, providing access to forest and field. Many are still used to provide a means of travel between home and school or market. But they are also used for recreation. What better way to spend a sunny summer Sunday afternoon than to stroll through the cool woods, more than likely ending up at a *Waldhaus*, or forest inn, for a half liter of the local beer or wine! It is a universal pastime, certainly a healthier one than screaming down the autobahn in search of who knows what.

As visitors to the continent—sometimes on business, sometimes on vacation—we have often wanted to spend a half day or day seeing something of the countryside, rather than taking one more sightseeing tour through town. Usually we did not have a car and so were restricted to going somewhere by train or tram or bus. More than once, we have gotten on the bus that seemed to go farthest out of town, ridden it to the end of the line, and then started walking. Sometimes this worked, and we found ourselves on some forest path leading to a promontory or tower that afforded rewarding views of the countryside. Other times we were not so lucky and ended up in just another suburb.

Eventually we learned to look first for a walker's guide or map, one that showed the trails and forests and mountains. It is no exaggeration to say that Europe is the most guidebooked area in the

1

world. Newsstands at the railroad station carry the local trail map (*Wanderkarte*), often several different ones. And it is a rare town that does not have a guidebook to the local paths. Unfortunately, these guidebooks are usually in the language of the area and are often difficult to translate even with a dictionary.

And so the genesis of this book. For the major cities and regions in and around the Alps, we have scouted out interesting day walks. They have been chosen to be accessible from the city by bus, tram, or rail, with travel time to trailhead one hour or less. Some start out with a gondola or chair-lift ride, reducing the time and effort required to reach the scenic high country. Some are gentle walks through field and forest; others are above timberline. Wherever they are, they will give you an opportunity to hike through some of the most scenic terrain in Europe with nothing more than a free day and suitable shoes and clothing. If you have more time, you might plan a longer trip, staying in one of the Alpine huts (see "Huts, hostels, and mountain inns").

A word about the organization of the book. On the assumption that you are likely to find yourself in one of the major cisalpine cities with that free day, we have organized the chapters around those cities. Nevertheless, the Alpine region is relatively compact and public transportation so good that many of the described walks are readily accessible from several of the hub cities.

For the most part, we have hiked the trails described. In a few cases (these are indicated in the text), we have included walks that have been recommended by friends or have been gleaned from other sources. The descriptions of these walks are less complete and detailed. But do not be deterred; trails are generally very well marked and signed. And the commercially available maps are kept up-to-date. Although the maps we have included in the text are sufficient, we suggest that you obtain a local map from newsstand or bookstore. With a good map in hand, you will find that you are soon striking out on your own, choosing a new destination, a new route.

Tourist information

The most underutilized sources of information on recreation in the Alps are the various national tourist offices, all of which have facilities in the United States and Canada. Write or call (well in advance of your departure date), asking for information on hiking in their country. It will help if you specify the city or region you are going to. They may be able to obtain maps and brochures for specific regions, but that will take time. And even if you don't end up with a gold mine of information, your inquiry will let them know that there is interest in Alpine hiking and may stimulate development of promotional materials.

The best place to write is the New York or Toronto office. The addresses are:

Austrian National Tourist Office: 545 Fifth Avenue, New York, NY 10017; 2 Bloor Street East, Suite 3330, Toronto, Ontario M4W 1A8.

French Government Tourist Office: 610 Fifth Avenue, New York, NY 10020; 1 Dundas Street West, Suite 2405, Toronto, Ontario M5G 123.

German National Tourist Office: 747 Third Avenue, New York, NY 10017; 2 Fundy, P.O. Box 417, Place Bonaventure, Montreal, P.Q. H5A 1B8.

Italian Government Travel Office: 630 Fifth Avenue, New York, NY 10020; 3 Place Ville Marie, Montreal, P.Q.

Swiss National Tourist Office: 608 Fifth Avenue, New York, NY 10020; Commerce Court, P.O. Box 215, Commerce Court Postal Station, Toronto, Ontario M5L 1E8.

Yugoslav National Tourist Office: Suite 210, 630 Fifth Avenue, New York, NY 10020; 377 Spadina Road, Toronto, Ontario M5P 2V7.

You can also write to the tourist office in the town or towns in the region you intend to visit. Ask for hotel lists and information on walking and outdoor recreation facilities.

Transportation

The walks in this book are all accessible by public transportation. That is not saying much, because almost every hamlet or roadhead in the Alpine region has a train, tram, or bus running to it. However, we have designed the walks so that trailheads can be reached within an hour from the main railroad stations in the various cities covered, with few exceptions. Railroads and buses need not be intimidating to the nonnative speaker. All major cities have transportation maps or brochures with instructions in several languages, including English, on how to use the trains and buses. Even many smaller towns have such a multilingual bus or tram guide. The best place to obtain transport maps is the local tourist office or information bureau. These maps are usually free or at nominal charge.

Bus lines have stops designated by signs, usually sporting an H for *Haltestelle*, literally "stopping place." Where appropriate, the maps accompanying the walks in this book indicate bus stops by a circled H, the same designator used on published hiking maps. The signs at bus stops almost always have timetables posted; European buses tend to run on time, so don't be late. In the mountains, buses run by the national postal services connect even the tiniest hamlets with the nearest city post office. Often, there will be only two round trips per day, one morning, one late afternoon, so it pays to obtain a timetable and plan your trip around the bus schedule.

If you miss the bus, hitchhiking is always possible. We don't recommend it, for European drivers are not as likely to stop as are American drivers. Nevertheless, there have been times when the choice was to walk a long distance on the road or put up the thumb. Sometimes the wait is long, but the compassionate driver eventually stops. Indeed, we have met very nice people this way.

Intercity train travel in Europe is fast, convenient, on time, and relatively inexpensive. So much has been said in praise of European rail travel that we won't repeat it here. There are some caveats, though, about which the train traveler should be aware. In many of the larger cities in and around the Alps, there is more than one main railroad station, although there will be only one designated as the *Hauptbahnhof*. In Vienna, for example, there is the Südbahnhof and the Franz-Josefs-Bahnhof as well as the Westbahnhof, the main station. And it is not too easy to get from one to the other. However, Vienna is one of the cities that has an excellent transportation brochure, *Offentliche Verkehrsmittel in Wien*, which lists all of the bus routes, tram routes, and train stations, with information in English. It costs five schillings, about twenty-five cents, and is widely available.

If you plan to do much train traveling, you should consider purchasing a Eurailpass. The ticket, available for first-class travel in all of the countries covered in this book except Yugoslavia, can be purchased for periods ranging from two weeks to three months. It is valid on all first-class and second-class trains and cars, although sleeping accommodations and some seat reservations carry extra charges. Sleeping accommodations are generally rather expensive, especially in first class. We have often found first-class cars to be sparsely populated and have had a compartment all to ourselves on night journeys.

For travelers under twenty-six years of age, Eurail Youthpass is available for second-class travel. It is substantially cheaper than the regular Eurailpass. Both passes must by purchased before leaving the United States and can be obtained through travel agents or direct from offices of the national railroads in the United States or Canada. The New York office of Germanrail is 747 Third Avenue, New York, NY 10017; in Canada, the address is 1290 Bay Street, Toronto, Ontario M5R 2C3.

A good pocket timetable listing main Intercity trains is available free from the offices handling Eurailpass sales; write for one. The Thomas Cook Continental Timetable is more comprehensive. It may be available through your travel agent or from Forsyth Travel Library, Box 2975, Shawnee Mission, KS 66201. It costs about sixteen dollars. In Europe, all of the national railroads publish comprehensive timetables. The Swiss *Offizielles Kursbuch*, for example, lists not only all Swiss trains and the main international trains, but also cable cars, postal buses, municipal buses, and even lake steamers. It is a four-dollar, 1500-page bargain, but scarcely something you want to carry with you.

A better choice is the *Auslandkursbuch*, published by the Deutsche Bundesbahn, the German railroad, which includes timetables for all but the most local of trains, country by country. It is available in railroad stations in Germany and elsewhere for three dollars.

Air travel in the Alpine region is best avoided. It is expensive and distances are so short that trains are often faster from city center to city center.

Geography of the Alpine region

The point where Italy, Switzerland, and France meet is just a few kilometers from the highest summit of the Alps—Mont Blanc. From here, the Alps stretch southward along the French-Italian border, diminishing in height until finally meeting the Mediterranean Sea near Nice. In the other direction, the Alps curve northeastward, then eastward, gradually dropping down to their eastern termination in the rolling hills and vineyards of the Vienna Woods.

Because the Alps were formed by the crushing pressure of two gigantic continental plates pushing toward each other from the north and south, many of the component mountain chains are oriented roughly east-west. This orientation has imposed a pattern on the main drainages. In the eastern Alps, the Inn, Salzach, and Enns rivers flow eastward before finding a break in the mountains permitting a northward turn toward the Danube.

Farther west, the headwaters of the Rhine follow the same pattern, although after reaching Lake Constance, the Rhine turns westward to flow toward the Atlantic Ocean. The Rhone, on the other hand, flows southwestward before turning north into Lake Geneva. Blocked by the pre-Alpine Jura Mountains, the Rhone finds its course to the Mediterranean near Marseilles. On the south side, waters from the southern scarp also flow more or less directly to the Mediterranean. Since these rivers are relatively short and have few tributaries, none reaches the great size of the Rhine or the Danube.

The Alps form a well-defined massif, rising sharply from surrounding lowlands: the Bavarian Plain on the north, the flat Po Valley on the south, the low country of France to the west, and the Hungarian plains to the east. The area was heavily glaciated during the Pleistocene, and many of the valleys show the characteristic U shape formed by glacial scouring. Glacial features abound: terminal moraines, lateral moraines, and, of course, the remnant glaciers themselves. The Aletsch Glacier in central Switzerland is the largest of these, covering an impressive 170 square kilometers with its frozen surface.

The central ranges are composed mostly of crystalline rocks, whereas the northern and southern ranges are largely of limestone. Despite the common bedrock, the limestone mountains display rather differing landscapes north and south. The Dolomites, named after the French geologist Gratet de Dolomieu, have many sheer-sided towers that rise abruptly from gentle terrain. Perhaps the most characteristic of these, Tre Cime (Three Pinnacles) form the backdrop for one of the described walks. The northern limestone Alps along the Austrian-German border have a rather different aspect, more typically Alpine. Much of the terrain displays the sinkhole topography characteristic of water-worn limestone.

Timberline is about 2000 meters above sea level, somewhat lower in the north, higher in the south. Since the major inner valleys and the plains surrounding the Alps are about 600 meters in elevation, timberline is rather readily reached by the day-hiker. Many of the cable tramways run from the valley floor to above timberline, sometimes in one gigantic leap. One is never very far from the Alpine tundra.

Climate

An auto trip across the Alps, from Altdorf in Switzerland, across St. Gotthard Pass to Como, Italy, takes about a half day to cover the 200 kilometers. In the summer, this may also take you from cloudy weather in Altdorf, through a cold rain in Andermatt, to bright, warm sunshine in Como. Indeed, the great difference between the weather and climate on the north and south sides is one of the typical features of Alpine weather. The flexible traveler can take advantage of this contrast: if the weather is bad on the side of the Alps you are on, journey to the other side and find improved weather.

The reason for this difference can be found in the height to which air must be forced to cross the Alpine massif. With typical north-westerly winds on the north side of the Alps, moist air from the Atlantic Ocean is forced upward. As it cools, the moisture condenses into cloud, finally producing rain (or snow) at higher elevations. But as the air is forced down the lee side, it warms and the clouds evaporate. The heat produced as the moisture condenses into rain makes the air warmer on the lee side as compared with the wind-ward side. So it is not uncommon to find the temperatures five to ten Fahrenheit degrees warmer on the lee side at the same elevation.

This flowing of air across the Alps is the cause of the celebrated (or cursed!) foehn. It is the same kind of warm, dry wind as the chinook that blows down the eastern slopes of the Front Range of the Rockies, or the Santa Ana in southern California. In the Alps, the foehn is blamed for all sorts of things, including higher auto-mobile accident rates and miscellaneous illnesses. In the summer, the north foehn predominates; in spring and autumn, the south foehn is more common, with the north slopes of the Alps subject to lee-side effects.

Because both sides of the Alps are open to the moist currents of air from the ocean, the summertime climate is characterized by rather frequent clouds, rain, and thunderstorms. The accompany-ing table presents climatic data for late spring (May), midsummer (July), and early fall (September). Differences between the north and south sides of the Alps are striking. Milan and Lugano tend to have fewer days with rain, fewer days with thunderstorms, and lower average cloudiness than the cities north of the mountains. Garmisch-Partenkirchen generally has the largest number of days with rain and the highest average cloudiness as compared with cities north or south of the main massif.

Vienna, the easternmost city in the table, shows the influence of being farthest from the ocean. It has fewer days with rain and thunderstorms than cities farther to the west, and is below or near the minimums of the regions south of the crest.

Snowfall and duration of the winter snowpack show great latitudinal and altitudinal variation. Regions in the lowlands south of the Alps generally have few winter snowstorms, and what does cover the ground rarely lasts very long. Munich, north of the Alps, averages twenty days of measurable snowfall for a total of 100 centimeters; Milan's average is fewer than nine days, with a total snowfall of less than 40 centimeters. In the lowlands, snow is not an

CLIMATIC DATA FOR ALPINE PEAKS AND CITIES

City	Elev. meters	May Temp ° C	Rain days	Tstm days	Cld %
Bolzano	265	16.4	8	1	—
Bourg-St. Maurice	865	12.6	—	—	—
Feldkirch	537	13.0	8	3	—
Garmisch	704	10.9	14	5	69
Geneva	405	14.1	9	3	53
Innsbruck	582	13.8	11	3	64
Klagenfurt	448	13.3	11	5	63
Lugano	276	15.4	13	3	57
Milan	147	17.9	9	2	57
Munich	551	12.2	13	5	53
Salzburg	435	13.2	15	6	65
Santis	2502	0.4	14	5	72
Sonnblick	3106	−3.8	15	1	81
Vienna	203	14.8	9	4	57
Zagreb	163	16.4	17	6	66
Zermatt	1610	8.9	11	1	—
Zugspitze	2960	−2.5	21	—	—
Zürich	569	12.7	13	5	63

NOTE: °F = °C (9/5) + 32

impediment to the walker in the spring, summer, and autumn months. At higher elevations, of course, the story is much different. Snowfall amounts increase to as much as 35 meters, representing 3.5 meters of melted precipitation. Indeed, above timberline, snow may occur any month of the year. Year-to-year variability is great, also: some years, trails above timberline may be impassable until July.

For the day-walker who stays at low elevations in the Alpine forelands (Munich and the Vienna Woods, for example), this means that walks are possible most of the year. Below-timberline mountain walks are usually possible from late spring through autumn. Above timberline, trail passability is more problematical, although the high routes we describe will generally be passable from July through September. In case of doubt, inquire at the local tourist office.

July				September			
Temp ° C	Rain days	Tstm days	Cld %	Temp ° C	Rain days	Tstm days	Cld %
21.7	9	6	—	18.6	6	1	—
17.7	—	—	—	14.5	—	—	—
18.3	10	6	—	14.4	9	1	—
16.0	16	7	68	12.4	12	2	59
19.9	7	7	43	15.8	9	3	52
18.1	14	8	61	14.6	10	2	55
18.6	11	9	54	14.1	8	3	57
21.4	10	5	42	17.4	9	3	47
24.1	6	5	43	19.1	6	2	51
17.2	14	7	54	13.3	11	2	48
17.8	16	8	62	14.0	12	2	55
5.6	17	8	71	3.5	13	3	63
1.6	18	7	78	−0.5	12	2	67
19.9	9	7	53	15.6	7	1	48
22.0	11	6	45	17.7	11	3	55
14.7	10	1	—	10.6	9	0	—
2.5	20	—	—	0.6	17	—	—
17.6	13	9	59	14.0	10	2	61

Plants and animals

Timberline in the Alps is close to the 2000-meter contour. In the southern portion of the range, the boundary is about 200 meters higher; in the north, about 300 meters lower. Below this level lies a zone comprised largely of coniferous trees: Arolla pine (*Pinus cembra*), mountain pine (*P. mugo*), and larch (*Larix decidua*). Typically, at the upper limit of tree growth, the trees become prostrate, forming the densely matted krummholz so characteristic of tree line. The most common timberline tree is Arolla pine (*Arve* in German, *pin arolle* in French, and *pino cembro* in Italian). It is a five-needle pine with erect, purple brown cones. On good sites, it will grow to a height of 25 meters.

The other high-altitude pine is mountain pine, a short, contorted tree rarely exceeding 5 meters in height. It can be identified by its egg-shaped cones and two-needle fascicles and can be found in rocky and stony places, often on scree slopes.

Another common near-timberline tree is the deciduous larch (*Lärche* in German, *meleze* in French, and *larice* in Italian). It forms one of the most beautiful of the high-altitude forests; its lacy, light green foliage allows lush undergrowth. Larch is a coniferous curiosity in that it loses its needles in the fall, leaving the tree looking dead. But not so; a new crop of leaves will appear in the spring.

The most ubiquitous tree in the lower reaches of the Alpine forest is Norway spruce, the quintessential European conifer. Widely planted as a timber tree, it grows naturally at elevations below 2200 meters, especially on north slopes. It can be identified most readily by its growth habit: tall (to 60 meters), sharply conical, with downward-sweeping branches that have been compared to a spaniel's tail. Another common species is the two-needle Scotch pine (*P. sylvestris*). At lower elevations, black pine (*P. nigra*) and silver fir (*Abies alba*) are present, if not common. The latter is distinguished by its upright cylindrical cones and flattish top.

In the Alpine forelands, at elevations below 1500 meters, mixed hardwood forests become common. The most noticeable of these is the pure beech forest, with its clean stems of smooth gray bark reaching up to a canopy of lacy, light green leaves. Underneath, the forest floor is often carpeted with ferns, so dense that the ground can not be seen. If you're lucky, you'll see an old beech forest on a misty morning; few woodland sights are more beautiful.

Above timberline lies the domain of the true Alpine plant. Here in the *Alp* (or *Alm*—both mean high meadow) and scree slope, in the nooks and crannies of boulder fields, along glacier-fed rivulets, you can find some seven hundred species of flowering plants. You will probably see edelweiss (*Leontopodium alpinum*) with its whitish woolly bracts surrounding the flower head. It is not as common as you might suppose and is absolutely protected. Don't pick any! Most Alpine flowers are protected to some degree. They are prettier where they are, so resist the urge to collect a vaseful, or even one to stick in your hat.

Some of the colors in the Alpine flowers must be seen to be believed. Deep red alpenrose—a rhododendron—covers acres and acres with its saturated color. Blue and purple gentians of various species are common throughout the region, as are somewhat rarer brown and yellow gentians. Common monkshood, spikes of purple hooded flowers, grace damp Alpine meadows. And, if you go high enough or early enough, you may find Alpine snowbells (*Soldanella alpina*) poking through the melting snowfields.

Although many of the Alpine flowers have counterparts in above-timberline areas in North America, many are quite different. If you really want to know their names and lineages, the only way is to carry a flower guide. Two useful ones are listed in the Bibliography, and many are available in Europe; but few are in English.

Wild animals are rather scarce in the Alps. The most common beasts are cows, sheep, and goats. For centuries, Alpine herdsmer have been moving their flocks to the high meadows for summer pasturage. Signs of this are everywhere, from primitive farm buildings that protected man and beast from summer storms, to hay barns scattered about. Indeed, most of the trails you will be traversing started out as stock trails and are used as such today. So, don't be surprised if you hear the deep-throated clank of cowbells or the higher tinkle of sheepbells no matter where you are. They are a ubiquitous part of the Alpine scene.

What is not so obvious is what grazing animals have done to tree line. Alpine ecologists believe that tree line has been lowered as much as 200 elevational meters as the result of centuries of heavy grazing. Although the lowering of the tree line has afforded more grazing area and has thus been beneficial to the cows and herdsmen, it has been less felicitous for the valley dwellers below, at least in the wintertime. These de-treed zones are preferred areas for the initiation of snow avalanches, many of which may end in the valley bottoms with disastrous results for the people living there. Sturdy metal structures have been built in many high meadows to hold fast the snow. And in many areas, there has been an attempt to control grazing to the point where trees can once again recapture the lower ends of the high meadows.

Despite the capture of Alpine meadows by domestic livestock, there are wild animals up there, and you may be lucky enough to see some. Chamois, deer, and ibex inhabit the high Alps. Marmots live in rocky crevices, and you may well hear their shrill cry even if you don't see them. *Ursus arctos*, the brown bear, is reputed to survive in parts of Switzerland, but don't count on seeing one. Wolves are completely gone; the last wolf was killed a half century ago.

Few poisonous plants or animals will be found, although the common viper inhabits lower elevations. It is rather shy and not likely to be encountered. Although not as poisonous as the rattlesnake, a bite can be serious and must be treated expeditiously. Although entomologists count twenty thousand species of insects in the Alps, we have never been bothered by any of them.

What to take and what to wear

Is it possible to pack "a few extras" in an already crowded suitcase for a day hike above the Alpine timberline? Must you take a full range of mountain hiking gear for a safe and enjoyable high-altitude walk? We think that it *is* possible by a judicious selection of lightweight multipurpose gear, much of which you will want to have with you anyway on any extended European vacation or business trip.

One of the problems with specifying a single list is that it cannot possibly be suitable for all of the hikes in all of the weather conditions that are likely to be found during an Alpine summer. Some of the walks can be taken with nothing more than ordinary tourist clothing, even with street shoes. On the other hand, above timberline you may encounter rough trails and stormy weather. So a certain amount of judgment is necessary when you are planning for a trip that is to include country or mountain walking. The list that follows should be adequate even for bad weather above timberline. However, it must be stated that summer weather can be severe in the Alps; prudence in cancelling a trip or in turning back if the weather turns bad is essential.

The most important item is a pair of sturdy and comfortable walking shoes. On rough mountain trails the best is, of course, a pair of light hiking boots. The recent trend toward light boots is a good one; there are many with lug soles that are suitable for even the roughest trails. They may not be as waterproof as heavy leather boots, but they are much lighter and can be crammed into a much smaller space. Indeed, we prefer a good lightweight boot of this sort for city sightseeing. Many are reasonably attractive, if not high style.

On the other hand, lightweight jogging shoes and similar rubber-and-canvas footwear are increasingly seen above timberline. With only a light day pack on your back, you may find them suitable for nearly any trail. Of course, you may have to put up with wet feet on occasion, but at least your shoes will dry out faster. They may not provide enough ankle support, though. The real point is that whatever shoes you find suitable for woodland walking at home will be suitable for day-hiking in the Alps.

If your boots fit properly, a single pair of medium-weight athletic socks should be adequate. Carry an extra pair, in case your feet get soaked.

Next most important is your outer clothing. A lightweight hooded windbreaker or anorak is essential for high-altitude hiking. It need not be waterproof, although a light Gore-Tex anorak may prove useful. The best are hip length. Rain protection, which is essential, is best provided by a light poncho. It has been our experience that even a Gore-Tex parka does not provide adequate protection in a prolonged rain. A hat with a brim provides protection from both sun and rain if it is reasonably waterproof. You can rely on the hood of your anorak or poncho to keep your head warm if the weather turns cold and windy. A pair of gloves or mittens should also be carried for any above-timberline walk.

Many Alpine hikers today wear the ubiquitous blue jeans. Needless to say, they should not be skintight, but comfortable for walking. Sturdy cotton chinos are also satisfactory. Some might wish to consider a pair of light but sturdy wool pants, but for day-hiking when you can get down from the mountains quickly, they are not really necessary. The one wool item you should have is a medium-weight wool sweater, good for cool evenings in the city as well as inclement weather in the mountains. Rain pants are worth considering if you insist on hiking in the rain, but we do not consider them essential, especially for below-timberline hiking.

A few miscellaneous items complete the list. Drinking water may be hard to come by, and you should carry a plastic water bottle sufficient for your day's needs. Carry a multipurpose pocketknife (if you are a wine-drinker, don't forget a corkscrew!), a small "disposable" flashlight, and a whistle. (The standard Alpine distress signal is six signals spaced evenly during one minute, a minute pause, then repeated.) Don't forget sunglasses and sunscreen, a few Band-Aids and moleskin, and a small roll of toilet paper.

All of this can be put in a 4-ounce nylon day pack that can be folded and stuffed into its own pocket. You really don't need anything heavier or more substantial.

Passports, visas, and customs

For an American or Canadian traveling to any of the Alpine countries, the only travel document needed is a valid passport. Visas are not required except for entry to Yugoslavia, where you can obtain a ninety-day tourist visa at the entry point.

Check your passport for the expiration date. If you do not have a passport, apply for one well in advance of your expected departure date. Although it may only take a few weeks to obtain one by mail, there is nothing worse than having all arrangements made and wondering if your passport will show up in time. Many U.S. post offices handle passport applications; an inquiry to your local postmaster will give you the information on where and how to apply. Don't forget that two standard passport photographs are required. When you have these taken, have the photographer provide you with several additional ones. Europeans are great for requiring photos on ski tickets and the like.

Customs regulations vary by country, of course, but none is onerous to the tourist bent on sightseeing and hiking. Still cameras (usually two), a movie camera, and reasonable amounts of film can be taken across borders without duty so long as they are for personal use. Actually, it is not the going that may prove troublesome, but the coming back. Be sure to have a U.S. Customs agent fill out an identification form on your cameras before you leave the States. This will prove that you did not buy the items overseas and will thus avoid potential problems on your return. We have never had any problems, but it takes just a few minutes to fill out the form at the airport before your departure. You usually have time to waste anyway if you arrive at the suggested two-hours-before-departure time.

One final word about passports: keep yours with you at all times. Some of our walks involve border crossings (at Geneva, for example). You will need your passport and it won't do you any good back at the hotel room.

Maps and guidebooks

Map and guidebook publishing is big in Europe; there are several major publishers and numerous local publishers. And each of the major sources has several series of maps, at different scales and in different formats. It is not unusual to be confronted with three or four different maps of a region, each one "newer" and "better" than the others. If you want a map to supplement the sketch maps accompanying the route descriptions, the best thing to do is to browse a bit. Make sure that the map covers the route completely and shows the trails clearly. Some are directed toward the skier and may not be as good for summer trails.

We recommend that you obtain a map, although our descriptions and sketches should be adequate. Most newsstands at railroad stations have a selection of trail maps for the local area. And many, if not all, bookstores carry a more complete selection.

The local tourist office, usually near the railroad station, often carries hikers' maps for the local area. It will sometimes have maps and brochures published by the local authorities that are free for the asking. At any rate, tourist-office personnel, who almost always speak English, can be very helpful in indicating where local maps and guidebooks can be obtained.

An annotated list of hikers' books on the Alps can be found in the Bibliography. In addition, at the beginning of each walk description, a list of maps and guidebooks specific to the area is given. Unless otherwise indicated, listed maps are at a scale of 1:50,000, or 2 centimeters per kilometer. Although the guidebooks are generally in the German language, the maps usually have legends in several languages, including English. The publishers of the commonly available maps and guidebooks will be referred to by abbreviation, as follows:

AK	Amtliche Kartenwerke (official map agency)
AV	Alpenvereinskarten (Alpine Club maps)
F&B	Freytag & Berndt (Vienna)
F-K&F	Fink-Kümmerly & Frey (Stuttgart) (guidebooks)
K&F	Kümmerly & Frey (Bern) (maps)
KOMP	Kompass-Karten, Fleischmann (Munich)
RV	RV Reise- und Verkehrsverlag (Stuttgart)

Especially in smaller towns, you can usually find a large poster-map in, on, or near the railroad station. These will show routes within walking distance of the station, many of which will not show up on published trail maps.

Huts, hostels, and mountain inns

The Alps are speckled with mountain huts and inns. Nearly every trail from the valley leads to some sort of hostelry. Many of these are privately owned and operated inns that cater primarily to day-hikers looking for a place to rest for lunch and a stein of beer or a soft drink. Others are run by the various Alpine clubs. These also cater to day-hikers but in addition offer overnight accommodations at reasonable rates. Many private huts also have a *Matratzenlager* (bunkroom) for overnighters.

Nearly all of the Alpine walks we describe pass by one or more of these high-mountain huts. Many of the walks are planned so that you will find a hut at lunchtime. There you will find soup and wurst and drinks of various sorts at surprisingly reasonable prices. Outside tables permit you to enjoy the scenery while munching a hot *Wurstl* and quaffing a beer or *Viertel* of the local wine. It is likely that you will have table mates from who knows where. It is a time for discussing trails and passes and best routes down. Most of the hikers you will meet speak at least some English, and they will most likely want to practice English with you. But do not be bashful: try out your high school French or German on them. They will appreciate your efforts.

All of our described hikes can be accomplished in one day, although some make for a rather long day indeed. Some lead to the high country with its promise of spectacular hiking just over the ridge. So, if you have a couple of days at your disposal, you might consider including an overnight at one of the huts. You won't need anything you haven't brought for your day hiking. Blankets and a pillow are included in the overnight fee. Sleeping accommodations range from large bunkrooms with wall-to-wall mattresses to quite comfortable private rooms with real beds. If you are fastidious, you might wish to include a sheet sleeping sack with your gear, similar to the ones required at youth hostels. Nylon ones weigh but a few ounces. They are designed with a flap that encloses a pillow. The only other extra you might bring (besides a toothbrush, of course!) is a pair of slippers. Hiking boots are *never* allowed in the sleeping rooms. Socks may be OK, but it is nice to have a pair of comfortable slippers to pad around in.

Just about all of the huts serve food, except for the really high and remote ones. Food preparation tends to be simple—wurst, schnitzel, spaghetti, and so forth. The food may not be gourmet, but then we have never had a meal in a hut that we didn't like. Breakfasts are typical continental breakfasts, with bread and rolls, lots of jam, and coffee. There is always a charge for breakfast, unlike the hotels and inns in the valleys. For the truly hungry, a more extensive breakfast menu is usually available. But orange juice tends to be expensive in the mountains.

It is customary to pack your own lunch materials, although it may be possible to purchase something suitable at breakfast. However, you really should never venture into the mountains without a substantial cache of lunch food—just in case.

Reservations are never necessary in the huts; indeed, they are rarely accepted. The tradition is always to find room for the hiker. This is as much a safety measure as it is a gesture of hospitality. Weather changes can be rapid and severe above timberline, and the huts are a major link in the mountain safety chain.

Mountain inns and huts are open during the tourist season, which may vary from place to place. Above timberline, the usual season is from the end of June to the middle or end of September. Many high huts are also open during the ski season, but nearly all are closed for a month or two in the fall and spring. Lower down, roadside and trailside inns may be open year-round. The only way to know for sure if the hut marked on a map as "open all year" is really open is to go to it. Almost as good, and really essential if you expect to depend on hut accommodations, is to inquire at the tourist office in the nearest town.

What will it cost to stay overnight in a hut? Prices vary from country to country, but a good rule of thumb is that meals and drinks will cost about the same as in local restaurants in town. Space in the *Matratzenlager* is very reasonable, the equivalent of a few dollars; and even private rooms, if available, are surprisingly reasonable—no high-mountain Hiltons, these. So, a weekend in the mountains can be not only pleasant, but also inexpensive.

Winter walking and ski touring

This book is mostly about summertime walking. However, there is no reason why you shouldn't get out into the countryside during the fall, winter, and spring months. Many of the described walks are quite suitable for off-season walking, especially those at low altitude. These include most of the walks around Munich, Vienna, and Geneva. The controlling factor is, of course, the weather. Even low-altitude walks can be less than fun if it is sleeting. Check the weather, check the tourist office for trail conditions, then take off if all seems well.

Caution and common sense are advisable, especially if you plan to go up to or near timberline. Remember that it can snow any month of the year above timberline. Four inches of snow will obliterate trails and cover paint blazes. We know from personal experience that a summer snowstorm can disorient the Alpine hiker extremely rapidly and make a hut only a few hundred meters away almost impossible to find.

Remember also that daylight lasts for a very short time in mid-winter at the latitude of the Alps. From mid-November to mid-January, the time from sunrise to sunset is nine hours or less; eight hours in Munich at the winter solstice.

Nevertheless, off-season hiking can be most enjoyable on a fine fall or winter day. Get an early start, take extra clothing and food, and be just a little more alert than you would be in the summer.

If snow is on the ground, consider ski touring. Cross-country skiing is slowly becoming popular in the Alps; most ski-resort areas have their quota of marked trails. Equipment rentals are somewhat easier to find than just a few years ago. Some of the trails we describe are suitable for skinny skis, at least in part. Les Voirons, for example, has marked ski trails that sometimes follow, sometimes diverge slightly from the hiking trails. Many trail maps show ski trails. Some areas have maps specifically oriented to the skier. Local tourist offices can be helpful in guiding you to suitable areas and suggesting suitable maps.

Other areas potentially suitable for ski touring include the lowland walks around Munich, the walks in the Vienna Woods, and the Geneva and Zürich areas in Switzerland.

Walk grading system

European trails are usually classified either as *Wanderweg*, a low-altitude path, or as *Bergweg*, a rough, high-altitude trail. The former are marked with yellow signs, whereas the latter have red/white/red stripes on trail markers and direction signs. For our purposes, we have chosen to expand this classification into five categories, based on the character of the footway and the altitude or severity of the weather that might be experienced. These categories are related to the kind of clothing and footwear that are appropriate and can be used as guides to the clothes you should bring with you.

Grade 1. Many of the described walks are at low elevation, through field or forest, on graded, nearly level paths. Some involve a certain amount of city walking, or traversing back roads that may or may not be paved. For these, comfortable street shoes are adequate, although there is a chance that they may become muddy. Some kind of rain protection is appropriate, for afternoon showers are common in the summer.

Grade 2. While still at low elevation, many paths are somewhat less "civilized." Grades may be moderate, with erosion and wear resulting in a somewhat rougher footway. Good walking shoes, perhaps with ankle support, are appropriate, if not absolutely necessary. Again, some rain protection should be taken if the weather is at all threatening.

Grade 3. Higher up, toward timberline, paths generally become rockier, with a rough footway, even when graded. Good hiking shoes with lug soles are recommended. At higher elevations, extra clothing should be taken.

Grade 4. At and above timberline, trails are mostly rocky, although they are often carefully graded and well constructed. Nevertheless, they are often narrow and steep and may require some rock scrambling. Sturdy shoes with lug soles are necessary. Above timberline, protection from a sudden storm is essential. The full list of clothing and gear described earlier in "What to wear" should be taken. These trails are not dangerous, except perhaps during bad weather, and can be negotiated by anyone with some mountain-hiking experience.

Grade 5. Because of the extreme steepness of much of the Alpine terrain, some of the above-timberline trails require what is called in German *Trittsicherheit*, sure-footedness. Trails cling to the sides of cliffs, are often cut into vertical faces, and may or may not be secured with cables or railings. Some trails may have iron ladders traversing exposed steep sections. Although not particularly dangerous for experienced hikers, they may pose hazards in bad weather. And they are not recommended for those with a fear of heights. Many Alpine routes fit into this category, but few of them are included in this book. Fortunately, many of the most spectacular views in the Alps can be found from more benign trails.

A word here about mountain safety. Hundreds of thousands of recreationists swarm through the Alps, winter and summer. Very few of them are involved in serious or life-threatening situations. High-country skiers face severe avalanche hazards, and rock-climbers are exposed to obvious dangers. But the day-hiker who starts a timberline walk on a warm and sunny summer day is obviously not exposed to this degree of hazard. Nevertheless, by taking a cable car for a 1000-meter ascent to the Alpine tundra, the hiker is transported to what may be a radically different climatic regime. Temperatures may be fifteen to twenty Fahrenheit degrees colder than in the valley below. Winds on exposed trails may bring the effective windchill temperature substantially lower. So what may seem a warm summer day in the valley may turn out to be a downright chilly or cold day on the mountain. If the trail is shrouded in cloud, or if rain or drizzle is falling, it may be absolutely miserable and can even pose the threat of hypothermia.

So, the prudent hiker ventures above timberline aware of the rapid changes in weather that can occur, and goes prepared. You should also check the weather forecast before starting out, even on a seemingly benign day. Be ready to change plans if severe weather threatens. Take a trail lower down, where a change to bad weather may only mean some discomfort. On the other hand, most of the trails described in this book are rather well populated and obviously easily accessible. If you keep an eye on the weather and stay alert to changing conditions—something you should do on any mountain hike—there is very little to worry about. Alpine weather can be bad, but it can also be very good. And when it is good, it can be very enjoyable indeed.

France &
Switzerland

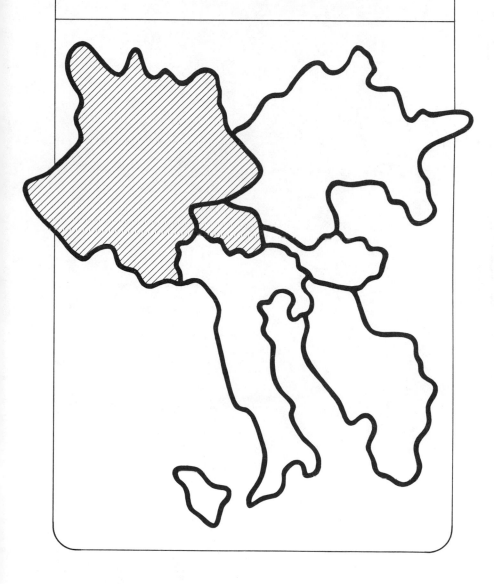

1. Chamonix and Mont Blanc

In the center of Chamonix stands a statue of Horace de Saussure, the great Swiss naturalist, with his gaze fixed on the towering summit of Mont Blanc (4807 meters). By his side stands the *Chamoniard* Balmat, his arm raised toward the summit as if to point out a possible route to the top, which he and Paccard had reached in 1786. It was a challenge de Saussure could not resist; in the following year he returned, assembled eighteen guides to carry his scientific equipment, and made it to the top. Chamonix and Mont Blanc have not been the same since. The climb to this highest of Alpine peaks created a sensation in the salons of England and Europe and ensured that Chamonix would become known as the mountain capital of the world.

Actually, the age of mountaineering did not really start until some seventy years later, in 1857, when the first Alpine Club was formed in London. Soon thereafter the names of Whymper, Mummery, and Coolidge became associated with Alpinism and the conquering of one Alpine peak after another. Even in the United States, Alpine fever infected would-be mountaineers. The Appalachian Mountain Club was formed in 1876. One of its first activities was to join with other Alpine clubs to honor Balmat and de Saussure with the Chamonix statue. Inscribed thereon: *"Érigé en 1877 avec le concours des Clubs Alpins français, suisse, italien, anglais, l'Appalachian Mountain Club de Boston, la Société des Touristes autrichiens et de l'Académie des Sciences de Paris."*

Horace de Saussure and his guide Balmat look toward Mont Blanc

Today, one can find members of all these clubs and others, and
many who are members of no club, flocking to Chamonix to follow
in de Saussure's footsteps in reality or imagination. It is a marvelous
place to be *in* the mountains. The narrow valley is flanked on both
sides by the famous Aiguilles, sharp needles pointing to the sky to
tempt the rock-climber. Glaciers push their way nearly to the valley
floor; some are accessible to the day-hiker or cable-car tourist. And
above all stands the monarch, Mont Blanc.

TRANSPORTATION

To the casual peruser of transportation maps, Chamonix seems
to be rather inaccessible. But that is something of an illusion. Direct
trains from Geneva, for example, make the trip in less than three
hours. That may be too long for a day trip (but not impossible, for a
train leaves the Eaux-Vives station in Geneva at about seven in the
morning, arriving in Chamonix before ten, with a return trip at

seventeen thirty). But Chamonix deserves more than a single day: at least a weekend. Go up on Friday night, return on Sunday night; you will not regret it. Accommodations are plentiful in the summer, and quite reasonable. We have come to town without reservations and found suitable accommodations without difficulty.

Transportation within the valley is provided by a bus line that runs up and down the valley, connecting all of the cable-car base stations and railroad stations. Service is frequent, about every half hour.

MAPS AND GUIDEBOOKS

The best hikers' map of the region is probably the *Massif du Mont Blanc* sheet (number 232) published by the Institut Géographique National at a scale of 1:25,000. Sheet 231 overlaps in the Chamonix region and includes country farther north. Both maps are tributes to the mapmaker's art and look almost like aerial photographs with added detail.

WEATHER AND CLIMATE

Chamonix lies in a deep valley that trends southwest-northeast. The surrounding mountains are among the highest in the entire Alpine chain. Chamonix is thus shielded from the sun a good part of the day, even in the summer when the sun ascends to its highest point in the heavens. Nevertheless, summer temperatures are relatively warm. Data from Bourg-St. Maurice, at a similar elevation and not far to the south, are presented in the climatic table and make an appropriate comparison. Temperatures are almost exactly the same as for Zürich.

Although comparable precipitation data were not available, it is likely that the number of rainy days is intermediate between the figures for Geneva and Zermatt. Thus about one-third of the days can be expected to have measurable rain in May, with only slightly fewer in July and September. Thunderstorms peak in July, with about seven probable. The best hiking weather is in September and early October, although snow becomes increasingly likely as the fall wears on. Snowfall is likely in any month at higher elevations.

Useful information

Tourist information

Office du Tourisme, Place de l'Église, 74400 Chamonix. Tel. (50) 53 00 24.

Maps, guidebooks, and trail information

Office de la Haut Montagne, Gérard Devouassoux, Maison de la Montagne, 74400 Chamonix. Tel. (50) 53 22 08.
Bureau des Guides, Maison de la Montagne, 74400 Chamonix. Tel. (50) 53 00 88. Conducts guided tours.
Club Alpin Français. Tel. (50) 53 16 03.

Local transportation

Chamonix Bus, Place de l'Église, 74400 Chamonix. Tel. (50) 53 05 55. Local buses run the length of the valley on a half-hourly schedule. Schedule available from the main terminal near the church in the center of town.
Note that the Swiss portion of the rail line from Chamonix to Martigny is privately owned. Eurailpass is not valid on the Swiss part.

Accommodations and restaurants

Central Booking Office. Tel. (50) 53 23 33. More than one hundred hotels, pensions, and dormitories.
Youth Hostel Chamonix, les Pelerins, 74400 Chamonix. Tel. (50) 53 14 52. One hundred thirty beds.
Camping. Nineteen private camping areas in the valley. Camping is not permitted outside commercial camping areas.
Restaurants. Brochure available from the tourist office lists nearly one hundred restaurants in Chamonix and surrounding towns.

Miscellaneous

Mountain Rescue Service. Tel. (50) 53 16 89.
Weather forecast. Tel. (50) 53 03 40.

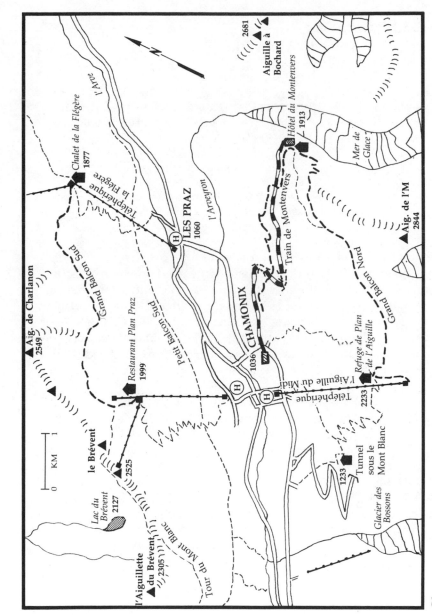

Chamonix

Grand Balcon Sud—
Part of the Tour du Mont Blanc

DIFFICULTY	Grade 3–4
DISTANCE	5 km
WALKING TIME	2 1/2 hours
MAPS	Institut Géographique National Carte Touristique 232, *Massif du Mont Blanc,* 1:25,000
	KOMP Wanderkarte 85, *Mont Blanc Massiv*
	Office du Tourisme de Chamonix–Mont Blanc, *Carte des promenades d'été en montagne*
GUIDEBOOK	K&F Wanderbuch Internationale Reihe 1, *Rund um Mont Blanc*

Chamonix has the reputation of being a place where only "real" mountain climbers go to test their mettle. Certainly one does find many such walking the streets, looking serious and somewhat distant, with great coils of ropes looped round their shoulders and their inner eyes fixed firmly on the towering Aiguilles. But Chamonix is at least as much for walkers, with miles and miles of trails that take no more than a pair of sturdy shoes and a light heart. Each side of the valley has its Petit Balcon well down in the timber and its Grand Balcon well above timberline.

One of the most spectacular of these Balcon walks is the Grand Balcon Sud, which here forms part of the Tour du Mont Blanc. But don't let the association with the rugged and demanding tour frighten you away from this walk. It is nearly level between the upper stations of two ski lifts and offers the most spectacular views of the Chamonix Aiguilles to be had anywhere in the vicinity. If the valley is hot, you can rely on the Grand Balcons being twenty Fahrenheit degrees cooler. So save this walk for a hot, sunny day with good visibility. And take plenty of film!

Easiest access to the Grand Balcon Sud is via the Téléphérique Flégère, which has its base station on the north edge of Les Praz de Chamonix, a ten-minute bus ride from Chamonix proper. Les Praz is also one train-stop from town. Either way, find the base station of the cable car, then enjoy the ten-minute ride to the top and the Hotel Flégère.

Aiguille du Midi

The route to Plan Praz, the southern terminus of our walk, is marked by signs at the end of the *téléphérique*. At the *sortie,* look for the sign that says "Plan Praz," to the right, then drop down a few meters and cross under the cableway, and start the contour trail

around the west side of the valley. From here there are views of the
Mer de Glace and the Grandes Jorasses as well as Mont Blanc itself.
The trail, here a broad dirt path, is marked with white/red blazes. It
soon passes under a chair lift. The trail then descends a little chimney
on rock steps, with an unnecessary iron railing, and through fields
strewn with wildflowers. Soon it drops down to the Charlanon, a
giant cirque, and the ruins of the Chalet de Charlanon near the trail
junction. If the weather threatens, you can go directly to Chamonix
from here.

The walk along here is a delightful promenade along a broad
bench, climbing rock ribs, dropping down to flower-filled tundra,
skirting the sheer cliffs that form the northwestern boundary of the
Arve Valley. The trail stays above timberline, and the eye is con-
stantly delighted with the seemingly endless spires and faces of the
Aiguilles across the valley. Due east, the Aiguille Vert dominates the
skyline. Directly below it, the snout of the Mer de Glace can be seen
(at least until the Montenvers Ridge intervenes). Farther south along
the main chain are the Aiguille du Midi with its *téléphérique*, and the
sharp spire of Mont Maudit, the ridge finally culminating in the
rounded top of Mont Blanc.

Near the Plan Praz end of the route there are signs of mining
activity. A mine road stretches upward, though you cannot see the
workings. Exercise caution here: the trail has been partially obliterated by the mine road. It follows the road for about 15 to 30 meters,
then branches left. You can see the white/red paint marks on the
rocks, so look carefully.

We follow the mine road up to the complex of ski mechanisms
that occupies Plan Praz. Here there are a signpost and red/white
markings on the rocks. Head down toward the hut that is at the top
of the chair lift. From the building follow the road down to the upper
station of the Téléférique du Brévent, which is of the type with small
gondolas that can grab the cable under the operator's control. This is
one of the few ski lifts of this type that we have seen in the Alps,
although they are fairly common in the United States.

The *téléphérique* deposits you at the upper end of town. It is a
short walk to the center of town, past the tourist office, then straight
down to the railway station.

If you prefer to walk, a good but zig-zaggy trail heads down an
old avalanche chute to the right of the cable line, ending up at the
base station of the *téléphérique*.

Grand Balcon Nord
and the Mer de Glace

DIFFICULTY	Grade 3–4
DISTANCE	10 km (train from Montenvers eliminates 4 km)
WALKING TIME	4 1/2 hours (2 1/2 hours if train is used)
MAPS	Institut Géographique National Carte Touristique 232, *Massif du Mont Blanc*, 1:25,000
	Office du Tourisme de Chamonix–Mont Blanc, *Carte des promenades d'été en montagne*
GUIDEBOOK	None

Most of the summer tourists who ride the Téléphérique de l'Aiguille du Midi stay on for at least the second section, which climbs dizzyingly to the summit of the Aiguille du Midi. Few debark at Plan de l'Aiguille, the first stop above the base station. We suggest that you do get off here and take the walk along the Grand Balcon Nord to Montenvers for a spectacular view of the Mer de Glace. The walk is a pleasant one, above timberline all the way, and nearly level until the drop down to the hotel at Montenvers. Here you can board the cog railway for a ride back to Chamonix, or take the woodsy and gentle trail back down.

Although both the *téléphérique* ride and the cog railway are among the most popular and crowded attractions in the Chamonix area, the trail connecting them, the Grand Balcon Nord, will be nearly empty of tourists. Such is the state of mountain sightseeing in the Alps today. But this works to our advantage, for it is quite easy to avoid most of the crowds by getting no more than a few hundred meters from the ends of the lifts and trains. So, if the day is warm and sunny, take the Midi cable and tread the path to Montenvers.

One note of warning: the ride up this particular *téléphérique* is so popular that you may have a substantial wait at the base unless you arrive quite early (i.e., before 0800 in the summer months).

If you are arriving in Chamonix by train, turn left upon leaving the station, follow along to the first street that passes under the rail line, then follow the street (and the crowds) to the base station. Here you may find two lines: one to purchase the ticket (one-way to Plan de l'Aiguille), the second for assignment to a particular departure. This will involve some waiting if you arrive around 0900. The lift is fast, and Chamonix drops away at an astounding rate once your gondola is under way.

Upon leaving the gondola, follow the signs to the refuge Chalet du Plan de l'Aiguille, a fifteen-minute walk straight downhill. (If you have time, take the short walk to a tiny tarn fifteen minutes away on a contour trail.) The valley walls are so steep here that you seem almost to be floating above the town. Although the Red Aiguilles across the valley are not as high and spectacular as the Chamonix Aiguilles, they are quite respectable and anywhere else would be the main attraction. Directly across the valley, you can see the Téléphérique du Brévent and just to the right, the Aiguille de Charlanon.

At the refuge, perhaps after stopping for a coffee or soft drink, take the signed and marked path toward Montenvers. The trail is graded and well maintained, and deviates little from the 2100-meter contour for most of the way. The trail crosses a clear stream shortly, with an abundance of Alpine willow with its fuzzy yellowish catkins. The slope is well watered and filled with wildflowers all summer long.

Several trails leave left for the valley, the one to Blaitière offering a suitable escape route down in case of inclement weather. In about 4 kilometers, we reach another trail junction; we take the right fork, which switchbacks up a steep slope to the 2200-meter contour. This is the only hard work of the trip. After reaching a broad ridge, the trail drops down into the valley of the Mer de Glace. We are still above timberline and have an unobstructed view of the upper reaches of the glacier, a sight many have traveled thousands of miles to see. Far below lies the Hotel Montenvers and the terminus of the cog railroad. From here the trail zig-zags sharply downward toward the hotel, with ever-changing views of the Mer de Glace.

On a fine summer day, there is likely to be a mob scene at the complex of restaurants, hotels, zoo, and what-have-you at the glacier overlook. You can even ride down a funicular railway to the glacier itself. But as with most such tourist attractions, most of the tourists stay with the mob; you have only to walk a few meters down the trail to get away from ninety-nine percent of the crowd. So, do not tarry long, but hit the trail back to Chamonix. It starts out on the south side of the tracks and drops gently toward tree line. Upon entering the trees, the trail switchbacks sharply down to the railroad tracks, crossing over to the north side.

The trail continues down through a fine larch forest, crosses several logged areas, and reaches a small restaurant, the Buvette Caillet, a quiet and shady spot for refreshment. Although we are still paralleling the railroad, we are quite some distance below it. We can hear it, if not see it. Along this very steep side slope, keep an eye out for old avalanche paths, and some not so old ones. Many of these run all the way from timberline to the valley. Even a solid stand of trees will not always keep the snow from sliding down the mountain.

The forest to this point has been almost pure larch. Below this level it turns to a mostly Norway spruce forest, which the trail now switchbacks down through. The grade all the while is not too steep for comfortable downhill walking. Near the bottom, the trail crosses an Alpine slide. If you are really tired, you can rent a sled and slide the rest of the way to the valley!

2. Geneva

There must be something called "Geneva pallor." At least we imagine that all those thousands of diplomats and bureaucrats who flock to the city at various times of the year for meetings and conferences and SALT talks and what-have-you spend all of their time in conference rooms and rarely see the light of day. If you are one of those, you are missing a great deal. For Geneva is a town of history, a town of lakes and parks, a town set in the middle of some of the finest outdoor recreation areas in all of Europe. Zermatt is only three hours away; Chamonix is even closer. And the fine hiking and skiing country of the Jura is a scant half hour away by car, bus, or train. So if you have a Saturday or Sunday off, and want to go walking in the mountains, the possibilities are virtually limitless.

Although there are many parks within the city limits of Geneva, they are all rather small and citified. You must leave the city to find places for walks of even moderate extent. Nevertheless, the walk along the south shore of Lake Geneva, starting from the Jardin Anglais, is a favorite with the Genevois. And the Jardin Botanique, at the end of the number 5 bus line, is worth a visit.

TRANSPORTATION

In common with every European city we have been in, Geneva has a first-rate transportation system. The bus and trolley-car network is extensive and efficient. Boats ply the lake and are pleasant to ride if you have the time. Fast trains connect Geneva with the rest of Switzerland and the rest of Europe. For local travel, you should obtain a copy of the *Plan de Genève—transports publics*. The main bus station (*gare routière*) is just off the Rue du Mont-Blanc, behind the English Church. Buses to outlying districts use this station. And the main docks are located along the Quai du Mont-Blanc at the north end of the Pont du Mont-Blanc.

MAPS AND GUIDEBOOKS

For some reason, there seem to be fewer good walkers' maps for the Geneva area than for most other regions of the Alps. About the only one that covers the immediate surroundings of Geneva at a useful scale is the official topographic map, number 270, at a scale of 1:50,000. We know of no English-language guidebook, although the Kompass Wanderführer *Schweizer Jura und Genfer See* (Lake Geneva) may be useful if you can read German.

WEATHER AND CLIMATE

Geneva has a relatively mild climate, partly because of its proximity to Lake Geneva. It snows only occasionally in the city, although the surrounding mountains are snow covered throughout the winter. Indeed, precipitation is surprisingly low; annual average is 86 centimeters spread rather uniformly throughout the year.

Temperatures are rather mild, also. Winter minimum temperatures average a degree or two below freezing during winter months. Summer temperatures can be oppressively high (average daily maximum in July is 25° C (77° F), especially when combined with the high humidities that are common in summer. Thus, a walk through the vineyards on a sunny summer afternoon can leave you limp and longing for the higher elevations. The lake breeze along the shore is most welcome, but its effect is not often felt more than a kilometer or so from the lake.

The climatic tables on pages 8 and 9 will provide good comparative data on this city's climate. Note particularly Geneva's climatic twin, Vienna.

Useful information

Tourist information

Office du Tourisme, 3 Place des Bergues. Tel. (022) 32 26 05.
Office du Tourisme du Canton de Vaud, 10 Avenue de la Gare, CH-1002
Lausanne. Tel. (021) 22 77 82.

Maps, guidebooks, and trail information

Club Alpin Suisse, 11 Grand Rue. Tel. (022) 24 67 00.
University Bookshop, Rue de la Corraterie.

Local transportation

Transports Public Genevois, la Jonction, 1211 Genève. Tel. (022) 21 08 44.
Publishes *Plan de Genève—transport publics,* showing all public transpor-
tation lines at a scale of 1:10,000. Information in English. Also, brochure
Transport Tickets gives complete fare information in English.

Accommodations and restaurants

Liste des Hôtels, available from the Geneva Tourist Office, lists one hundred
fifty hotels.
Liste des Restaurants, available from the Geneva Tourist Office, lists some
of the hundreds of eating places in Geneva.
Youth Hostel, Rue des Plantaporrets, 1205 Genève. Tel. (022) 29 06 19. Two
hundred sixty-six beds.
Naturfreundehaus/St.-Cergue. Tel. (022) 61 10 46.
Camping. Three camping areas in Geneva: Bois de la Bâtie, Conches, and
Pointe à la Bise. Check tourist office for further information.

Miscellaneous

American Embassy (branch office), 11 Route de Pregny, CH-1292 Cham-
besy/Genève. Tel. (022) 99 02 11.
Canadian Mission, Consular Section, 10A Avenue du Bude, CH-1201
Genève. Tel. (022) 34 19 50.
Weather forecast. Tel. 162.

La Dôle—
A high point of the Swiss Jura Mountains

DIFFICULTY	Grade 2–3
DISTANCE	14 km, possibility of 4 km shortcut
WALKING TIME	4 hours
MAP	Office du Tourisme de St.-Cergue, *St.-Cergue*, 1:25,000
GUIDEBOOK	None

The crest of the Swiss Jura, stretching northeastward from La Dôle just north of Geneva to the Lagern near Baden, effectively forms the northwestern boundary of Switzerland. Between the Jura's calcareous folds and the steep slopes of the pre-Alps lies a broad undulating plain, the Central Plateau, formed from glacial debris washed down from the Alps. Although the plain is rather heavily dissected by the Aare River and its tributaries, it is the agricultural heartland of Switzerland. Not particularly well suited to cropping, the land is ideal for dairy farming. This is the land of Gruyère and Emmentaler cheeses. Here also lie Switzerland's largest cities—Geneva, Bern, Lucerne, Zürich.

The Jura form a natural barrier between the low country to the west and the Swiss *Mittelland* and played an important part in the early history of the Confederation. Although much lower than the majestic Alps to the south, the Jura formed a kind of first line of defense.

The southern culmination of the Swiss Jura is La Dôle, a shining calcareous peak 30 kilometers due north of Geneva. Although only 1677 meters high, it is a more impressive mountain than its height might indicate. The summit is 1300 meters above Lake Geneva. It is high enough to sport a major ski resort with seven lifts and tows and a maximum 450-meter drop. Although the slopes swarm with skiers in the winter, summer brings a more tranquil time. La Dôle makes a fine destination for a day trip from Geneva. When Geneva swelters in the summer sun, the open slopes of the Dole summit may be a breezy fifteen Fahrenheit degrees cooler.

Furthermore, the trip to St.-Cergue, the starting point, involves a delightful narrow-gauge electric trolley from Nyon on the lake. We recommend this journey whether or not you want to climb La Dôle— it is a fun ride.

La Dôle

Station and narrow-gauge trolley at St.-Cergue

The journey starts at the main railroad station in Geneva, on any of the numerous Lausanne trains that stop in Nyon. (Most do, but check the schedules, for the Intercity trains do not stop until Lausanne.) It is a fifteen-minute ride to Nyon. Immediately in front of the Nyon station, board the red cars of the Chemin de fer Nyon–St.-Cergue–Morez. The connection is tight for some trains—don't dawdle! The little train winds through the city, then through fields overlooking Lake Geneva, finally climbing through woods to St.-Cergue, a journey of about forty minutes.

St.-Cergue (1041 meters) is a small resort town that boasts a sizable youth hostel and a Nature Friends house in addition to a number of hotels. It is busiest in winter, for there are several ski lifts in the area, one of which we utilize for the hike.

From the railroad station, head south to the main intersection. A few meters beyond, a trail (sign) branches right and heads westward, paralleling the road and rail line, which are on your right. The route works its way through town, past two small ski lifts, and joins a paved road for a short distance. Signs indicate a branch left through fields to the base station of the La Barillette chair lift. (If you miss this trail, just follow the road to the lift.) Unless you like to climb along ski slopes, take the lift. It gets you up the 300 least interesting meters of the walk in a couple of minutes.

The view from the top of the lift is grand, but the better views are yet to come. There is a restaurant at the top of the lift, a good place for lunch or a snack. (There is also a new Alpine slide, if you are into that sort of thing!) The path west to the summit of La Barillette is well marked and gentle. The summit is hard to miss: there are several buildings and a giant TV tower on top. The route does not go over the top, but contours the south side on a service road, crosses the paved road, and heads across a field. The ridge here is nearly flat and is criss-crossed with trails, some marked, others not. The route is not difficult to find, however. Cross a broad saddle and follow the trail that climbs the south slope of the Pointe de Poêle Chaud, a well-defined knoll on your right.

The trail reaches a saddle and trail junction on the main ridge of La Dôle a few meters from a privately owned hut that does not offer public service. The trail (part of European Long-distance Footpath E4) now swings around to the west side of the ridge, climbing rather steeply to the broad, grassy summit. There is a military radar building on the very top, and a cable lift that serves it dropping off to the east. Several ski lifts also terminate on or near the ridgetop. Despite the intrusion of the structures, the views from the top are nothing short of spectacular. The main chain of the Alps can be seen to the south, with Mont Blanc clearly discernible. The great trench of Lake Geneva lies before you, although it must be said that haze and pollution may make that view something less than spectacular. The summit is very close to the French border—about 2 kilometers south and west. Indeed, the bottom stations of the ski lifts are just a few meters from the border.

For the return journey, follow the top of the eastern cliffs back to the trail junction and pick up the trail down the northwest slopes. It parallels the chair lift, following ski trails—not very well marked, but easy to follow. Near the bottom, the trail diverges right along a dirt road past a small restaurant. In about a kilometer, it joins another main trail, E2, and heads eastward along the edge of the woods. The road and railroad become visible soon. A trail diverges left across fields to La Givrine, where the narrow-gauge railroad to St.-Cergue and Nyon can be boarded. If you miss this trail junction, you can head across the open fields directly to La Givrine.

If you elect to walk back to St.-Cergue, take the forest road out of sight of the highway. It follows a level route and eventually reaches the houses at the upper end of St.-Cergue. City streets are followed down to town and the railroad station.

Les Voirons—
The French side of Lake Geneva

DIFFICULTY	Grade 2
DISTANCE	13 km
WALKING TIME	5 hours
MAP	Didier & Richard 3, *Massifs du Chablais, Faucigny et Genevois*
GUIDEBOOK	Annemasse Tourist Office, *Annemasse et environs. Promenades pédestres dans le Salève et les Voirons.* Available free from the Annemasse Tourist Office in City Hall

On the south shore of Lake Geneva, a series of low wooded ridges trend more or less north-south. Two of these are easily accessible from Geneva: Mont Salève in Switzerland and Les Voirons, just across the border in France. Mont Salève is the more popular of the two; it sports a dense network of trails, roads, restaurants, and even a cable car to transport tourists in cabined comfort, avoiding the 600-meter climb. Les Voirons has its trails, too; but they are less frequented. There is no cable car to the top, no restaurants. But there is a day's worth of good walking in a very rural setting, with good views of the lake and of the Alps just a few kilometers away.

Starting point for our trip is the busy village of Bonne. There is a direct bus from Geneva to Bonne that leaves the *gare routière*, the main bus station in Geneva (just off the Rue du Mont-Blanc, behind the English Church) at 0815. This is the SAT (Société Annemassienne de Transports) bus marked "Fer à Cheval," arriving in Bonne at 0900. (Don't forget your passport; Bonne is in France.) Get off the bus in the center of Bonne and walk back along the road 100 meters to the first street north (right) toward the mountain. Here there is a road sign to Le Meure, and a few meters up the street there is a white/red paint blaze. Follow the white/red paint markers on rocks and posts straight up the hill. We pass a new school and reach an intersection marked with a double white/red paint blaze on an electric light pole. Turn right here and follow the road on up. In 100 meters another double paint mark indicates a left turn up a gravel track. After 100 meters the dirt road swings left and a path leads through the woods, following a little stream bed. The route follows roads and old paths and is somewhat tortuous, but is well marked with white/red paint marks.

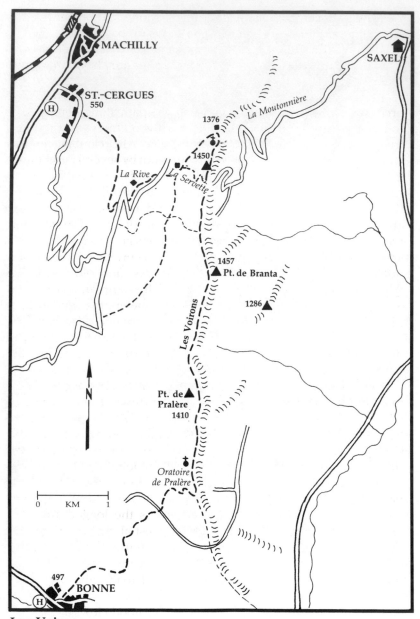

Les Voirons

The path climbs steadily through meadows and orchards. After reaching a paved road, the way continues up past a sign, "Sud La Chat." Pay attention to the double paint blazes that indicate marked changes in direction. Some of these changes are also marked with red arrows.

After about an hour's climb, the trail finally leaves the fields and orchards and enters the woods. While the path along here appears to be well trod, it follows through a hardwood forest, mostly small trees, but occasionally larger Norway spruce. After climbing through woods for a half kilometer, the trail comes out by several farmhouses, meets a narrow paved road, jogs left about 50 meters, then turns right and enters a gravel track. It then climbs through an old orchard and again meets the paved farm road and a power line, turns left and then, in about 100 meters, right again. Along this stretch there are fine views of the valley below with its mosaic of farms and woods and scattered houses. Along here there is a curious mixture of new houses, perhaps summer recreation houses, and old farms. The Alps are also visible along the skyline to the south and east.

The pavement soon ends, and in 100 meters the trail diverges right from the now-gravel road and enters the woods. The path now leads through a fine old Norway spruce stand, some trees 1 meter in diameter. Here we enter a game preserve (*reserve de chasse*). The paint blazes here consist of a red stripe on a white background.

After an hour of climbing up long switchbacks, we reach the main ridge and the trail turns left, or northward. After climbing along the westward slope of the ridge, the trail finally comes out into an open grassy area and climbs to a minor summit, which has a little shrine. There are fine views of the Alps from this point. Along the ridge the path may be obliterated by recent logging; however, it is generally not difficult to pick up by staying close to the ridgeline and paying attention to the occasional paint blazes and to the beaten path, which often can be followed across the logged area. The important thing is to stay pretty much west along the crest of the ridge and not be led astray eastward, down into the logged areas. (The logging attracts wildlife; when we were there, we saw a lovely doe.) On a broad reach of the ridge, a logging road comes in from the right, which we follow along the ridge. The road passes through an old logged area with many wildflowers and good views of the Alps. There is also a profusion of paint blazes of various sorts, some marking boundaries, some marking trails. There is little difficulty in following the main trail along the ridgetop. Along this stretch, look for a grove of huge Norway spruce, including one that is over 1 meter in diameter. The logging road eventually diverges right, whereas the trail sticks to the ridge (here marked white/red and red dot). Incidentally, the red dot marks a cross-country ski route, whereas the blue dot indicates a hiking trail. The ridge has both a ski trail and a hiking trail that at times share the same trailway, at times diverge. But they both share the ridgetop for its entire length.

This trail has been distinguished by its profusion of paint blazes and its lack of trail signs; but now one appears. It points south to Pointe de Branta and Oratoire de Pralère (the little shrine we passed a while back) and north to Le Signal and Le Prieure La Chapelle, which we come to soon. At this point, a trail heads west (left) off the ridge, marked with yellow paint blazes. It is a possible shortcut if time is short; it avoids the loop around the north end of the ridge. From the rocky promontory at this point there is a fine view of Lake Geneva to the north. A second trail heading west off the ridge is soon reached.

The trail over the highest point of the ridge (Le Signal) diverges left and is marked with both blue and red paint blazes. The unremarkable summit is marked by a sign, "Signal des Voirons, alt. 1480 m." After the summit the trail drops fairly sharply downward along the ridge, with good views to the north.

In a few minutes we come to La Chapelle, which apparently is a rarely used chapel, along with another building. At the trail junction here, take the trail to the left, marked red and yellow with a signpost, "La Servette de Voirons." But before you do, take time to visit the little chapel. The interior is spartan, with a stone altar, a statue of the Virgin Mary, and a bell rope. But where is the bell ringer? The house looks almost abandoned, but not quite, as if somebody is camping there. It seems, though, that somebody does ring the chapel bell and take care of the chapel. Perhaps you will see the bell ringer when you are there. At any rate, it is a cool retreat on a hot summer day.

From the chapel, the trail heads down rather steeply, switchbacking down the steep slope on a well-constructed footpath. We now pass through a dense Norway spruce forest that alternates with a light beech forest, producing extraordinary contrasts in the quality and quantity of light beneath the two canopies. Soon the trail meets and crosses a new gravel logging road. This crossing was rather

Chapel at Les Voirons

obscure when we were there. Walk left along the road about 100 meters and find a trail that drops right off the road and rejoins the regular path. Follow this left for 100 meters to La Servette, an abandoned farm or logging site. The piped spring water is cold and refreshing, the first and only water on the entire trip.

Below La Servette, the trail crosses logging roads and becomes difficult to follow. However, you can stay on the gravel road, which eventually turns into a paved road and zig-zags its way down to the main highway south of the village of St.-Cergue. The bus to Annemasse and Geneva runs along this road.

Mont Salève—
The most beautiful outlook near Geneva

DIFFICULTY	Grade 2
DISTANCE	14 km
WALKING TIME	5 hours (3 hours if cable car is used)
MAP	Didier & Richard 3, *Massifs du Chablais, Faucigny et Genevois*
GUIDEBOOKS	Annemasse Tourist Office, *Annemasse et environs. Promenades pédestres dans le Salève et les Voirons.* Available free from the Annemasse Tourist Office in City Hall K&F Schweitzer Wanderbuch 41, *Schweiz— die 50 schönsten Wanderungen.* Trip 38

Mont Salève and Les Voirons are similar mountains: they are both long ridges stretching in a southwest-northeast direction; they are both a few kilometers southeast of the city; and both are readily accessible by public transportation. But there the similarity ends. Les Voirons is a "wilderness" mountain with few trails and fewer roads. Mont Salève is an "urban" mountain, complete with cable car, roads, and numerous restaurants and hostelries along the summit ridge. Nevertheless, it does have magnificent views of the city and lake of Geneva, and is so accessible that it makes an ideal half-day or day walk on a good, clear day.

It is readily accessible by the number 8 bus from Rond-Pointe de Rive in Geneva, which in turn can be reached by the number 5 bus from the Cornavin station. The destination is Veyrier at the end of the line and hard on the French border. From the bus stop in Veyrier, head south toward Pas de l'Échelle, crossing the border at the toll station in a few meters (don't forget your passport). Just after passing under the railroad, the road to the base station of the Téléphérique du Salève swings right, whereas the path up the steep scarp of Mont Salève heads straight toward the mountain. It climbs rather steeply to the gap between Petit Salève on the left and the main ridge on the right.

At the gap, a road leads straight ahead to the little town of Monnetier-Mornex, worth a detour. From this road, a path leads southwest (right) up the ridge, along the Balcon du Léman. The path crosses the ridge road several times before reaching the Au-

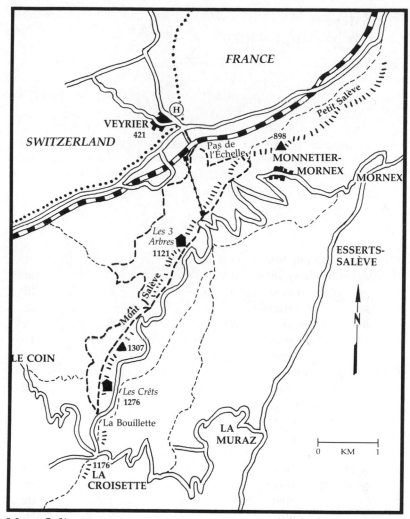

Mont Salève

berge Les Tres Arbres, where refreshments can be obtained. From here, the path follows the main ridge with magnificent views of the lake and city of Geneva, and, on a clear day, the massif of Mont Blanc and the Savoie Mountains.

About a kilometer and a half from the restaurant, we reach a trail junction at the head of the Grand Gorge. If time is short, you can head down from here, but we continue along the ridge to Les Crêts. Here the trail bends right (north) and heads toward the rim of the plateau, which it follows back to the trail junction at the head of the Grand Gorge. The trail heads down through the gorge, then switchbacks its way to the foot of the scarp. Here, at a road and trail junction, follow the footpath northward back to the lower end of the cable car and Pas de l'Échelle.

There are numerous paths on Mont Salève, and many variations of the described trip are possible. However, the best public-transport access is Veyrier. With all the roads and marked trails, it is difficult to get lost on this mountain. Nevertheless, if you wish to explore the variants, the Didier & Richard map is a great help.

3. Zermatt

Zermatt is, perhaps, the quintessential Swiss tourist town. Ever since Edward Whymper and his guides and colleagues conquered the Matterhorn in 1865, the town has been the chosen destination of mountain lovers and mountain climbers from all over the world. And there is something magic about the Matterhorn. Its upper slopes really do appear to be giant overhangs, an optical illusion that no knowledge seems able to dispel. It looks absolutely unclimbable, but the truth is, of course, that Matterhorn guides will lead anyone in good physical condition to the top.

Of course, few Zermatt visitors make the trip; most are content to wander the more gentle trails that abound along the lower slopes. Many of these are reachable by cable car or chair lift, so you can take a long day's trip above timberline without the necessity for a long and tiring climb through the forest. The hikers' map of the Zermatt region, published by the Zermatt Tourist Office, lists forty-eight routes suitable for nonclimbers. To be sure, some of these involve glacier crossings that should not be attempted by the inexperienced hiker. Glacier crossings can be extremely dangerous, especially when covered by fresh snow, which is possible any time of the year. If you are bent on that, you can hire a guide or join a guided hike organized by the Zermatt Guide Association.

But there are so many fine walks on marked trails that hiring a guide is scarcely necessary for the day-hiker. We describe several of

Zermatt

the more common and more spectacular walks, but we urge you to obtain a copy of the map described above and plan your own trips. The map is based on the fabulous sheets of the Swiss Federal Topographic Map series with red overprinting to indicate the hikers' trails. Best of all, the map back has a brief description of each marked path in English as well as German.

TRANSPORTATION

Zermatt is not the most accessible Swiss town and it is not really suitable for a day hike from any of the major cities. By train from Brig, at the junction of the Simplon route and the main line through the Rhone Valley, the journey is nearly two hours by cog railway. And Brig itself is nearly two hours from Lausanne by fast Intercity train. If you are traveling by car, you can't get all the way to Zermatt, anyway. You will have to leave your car at Visp or Täsch or somewhere in between and take the train. So, you should plan to spend a few days in Zermatt. Anything less would be a frustrating disappointment.

Fortunately, there is no lack of suitable places to stay; and accommodations are readily obtained on short notice in the summer season. Winter is still the big season, and there is excess capacity at other times of the year. The tourist office is just south of the railroad station. It has an illuminated list of hotels: those with space available are indicated by green lights. There are several quite reasonable and very comfortable places that cater to hikers. The youth hostel has 146 beds, and the Nature Friends house (Naturfreundehaus) is a large and modern hostelry with private rooms, open to the public so long as there is room.

MAPS AND GUIDEBOOKS

There is no shortage of maps and guidebooks to trails in the Zermatt area. The Zermatt Tourist Office has made certain that much of the material is published in English as well as German. For example, they have taken the Swiss federal map of the Zermatt area (number 5006) and added trails overprinted in red and filled the backside with short trail descriptions in both languages. The tourist office also publishes a pictorial aerial map that contains trail information in English, French, and German. These are available at the tourist office right next to the railroad station.

Guidebooks are rather more scarce. If you can read German, try the Kümmerly & Frey Schweizer Wanderbuch 8, *Vispertäler*. The Sierra Club totebook *Footloose in the Swiss Alps* contains a chapter on Zermatt. Both of these are available at the bookstore on the main street in Zermatt, about a block from the railroad station.

WEATHER AND CLIMATE

Zermatt features year-round skiing on the Theodul Glacier. This doesn't mean that the weather is always cold in Zermatt. It can be quite warm in the summer, especially in town. Daily average maximum temperature in July is 19° C (66° F) and the highest maximum on record is 30° C (85° F), not exactly tropical. At high elevations, of course, temperatures are lower, corresponding to the average 6 Celsius-degrees-per-1000-meter decrease (3 Fahrenheit degrees per 1000 feet). In winter months, average minimum temperatures are close to −7° C (20° F).

It is a rather cloudy area, but precipitation is not great, the anr.ual amount being 66 centimeters spread rather evenly through the year. At higher elevations, precipitation is somewhat more, with snow possible any time of year above timberline. Thunderstorms are rare, averaging about two per year.

Useful information

Tourist information

Verkehrsbüro, Bahnhofplatz. Tel. (028) 67 10 31.
Union Valaisanne du Tourisme, CH-1951 Sion 1. Tel. (027) 22 21 02. Tourist
    information for the canton of Valais.

Maps, guidebooks, and trail information

Association Valaisanne de Tourisme Pédestre, Union Valaisanne du Tour-
    isme, CH-1951 Sion 1. Tel. (027) 22 21 022. Sells maps and guidebooks.
    English spoken.
Buchhandlung Zermatt. On main street, south of railroad station. Full line
    of maps and guidebooks.
Bergführerbüro (Mountain Guide Office). Tel. (028) 67 34 56.

Local transportation

No tourist automobiles are permitted in Zermatt. Local transportation is by
    electric taxi, horse-drawn taxi, or walking.

Accommodations

Numerous hotels and pensions at all price levels. Electric map at tourist office on Bahnhofplatz shows hotels that have available accommodations.
Youth Hostel. Tel. (028) 67 23 20. One hundred forty-six beds.
Naturfreunde-Ferienheim Zermatt. Tel. (028) 67 27 88.

Miscellaneous

Weather forecast. Tel. 162.
Rettungsobmann SAC (Mountain Rescue Service). Bruno Jelk, Bergführer. Tel. (028) 67 22 82.

A walk in the shadow of the Matterhorn

DIFFICULTY	Grade 3–4, graded path, above timberline
DISTANCE	9 km
WALKING TIME	3–4 hours
MAP	Zermatt Tourist Office, *Zermatt Exkursionskarte* (contains brief trail descriptions in English)
GUIDEBOOK	None

No mountain in the Alps inspires as much awe as the Matterhorn. From some angles, the sheer upper faces actually appear to overhang the lower slopes. The illusion is powerful, even if you know that it is just an illusion. The view from close up may dispel that illusion but creates another equally powerful sense of majesty. The mountain appears to be sculpted from a single block of stone by some giant hand wielding a massive chisel. It is almost too perfect. But of course it *is* a perfect mountain and shows its perfection from every angle, every side.

The walk along the north face provides an intimacy with the mountain that complements the more distant, more traditional views. The walk is one that is made readily in just a few hours, using the gondola from Winkelmatten to Furi and on to Schwarzsee, eliminating a somewhat tedious 1000 meters of climb. From the center of

Schwarzsee and Trift

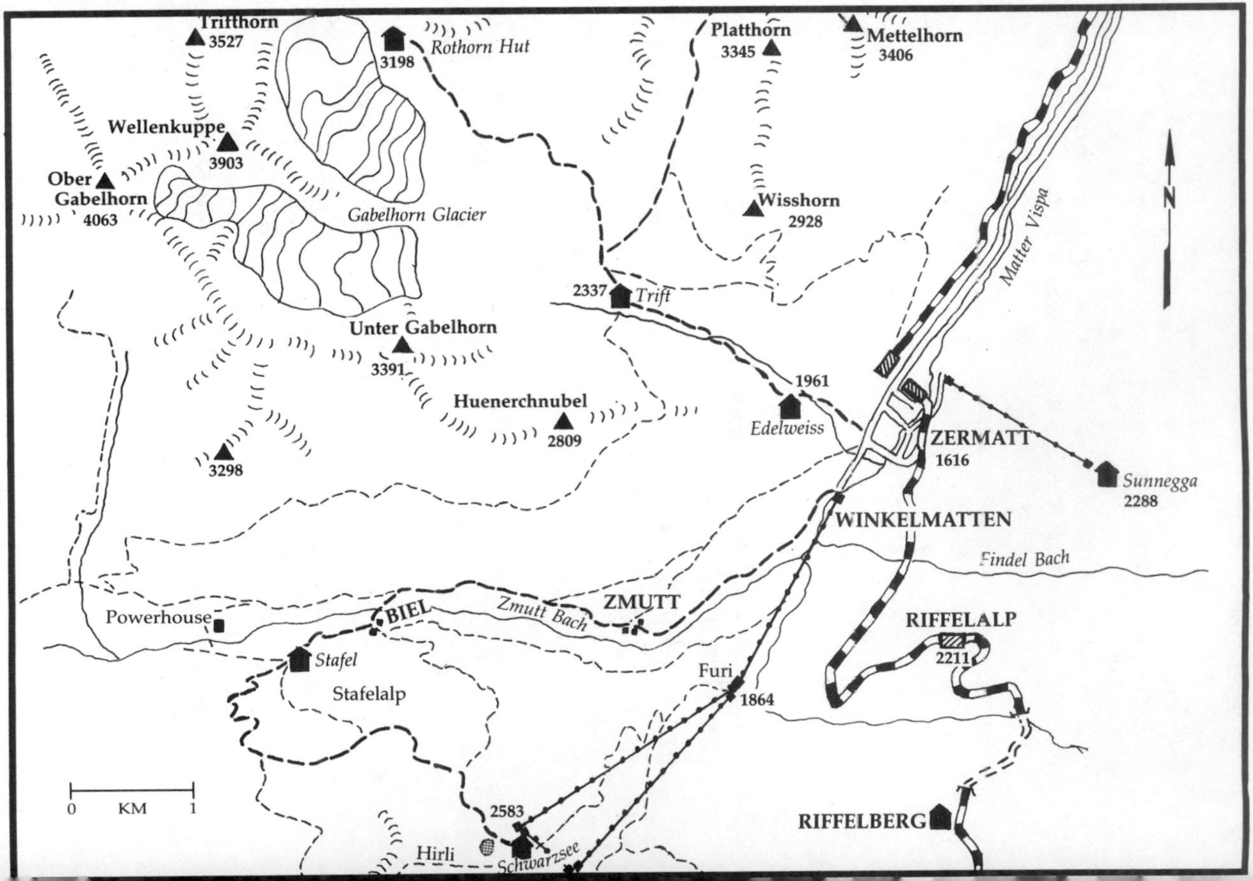

Mettelhorn
3406

Platthorn
3345

Wisshorn
2928

Trifthorn
3527

Wellenkuppe
3903

Ober
Gabelhorn
4063

Rothorn Hut
3198

Gabelhorn Glacier

Unter Gabelhorn
3391

Huenerchnubel
2809

3298

Trift
2337

1961

Edelweiss

Matter Vispa

ZERMATT
1616

Sunnegga
2288

WINKELMATTEN

Findel Bach

RIFFELALP
2211

RIFFELBERG

Furi
1864

ZMUTT

Zmutt Bach

BIEL

Stafel

Stafelalp

Powerhouse

2583

Hirli

Schwarzsee

N

0   KM   1

Zermatt, follow the signs to the Muttseilbahn Schwarzsee. The first twinned lifts carry you to Furi. From there, take the lift to Schwarzsee if it is running; otherwise, take the one to Furgg, and from there a short lift to Schwarzsee. (There is no shortage of lifts in Zermatt!)

At the top, there is the usual restaurant and hotel, which can be readily bypassed. But tarry a few minutes for the view of the Monte Rosa massif and, of course, the Matterhorn itself. Just to the west of the hotel, a trail sign indicates the way to the Schwarzsee, visible just below. The trail winds down between the two upper lakes, passing to the right of the tiny chapel, and past another tiny tarn, all the while heading toward the Zmutt Valley. The mountain immediately across the valley is the Unter Gabelhorn.

The path swings westward, crossing Stafelalp more or less on the contour before heading down to the Hotel Stafel. There are several paths traversing Stafelalp, but all of those leading downward eventually end up at the hotel. All the while, you have been traversing the north slope of the Matterhorn; you should stop now and then to view the ever-changing aspect of the mountain.

At Stafel, you have a choice: take the trail up-valley to the waterworks and electrical generating plant, crossing over to the north side of the valley at that point; or follow the road down-valley a half

The village of Zmutt

kilometer to Biel and cross over to the north side there. The up-valley route is about 1 1/2 kilometers longer, but affords interesting views of the barren terminal moraines of the Zmutt Glacier. Since there are numerous trails and service roads in the area, you must pay close attention to the trail signs.

Valaisian slate roof

After crossing the river, you join the Schönbiel trail (marked with orange paint) and follow it down-valley. The trail is well graded and maintained and much used. This north slope of the Zmutt Valley supports a profusion of wildflowers, an irresistible invitation to belly-down with the camera and run great quantities of film through the sprockets. Ahead you can see the tiny cluster of buildings that is Zmutt, a quintessential Valaisian farm community with slate roofs glinting in the sun and tiny barns sitting on elevated stone discs to keep four-footed creatures on the ground where they belong. Today, nearly every building seems to house a restaurant. A word of caution: be sure your order is clearly understood by the waiter or waitress; somehow they seem to have a way of misinterpreting your tentative German. Nevertheless, it is a delightful stop on a warm afternoon. And the view of the Matterhorn is certain to please.

At the second group of buildings, a choice presents itself: take the high road left to Hubel and Herbrigg; or follow the cobbled cart track that once was the main road between Zermatt and Zmutt. Either way brings you back to town in about an hour or hour and a half.

Views of Monte Rosa, Switzerland's highest peak

DIFFICULTY	Grade 4
DISTANCE	10 km
WALKING TIME	4 hours
MAPS	AK 1348, *Zermatt*, 1:25,000
	Zermatt Tourist Office, *Zermatt Exkursionskarte*
	(contains brief trail descriptions in English)
GUIDEBOOKS	Reifsnyder, William E. *Footloose in the Swiss Alps.*
	San Francisco: Sierra Club Books, 1974. The walk
	up from Zermatt to Gornergrat is described
	K&F Schweizer Wanderbuch 8, *Vispertäler*

The Gornergratbahn, the cog railway connecting Zermatt with the Gorner Ridge, ranks as one of the seven wonders of the tourist world, according to the Kümmerly & Frey *Wanderbuch* listed above. One may argue about its rank, but it is certainly one of the most

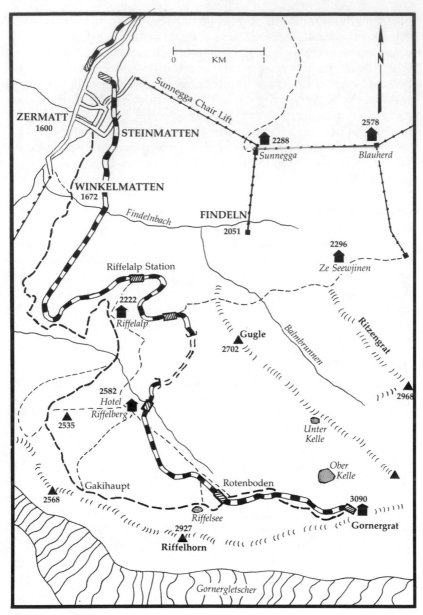

Gornergrat

spectacular cog railways we have ever been on. The top station is 5000 meters in a direct line from the center of Zermatt and 1500 meters higher. The track is 7 kilometers long, which makes the average grade better than twenty percent! It is a spectacular ride and one that makes the walk between Gornergrat and Zermatt possible for day-hikers who want to spend more time enjoying the views and less time struggling up a long and steep trail. We recommend, therefore, that you take the train up and walk down. This way you will face the Matterhorn most of the way. This strategy will maximize the likelihood that you will actually see the summit, which most of the time is shrouded in swirling mists.

Indeed, this is a trip you should save for good weather. The view from the Gornergrat is so spectacular that the very best day should be reserved for it. From the station in Zermatt (opposite the main rail station), the train grinds its way steeply upward, soon crossing the narrow defile of the Findelenbach on a high bridge. Above the Riffelalp station, the track is above timberline, affording ever-changing views of the Matterhorn and the high peaks on every side. But the real view is from the top; no fewer than twenty-seven *Viertausender*, peaks higher than 4000 meters, are visible from this vantage point. Far below lies the Gorner Glacier; if you look sharply, you will be able to see the Monte Rosa hut on a point of land that lies

The Gorner Glacier

The Matterhorn

between the main glacier and the tributary Grenz Glacier. Towering
above this sea of ice and rock lies the massive dome of Monte Rosa
itself, at 4634 meters the highest peak in Switzerland.

To the west, the pyramid of the Matterhorn dominates the skyline, but is somehow less impressive than when seen from a lower
elevation. No matter in which direction the eye roves, it is filled with
the incredible array of peaks and glaciers and steep-walled valleys.
It is easy to understand why this region has been the premier climbing attraction of the Alps for more than a century, for the sheer
beauty and wonder of it.

From the Gornergrat, a gondola cableway proceeds to the
Stockhorn, but the view from there is scarcely more grand than that

from the Gornergrat itself. But our sights are now set on the downward journey. From the railroad station, a broad trail (no sign!) heads downward, staying on the south side of the tracks. Just beyond a small knoll to the left, avoid the trail branching to the right crossing the rail line. Continuing straight ahead, the trail zig-zags sharply down a ridge, crosses the tracks, and passes a signed trail junction. From here, the trail follows the tracks on the north side to the Rotenboden station (2815 meters).

From here you have the choice of taking the direct path to Riffelalp via Riffelberg or, as we suggest, taking the trail to Gakihaupt that veers away from the tracks and follows the ridge above the glacier. This is rather more scenic and somewhat less traveled. The trail drops down to a group of rocky tarns, past a four-way trail junction. The ponds make fine reflecting pools for the Matterhorn, an invitation to stop for picture taking. All along here, there are multiple pathways, indication of the heavy use this region has sustained over the years. But the way down is clear and pathfinding poses no problems. The route follows the brook that drains the lowest lake. The main problem is deciding just when and where the best view of the Matterhorn is to be had. Be sure you have lots of film!

At Gakihaupt, a marked trail diverges right to Riffelberg. Shortly beyond this junction, the brook disappears down a cliff to the glacier far below, while the trail swings northward away from the ridge. It now crosses an extremely steep, grassy slope with extensive views of the Mattertal and its farms and villages. Soon the buildings at Riffelalp come into view. The first hotel here was built by Alexander Seiler, founder of the Seiler hotel dynasty. Unfortunately, it burned to the ground on February 16, 1961.

From here, you can go straight ahead to the Riffelalp station and follow a marked trail down to Winkelmatten and Zermatt, or take the trail left (as we did) that takes a somewhat more circuitous but more scenic route. If you are hungry or thirsty, there is a small restaurant here. The trail quickly enters a fine larch forest, reaches another trail junction (follow signs to Winkelmatten), and continues down to a portal of the cog railway. We seem to be on the wrong side of the tracks, but that is because we crossed over the tunnel without realizing it. The trail swings back to the right, zig-zags down through the forest, and soon reaches and crosses a paved road (sign). Stay on the trail, which eventually reaches and follows a dirt track to Winkelmatten and Zermatt.

Up the Trift Valley
to Trift and the Mettelhorn

DIFFICULTY	Grade 5
DISTANCE	5 km (Trift) or 13 km (Mettelhorn)
WALKING TIME	3 hours (Trift) or 8 hours (Mettelhorn)
MAP	Zermatt Tourist Office, *Zermatt Exkursionskarte* (contains brief trail descriptions in English)
GUIDEBOOK	None

Jack and Ann Middleton, hikers and climbers with many years' experience on Zermatt trails and peaks, recommended this scramble. It is a long day's climb, with a short stretch of glacier to cross, and some rock scrambling, but without any technical climbing. Anyone with some experience on steep, rocky trails should find that this climb will pose no problems; nevertheless, *Trittsicherheit*—surefootedness—is required. The climb is a long one and will take a full day to negotiate the 1800 meters of vertical rise. So, get an early start if you plan to reach the summit.

If you don't have a full day, the views from the Trift Valley are exceptional. The walk to the mountain hotel at Trift will take only two hours; the vertical climb is 720 meters.

From the railroad station, go right up the main street to the Hotel de la Poste, then take the road right (sign) toward the sharp defile of the Trift Bach. The trail zig-zags sharply up the north side of the brook, then crosses over and quickly reaches the recently refurbished Edelweiss Restaurant (marked Alterhaupt on the Zermatt map). This is about 350 meters above the town. The trail continues up the valley, crosses over to the north side, and reaches the alp at Trift at an elevation of 2337 meters.

For the climb up the Mettelhorn, continue on the trail up-valley a few hundred meters to a small plateau and trail junction, at which the trail to Rothornhütte branches left. (This is a good, marked path that leads to a hut operated by the Swiss Alpine Club; it is a suitable alternative to the Mettelhorn climb). From the junction, the trail to the summit turns eastward and climbs through the Triftkumme, a great glacial cirque that culminates at a saddle at an elevation of 3166 meters. From here, the summit of the Mettelhorn is visible to the east. The route crosses a small glacier and climbs to the top on a narrow and rocky pathway that requires surefootedness.

The view from the top is panoramic, in many ways more spectacular than that from the higher peaks. To the north, the great tower of the Weisshorn, some 1000 meters higher, dominates the skyline. To the west, the lower but closer Zinalrothorn spawns the Hohlicht Glacier. Stretched along the Italian border to the south are the Matterhorn, Breithorn, and the Monte Rosa massif—a full circle of 4000-meter peaks, a truly magnificent spectacle.

The route down follows the route up, at least to Trift. From there, an alternative path to Zermatt branches north to Balmen via Schweifinen. It is a kilometer or so longer, but offers a new set of views to the north and east.

4. Interlaken and the Berner Oberland

Interlaken must be close to the centroid of Switzerland. Go 150 kilometers in any direction and you will be in another country. Interlaken occupies a felicitous location between two attractive lakes, the Thunersee and the Brienzersee. The town grew up "between the lakes" from its beginning as an Augustine monastery in the twelfth century (traces of the monastery are still visible at the castle). If this were all, Interlaken would be a tourist mecca, but it has much, much more: it is the gateway to one of the most popular tourist areas in all of central Europe—the great north flank of the Berner Oberland and the Yosemite-like Lauterbrunnen Valley just below. One of the "obligatory" tours for anyone visiting the tourist attractions in Switzerland is the cog-railway ride to the Jungfraujoch, the high pass between the Jungfrau and the Mönch.

One of the attractions of this rather expensive ride is the stop at the Eigerwand. After burrowing through the solid rock of the Eiger for several kilometers, the train stops to permit passengers to walk a few meters to a lookout cut into the very center of the Eiger north face. It gives one an eerie feeling to be at this most dangerous location, where many climbers attempted and failed to scale the wall before final victory in 1938. Two Germans and two Austrians in separate parties that joined and pooled efforts during the climb finally surmounted the sheer face. It was an event that was highly regarded by Hitler as exemplifying the superiority of the "master race." Be that as it may, there is no gainsaying the extraordinary difficulty of the climb, something one can begin to appreciate when peering out of the hole cut by the railroad men.

But we are not Eiger climbers and there is much that the day-walker can find in the area—so much so that you could take hikes for days and not repeat your route. Not all of the mountains are as high and steep as the Bernese giants. Many lower summits are surrounded by sloping benches that make for long and eminently satisfying ski runs. This also means that there are numerous ski lifts that run in the summer as well to help hikers scale the heights.

TRANSPORTATION

Interlaken lies on a spur line about 40 kilometers east of the main Bern–Milan route. Spur lines also run from Interlaken to Lauterbrunnen, up to Kleine Scheidegg, and over to Grindelwald. Starting point for the trains to Lauterbrunnen and the Jungfrau region is the Interlaken Ost (east) Bahnhof. There is a large parking lot at this station, if you have arrived by car. Buses run along all the major roads.

Indeed, the tourist can spend many hours just riding trains and tramways. But that is not our goal. The rails and cables provide access to a vast above-timberline expanse where, in summer, the hiker is king (or queen). So if your plans include or permit a few days of hiking in the vicinity of Interlaken, read on. We will take you on a long, long chair lift out of Grindelwald for a walk that includes a pretty mountain tarn and extensive views of the high peaks; a tramway ride to the broad ridge between Lauterbrunnen and Grindelwald and a level walk to Kleine Scheidegg; and a less frequented but nevertheless rewarding walk on a ridge high above Brienzersee. The possibilities are endless; once you get started, you may find it difficult to stop.

MAPS AND GUIDEBOOKS

As with most of the heavily touristed areas of the Alps, maps and guidebooks for the Berner Oberland abound. *Geo-Katalog*, a comprehensive catalog, lists twelve maps and thirteen guidebooks.

Many of them will be on sale in local bookstores, and the best thing to do is to browse and buy one that looks suitable. There are also English-language guides, mostly for rock-climbers. The English Alpine Club publishes *Selected Climbs in the Bernese Alps*, which contains some material of interest to mere walkers. *Footloose in the Swiss Alps*, a Sierra Club totebook, contains a chapter that includes the area around Lauterbrunnen and Grindelwald.

WEATHER AND CLIMATE

Because of the complex topography surrounding Interlaken, it is rather difficult to characterize its climate in simple terms. For example, the annual precipitation in the city is about 1.5 meters; only a few kilometers away, along the upper slopes of the Bernese Oberland, annual precipitation increases to 3 meters or more. Especially in this region, topography and elevation exert profound control over climate. Each valley has its own local climate.

The climate of Interlaken itself, situated on the narrow neck of land separating Thunersee from Brienzersee, has been characterized by the Swiss Meteorological Service as "on the whole mild and only slightly stimulating in its effects, as one would expect from its comparatively low altitude. Climatic conditions are especially good towards autumn." Indeed, Interlaken has a reputation as a health resort and is visited frequently for its benign and therapeutic climate, especially in summer and autumn. In terms of sunshine duration, it is intermediate between the gloomy North German Plain to the north and the sunny Rhone Valley and the south-facing slopes south of the main Alpine crest.

By contrast, Wengen, situated on a bench overlooking Lauterbrunnen Valley, has a climate characterized as somewhat more stressful. Wengen is substantially colder both summer and winter and has substantially greater precipitation, more of it falling as snow in winter months. Hiking at higher elevations (Wengen is at an elevation of 1300 meters compared with Interlaken's 600 meters) is thus restricted to summer and early fall months in the higher elevations. Because of the relatively drier and sunnier weather in early fall, September is an ideal month for hikers, although you should be mindful of the possibility of early fall snowstorms.

Useful information

Tourist information

Verkehrsverein Berner Oberland. Jungfraustrasse 36, CH-3800 Interlaken. Tel. 22 26 21. This regional tourist office has numerous publications on hiking in the Berner Oberland that are free for the asking.
Verkehrsbüro Grindelwald. Tel. 53 12 12.
Verkehrsbüro Interlaken. Tel. 22 21 21.
Verkehrsbüro Lauterbrunnen. Tel. 55 19 55.

Maps, guidebooks, and trail information

Berner Wanderwege. Sekretariat, Nordring 10a, Postfach 263, CH-3000 Bern 25. Tel. 42 37 66.

Local transportation

Berner Oberland Bahn (BOB). Interlaken Ost Bahnhof. Operates trains from Interlaken to Lauterbrunnen and Grindelwald. One of the numerous private railways in this region. Note that the Eurailpass is generally not valid for transportation on these private railroads.
Wengernalp Bahn (WAB). Private cog railway connects Lauterbrunnen with Grindelwald via Wengen and Kleine Scheidegg.
Jungfrau Bahn (JB). Private cog railway runs between Kleine Scheidegg and Jungfraujoch, mostly through tunnel.
Postal bus Lauterbrunnen–Stechelberg. Postal bus on hourly schedule connects points in the Lauterbrunnen Valley.

Accommodations

Youth hostels. Interlaken–Böningen Youth Hostel, Aareweg am See, 3806 Böningen. Tel. 22 32 53. Gimmelwald–Mürren Youth Hostel, near Restaurant Schilthorn, 3801 Gimmelwald. Tel. 55 17 04.
Nature Friends Houses. Naturfreundehaus Alpenhof, 3801 Stechelberg. Tel. 55 12 02. Naturfreundehaus Grindelwald, Terassenweg, Grindelwald.

Miscellaneous

Weather forecast. Tel. 162.

Kleine Scheidegg
and the north face of the Eiger

DIFFICULTY	Grade 3
DISTANCE	4–12 km
WALKING TIME	1 1/2–4 hours
MAP	AK 5004, *Berner Oberland*
	Exkursionskarte *Lauterbrunnen–Mürren–Wengen*, 1:33,333. Available from Lauterbrunnen Tourist Office. Trail descriptions in English, German, and French
GUIDEBOOKS	K&F Berner Wanderbuch 6, *Lütschinentäler* (yellow series)
	Reifsnyder, W. E. *Footloose in the Swiss Alps.* San Francisco: Sierra Club Books, 1974. Chapter 7, "From Montreux to Muotathal."

If there is a classic ramble in Switzerland, it must be the walk from Lauterbrunnen (or Wengen) to Kleine Scheidegg. The walk is usually combined with a ride on the Jungfraubahn cog railroad. Many tourists take the train to the Jungfraubahn for a closeup view of the glaciers, then debark at Kleine Scheidegg on the return trip and walk down on the trail that parallels the railroad. This is an extraordinary experience, so close to the fantastic north wall of the Eiger, with the towering giants of Mönch and Jungfrau scarcely less imposing and formidable. The walk will take about two and a half hours, all downhill on a broad, graded path. By all means do this if you are planning to ride the train to the Jungfraujoch.

But if you have already taken this trip and are looking for another fine walk in the vicinity, try this variation: ride the Männlichen ski lift from Wengen, then walk the trail south to Kleine Scheidegg, and walk back to Wengen or Lauterbrunnen on a less used but more scenic trail along the slope of the Trümmelbach.

If you are traveling by train from Interlaken, transfer at Lauterbrunnen to the Jungfraubahn after purchasing a ticket to Wengen. Wengen may have been the quintessential Swiss Alpine town in days past. Now it is a modern ski resort town, although it has managed to maintain a good deal of its earlier charm. At any rate, we won't tarry long. Head uphill to the base station of the Männlichen cable car, purchase a one-way ticket to the top, and you're on your way.

Jungfrau over Kleine Scheidegg

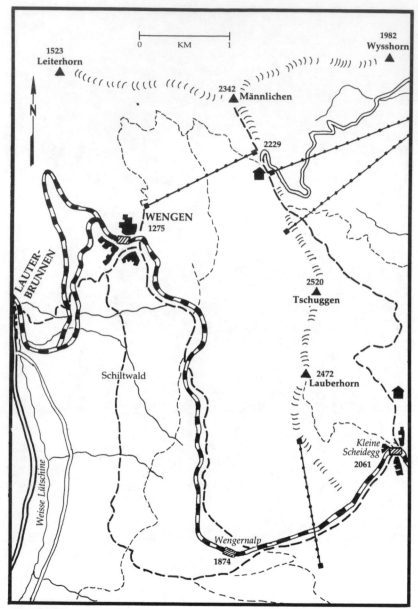

Männlichen and Kleine Scheidegg

There is a veritable city on top of the Männlichen Ridge. Ski lifts come up from both Grindelwald and Wengen. Aside from the ski lift structures, there is a large hotel and restaurant. Nevertheless, the broad, flat summit offers fine views of the mountains around, especially of the main peaks of the Bernese Oberland, and of the Lütschine valleys. The short walk north to the summit of Männlichen, a climb of only 100 meters, is worth the effort for the expanded 360-degree view.

Retracing the path to the lifts, continue southward on the well-graded trail directly toward Tschuggen, a craggy 2500-meter peak. The trail contours around the left side of the peak and soon passes under the cables of a chair lift. Soon the trail reaches a junction, with the right branch heading up the slopes of the Lauberhorn, another rounded summit with a ski lift to the top. Near the junction, there is a tiny restaurant, the Grindelwaldblick, perched on a rock with a straight-on view of the Eiger north wall. In a few minutes, the trail arrives at the hotels and railroad station at Kleine Scheidegg. The walk so far should have taken only about an hour.

The trail to Wengen and Lauterbrunnen starts out at the west end of the train platform, follows the tracks, and passes through the railroad yard (good signs throughout). The route, a broad gravel track, winds down first just below the railroad with extensive views of the north wall of the main range of the Bernese Oberland. To the left, high above at the Jungfraujoch, you can see the observatory glistening in the sun. Numerous glaciers cling to the north face here. On a warm summer day you can hear the crashing of great blocks of ice that break off the forward edges and tumble down the near-vertical slopes.

Just before the railroad station at Wengernalp, there is a spring with good water; a hundred meters past it is a trail junction. The normal route to Wengen passes underneath the railroad and more or less parallels the tracks on the upper side. We recommend a somewhat less traveled and more scenic route. From the trail junction, take the trail straight down the hill, marked "Mettlanalp 20 minutes." This path zig-zags rather steeply at first down the meadow, then heads on a straight line for the valley. Just below, on the other side of the valley, you can see the little town of Mürren. The path soon enters a grove of Norway spruce trees. The dark spruce make a beautiful contrast with the glistening white snow of the glaciers on the north side of the Jungfrau.

The trail, now a narrow gravel path, soon crosses a farm road. At Mettla, the trail enters a big meadow with fine views of the Lauterbrunnen Valley directly ahead. We are still close by the wall of the Jungfrau, and you should stop here occasionally and look back at the ever-changing aspect of the Eiger and the Mönch. The road is intersected again and the trail follows it, makes a switchback, and heads north toward Wengen. Here there is a signpost indicating that the left-hand trail at the trail junction at Wengernalp, which went to Biglenalp, has rejoined our path.

The trail now continues along a one-track gravel road, past the building at Mettlanalp. Just after the road turns northward, it reaches a trail junction, and a trail branches left away from the road with a trail sign indicating "Wengenstation 1 hour 10 minutes." Take the route left down the hill and soon reach, at the foot of the slope, another trail sign at a four-way trail intersection. Follow the sign to Wengen Station, crossing over the road and entering the woods. The trail winds downward, staying very close to the edge of the valley wall, following a fence line. Although most of the trail is in the woods, there are occasional viewpoints from which you can see the village of Lauterbrunnen far below. Indeed, one such viewpoint is built right at the top of a vertical cliff, and you can look straight down on the village. Wengen is also visible ahead just a little bit below the elevation along the trail here.

After crossing a small brook, we reach a viewpoint about 20 meters off the trail. A sign here tells us that we are on the right trail. After switchbacking down the slope and crossing a small brook, we meet another trail, unmarked, coming in from the left. We continue straight ahead toward Wengen. The trail now levels off and contours to the outskirts of the village, passing through meadows and by picturesque barns with views of the valley below and Wengen directly ahead. At the first dwellings—Schiltwald (1310 meters)—we reach a trail junction, which indicates that Wengen Station is twenty-five minutes directly ahead, or thirty minutes to the left, a trail that goes down. We'll follow straight ahead.

Soon we reach another junction, which indicates Wengen Station to the right. We pass Mary's Cafe and reach another intersection, which indicates a path to Lauterbrunnen to the left. Here you have a choice: walk through village streets to the railroad station in Wengen, or head on down to Lauterbrunnen. Trains are frequent, about every half hour, and there are good connections for Interlaken.

From First to Faulhorn

DIFFICULTY	Grade 4
DISTANCE	12 km
WALKING TIME	5 hours
MAPS	AK 5004, *Berner Oberland*
	K&F Exkursionskarte *Grindelwald*, 1:35,000
	Walking Map *Grindelwald*, 1:25,000. Available
	from Grindelwald Tourist Office
GUIDEBOOK	K&F Berner Wanderbuch 6, *Lütschinentäler*
	(yellow series)

"The longest chair lift in Europe" takes the Alpine hiker from the center of Grindelwald to the top of the First ("the ridge"), a 4-kilometer trip lasting thirty minutes and gaining 1100 meters in elevation. The short ride takes you from the bustle of touristy Grindelwald to peaceful Alpine meadows. The chairs are somewhat curious, for they face sideways. But this is rather a plus, for you are not looking into the hillside, but out toward the valley and across to the incredible view of the main wall of the Bernese Oberland—from the cliffs of the Wetterhorn, brooding over Grindelwald, to the Eiger, Mönch, and Jungfrau, and the peaks to the west.

The First chair lift is constructed in four sections. The chairs are not permanently fixed to the cable, but grip it like the platters of a Poma lift. At the junctions of the sections, a clever switching device enables the operator to switch the chairs from one section to another, so you stay on the same chair for the entire journey.

The top of First sits in a high meadow well above timberline at 2200 meters. The views of Grosse Scheidegg and Kleine Scheidegg and the mountains to the south are superb, although on a hazy day with early morning sun in the south the detail of the mountains is somewhat obscured. At the top, find the trail sign indicating the route to Bachsee and Faulhorn.

It is easy to see why skiers are enthusiastic about this run. Great open slopes extend all the way to Grindelwald. The runs are not as intimidating as those from the Hafelekar above Innsbruck, for example, yet they will challenge the moderate skier and provide hours of exhilarating running.

The trail to Bachsee leads straight ahead away from the Firstbahn, through a gate, and down into a little saddle with a trail sign.

At the end of the road below in the direction of Kleine Scheidegg lies Bachlager, a little group of farmhouses. Just below you can see a fine waterfall. For a short distance the path, marked white/red/white on the rocks, parallels a Poma lift that has two unusual right-angle

The view from the First chairlift

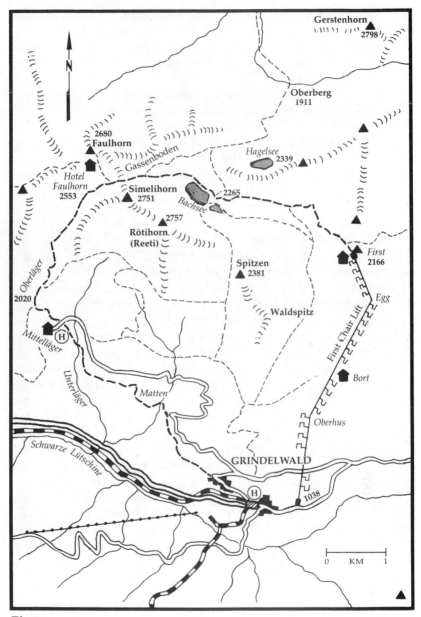

First

bends along its route. The path here has been severely eroded, apparently by a combination of human waffle-stompers and bovine hooves. At one time it appears to have been graded and paved with large flat stones, but the years have taken their toll and it now is extremely badly eroded.

On rounding a minor ridge, the trail changes direction and now heads north. This is the marked paint-blazed trail. Avoid the trail that heads to the left on the contour; our trail climbs slightly. The Poma lift takes yet another curve before reaching its top. All along this way, the views toward the forbidding north face of the Eiger and the string of mountains forming the main massif of the Bernese Oberland are visible in all their glory. Just beyond a fence, the trail that branched left comes in from the left, at a small shelter hut, the Hermehütte.

At a signed trail junction, a *Bergweg* branches right to Hagelsee, a tiny tarn over the ridge to the right. In five minutes we reach the two tiny ponds that form Bachsee at another trail junction. At this point the trail from Waldspitz enters from the left. (If time is short, you can take this trail back to Grindelwald, a three-hour walk.)

In 200 meters, between the two lakes, we reach another small hut and trail junction. The sign points the way ahead to Faulhorn and Schynige Platte, around the north side of the lake. The two tiny lakes provide a beautiful setting for the profusion of Alpine flowers that grow in the wet meadows nearby. At 2430 meters above sea level, we pass the Bergenahütte, a small shelter hut. A hundred meters beyond, we meet a trail junction. The trail to the right goes to Tierwang and Oberberg.

Just before reaching the pass, we come upon an open lean-to made of rock with a wood roof in a bad state of repair. At the height of land there is a trail junction and a sign. Here we head toward the Faulhorn and in a few minutes we can see the top of the mountain with its famous and rather imposing hotel. Just before the switch-back trail to the summit, we reach a trail junction, where the trail to Schynige Platte diverges left, essentially on the contour. After a short, sharp climb, we arrive at the hotel, where refreshments and overnight accommodations are available.

For the walk back to Grindelwald we retrace our steps from Faulhorn to the col and trail sign. We now follow the trail right to Bussalp. Near the col there are large permanent snowfields on which you can practice glissading with little fear of running off a steep cliff.

Here the route is marked with red paint blazes as well as yellow markings. We drop quickly down into the upper end of Bussalp and head toward the peaks of the Bernese Oberland. In contrast to the rather heavily used path from the First chair lift to the Faulhorn, this high basin and meadow are quite isolated and quiet with few visitors except for the ever-present cows.

This part of the walk is a feast of delights: clusters of summer farmhouses set in broad meadows; fields of Alpine flowers; and, across the valley, ever-changing views of the Eiger, Mönch, and Jungfrau. Here too, we see the Grindelwald Glacier in its entirety every time we lift our eyes from the trail. In about an hour, we reach the farm buildings at Oberläger, with its good spring with clear, ice-cold water. The trail passes between the buildings and reaches a trail sign.

We now follow a gravel road to a second group of houses and another spring. Here a trail sign indicates the trail to Burg, a promontory with a renowned view. We take the road down to the left, which is now paved. By paying attention to the red and white blazes you can short-cut the road by taking paths across the fields. The path is steeper of course, the road longer, a choice of shorter time versus wear and tear on the knees. The post office and bus station at Mittelläger are plainly visible below. The trail reaches them quickly after zig-zagging down through the meadows. Where the trail meets the paved road again, close to the bus station, there is another trail sign indicating we're at Bussalp Mittelläger. There is a restaurant at the bus station. Postal buses leave for Grindelwald approximately hourly in the late afternoon; check the posted schedule. On a fine day this is a great place to relax while waiting for the bus, or to take a respite before continuing the walk. The veranda of the restaurant faces the range from the Wetterhorn on the left, past Berglistock to the sharp spire of the Schreckhorn, and on to the Eiger north wall. You can just see the Mönch behind the Eiger. The Jungfrau is impressive, just to the right of the Mönch. This is a sight you will long remember, one that is not surpassed anywhere in Switzerland.

The trail to Grindelwald takes off at the intersection about 100 meters from the bus station and heads down through the meadow, always keeping below the road. At first it drops rather steeply in the meadow, then continues through the meadow a little more gradually, marked here by yellow blazes on the rocks (since this is no

Waterfall near Grindelwald

longer a *Bergweg* but a *Wanderweg*). Dark Norway spruce trees surround the large meadow and lush green grass. The upper stations of the Männlichen chair lifts are visible off to the right; then to the left, the little peak of the Tschuggen; then Kleine Scheidegg and the long north wall of the Bernese Oberland.

The trail continues down along the edge of the meadow to a gate in a wall and a *Wanderweg* sign. It crosses the brook and comes to another trail sign that indicates that the path goes to the right, parallel to the brook, which is what we follow. It soon crosses a gravel road, which it then more or less parallels for about 200 meters, then joins it and follows it to a barn. From here, the path continues straight down the hill. Now the route passes pretty much along the edge of the forest with meadows off to the right and picturesque high mountain barns in the meadows and views of the Eiger and Kleine Scheidegg. Once again the trail meets a gravel road at its end and follows this on down through the forest. The gravel track becomes a narrow paved road and continues to wind down toward Grindelwald past some beautiful trees and high mountain barns. The route leads past several interesting waterfalls. It soon meets the route that the postal bus takes and we follow this road on down.

We are now in the outskirts of Grindelwald, and there are several routes down, all of which eventually lead to the city center. If you take the Terassenweg, you will pass the Grindelwald youth hostel; just beyond, the street to the right leads down to the main street.

Alternative routes. There are several possibilities for shortening this walk. The first leads down from the top of the First chair lift. It follows ski routes and a paved access road and is not as scenic as the longer route, but is useful if time is short. The walk down takes about two and a half hours. From the top of the lift, you can also take the trail to Grosse Scheidegg, about one and a half hours, and there take the bus back to Grindelwald, or walk down the road. Total time for this walk is about four hours. At Bachsee, a good, marked trail leads to Bachläger and Waldspitz and thence down to Grindelwald. From the top of First, this will take about three and a half hours. From the First station, you can also take the trail direct to Bachläger and down, a walk of about three hours.

A panoramic view
of the Berner Oberland

DIFFICULTY	Grade 4
DISTANCE	10 km
WALKING TIME	4 hours
MAP	AK 1209, *Brienz*, 1:25,000
GUIDEBOOKS	K&F Berner Wanderbuch 9, *Brienzersee* (yellow series)
	K&F Schweizer Wanderbuch 41, *Schweiz— die 50 schönsten Wanderungen*

Brienzer Rothorn

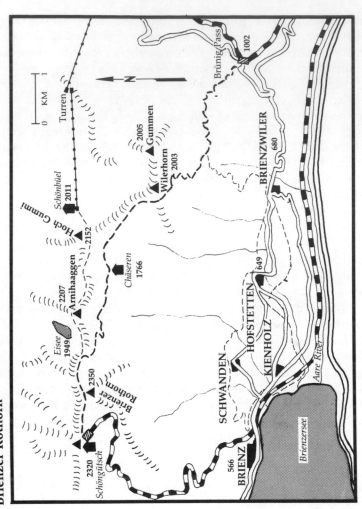

0 KM 1

N

Turren

Schönbiel 2011

Hoch Gummi

2152

Arnihaaggen 2207

Eisee 1949

2350

Brienzer Rothorn

2320

Schöngütsch

Chäseren 1766

Gummen 2005

Wilerhorn 2003

Brünig Pass 1002

BRIENZWILER 680

HOFSTETTEN 649

KIENHOLZ

SCHWANDEN

BRIENZ 566

Brienzersee

Aare River

Brienz is a city of wood-carvers. Most of the carved wooden bears one finds in the shops in Bern and Lucerne have their origin in the woodworking shops in Brienz. The town also has a lake that carries its name, and a magnificent waterfall, Giessbachfall, across the lake, which can be visited by boat and funicular. Tours leave from the main platform of the Brienz *Bahnhof*. But for us, the main attraction is the cog railway that climbs the Brienzer Rothorn at a spectacular maximum grade of twenty-five percent. The top of the rail line, at 2244 meters above sea level, is well above timberline and only 100 meters below the summit itself. It is also starting point for a marvelous high-route walk that keeps the main wall of the Berner Oberland always in view.

Brienz is on the main rail line between Interlaken and Lucerne with hourly service. From Interlaken, the ride is short, about twenty minutes; from Lucerne, it is about an hour longer, still feasible for a day trip. The cog railway starts from the main rail station in Brienz; the trip is an hour long. The train climbs in twists and turns that provide ever-changing views of the shimmering sea green Brienzersee, made that way by suspended minerals ground by the glaciers and carried to the lake by the Aare and Lütschine rivers.

The top station of the cog railway has the obligatory mountain restaurant, which in this case is reputed to be quite good. It is certainly worth tarrying here for at least a few minutes to absorb the view. The trail to the summit of the Brienzer Rothorn traverses the crest, climbing a mere 105 meters to reach the top. The view is truly panoramic: the Schwarzwald to the north; the low ridges of the Jura Mountains to the west; and the great sweep of the Alps to the south and east. It is a sight not soon to be forgotten.

From here, it is all downhill (or almost all). We are on the sunny south side of the mountain, the trail is good with gentle grades, and the views are ever-changing. What more could you ask? Well, if you ask for a stopping place for lunch, that can be arranged.

Near the halfway point stands the Chaserenhütten, with food, drink, and overnight accommodations. The trail continues on the contour around the west ridge of the Wilerhorn, a peak that barely makes it to 2000 meters. Soon the route turns south and switchbacks its way down the south slope of the Wilerhorn. At the little farm community of Wiler-Vorsasse, you have a choice: either head southward, zig-zagging downward to Brienzwiler and thence back to Brienz; or continue eastward to Brunig Pass, which is on the main line from Lucerne to Brienz. To either city, the train ride is fifty minutes.

If you are not feeling quite so adventurous or if the weather is bad above timberline, then walk to Brienzwiler, listed in *The 50 Most Beautiful Walks in Switzerland*. We won't vouch for that, but it certainly is a pleasant walk through forests and picturesque villages. From the Brienz Bahnhof, ascend the zig-zag path through the forest to Flueberg. Thence a path leads through beautiful meadows to Glyssen and, for a short distance on the road, to Unter Schwanden. Continue to Ober Schwanden and a fine view of Brienz Lake.

After crossing the Lammbach bridge, turn left. Here you can see something of the awesome power of nature on a rampage, the rubble of massive rock and mud torrents that destroyed the village of Kienholz some four hundred years ago. In 1896, a destructive mud slide was the impetus for the construction of massive torrent-control devices along the river bed. Shortly we pass through the village of Schried, then along the north side of the valley of the Fallbach to the valley town of Brienzwiler. Here there is a fine open-air museum with reconstructed buildings indigenous to various parts of rural Switzerland. It is worth a visit.

At western end of the tiny Weissensee, turn right and cross the highway at Hofstetten. Then, in about 150 meters, swing left to a meadow path that drops down to Balm. Continue to the shore of the lake, then head northward back to Brienz. This is a pleasant Grade 2 walk of about 11 kilometers, mostly through meadows and along farm roads.

5. Zürich

Zürich lies at the north end of Zürich Lake, in the valley formed by the ridges of Uetliberg on the west and Zürichberg and Adlisberg on the east. These are scarcely more than hills—the former is 874 meters high, the latter 676 meters and 701 meters, respectively—but they make for pleasant walking near town. Uetliberg even has a railroad to the top, if you want to forego the exercise getting there and spend the effort walking the numerous trails on the mountain.

The train to Uetliberg leaves the Selnau Bahnhof, about ten blocks south of the *Hauptbahnhof* near the Sihl River. It is a short run through woods to the end station, just below the summit. From the station, a path leads to the summit and a lookout and restaurant. A path leads southward over the summit ridge to various lookout points and other restaurants. It is a popular walk, worthwhile for the views of the Alps as well as Zürich and its lake.

On the other side of the city, the somewhat lower Zürichberg also offers pleasant walks and a possible tour of the Zoological Garden. Take the number 6 tram from the *Hauptbahnhof* to the end of the line at the zoo. From here there are trails up Zürichberg to the north and Adlisberg to the south, enough to keep you busy for a few minutes or a few hours.

But for longer walks, we suggest the modest climb to the top of Albishorn (the highest point of the ridge, the northernmost peak of which is Uetliberg) or a more adventurous climb to the summit of the Rigi, a forty-minute train ride from Zürich.

TRANSPORTATION

The city transportation system in Zürich is first rate, in common with most European cities. Most lines originate at the *Hauptbahnhof*. A brochure, *Bus Tram Information*, explains the tariff rules in five languages. But unlike some cities, several of the rail lines leading to the suburbs are privately owned, and not connected physically or farewise with the city system. These include the Forchbahn and the Sihltal-Zürich-Uetliberg-Bahn, about which more later.

MAPS AND GUIDEBOOKS

A good place to obtain maps and guidebooks for Zürich and surroundings and, indeed, for all Switzerland, is Adolph Barth & Co., Bahnhofstrasse 94, just a few yards from the railroad station. Kümmerly & Frey publishes a map, *Kanton Zürich—Chumm Use und Lueg*, that shows trails in the countryside around Zürich at a suitable scale of 1:50,000. A brochure, *Freizeit und Erholung im Kanton Zürich* ("leisure time and recreation in the canton of Zürich"), published by the Zürcher Kantonbank, is keyed to the map. It is available from offices of the bank and from the tourist office. The two private railroads publish brochures and maps, *Mit der Forchbahn hinaus in die Natur* ("out to nature with the Forchbahn") and the SZU/LAF Wanderkarte. The state railroad publishes a brochure, *Rundfahrt- und Wanderbillette Zürich* ("round-trip and hikers' tickets"), that describes in maps and German text numerous hiking trails accessible from Zürich. It is best used with a good map, such as the *Kanton Zürich* map described above. The Kümmerly & Frey Schweizer Wanderbuch 41, *Schweiz—die 50 schönsten Wanderungen*, describes a number of walks in the Zürich area.

WEATHER AND CLIMATE

Zürich lies in the Swiss *Mittelland*, a region of farms and wooded hills. Since it lies at the rather low elevation of 400 meters, winters are relatively mild with little persistent snow. Summers are warm and rather humid, with rain occurring on an average of thirteen July days. Thunderstorms are common in the height of the summer, with nine July days rumbling with thunder. Hiking is thus possible most of the year, except for the periods when snow is on the ground. Of course, the higher you go, the more likely you are to find snow on the ground throughout the winter.

Useful information

Tourist information

Verkehrsverein Zürich, *Hauptbahnhof*. Tel. (051) 25 67 00. In the main hall of the railroad station.

Maps, guidebooks, and trail information

Züricherische Arbeitsgemeinschaft für Wanderwege, Eggweg 5, CH-8620 Wetzikon. Tel. (01) 930 20 36. Trail information for the Zürich area.
Several bookstores on Bahnhof Strasse near the station carry hiking maps and guidebooks.

Local transportation

Verkehrsbetrieben Zürich (VBZ) operates buses and trams in the city. Purchase tickets at automats located at most bus and tram stops. Honor system is used; you may be asked for your ticket by a wandering checker. Information booklets and maps in English available at tourist office.
Sihltal–Zürich–Uetliberg Bahn (SZU) runs commuter trains south through the Sihltal from Zürich–Selnau station. Leads to good hiking country (see Albishorn walk). Published hikers' map available at SZU stations.
Forchbahn (FB), privately operated tram, connects downtown Zürich with the hill country east of Zürichsee. Trams leave the terminal at Stadelhofer Platz near the north end of the lake, a few blocks east of the Quai Bridge. Publishes a pamphlet, *Mit der Forchbahn hinaus in die Natur,* that describes numerous walks accessible from FB stations.
Fly-Rail is the special train service from the main terminal at the Zürich Airport to downtown. It is fast and convenient. It is also possible to board many Intercity trains right at the airport, and to check baggage to or from the airport baggage room. It is also possible to check your flight luggage from most Swiss railway stations through to your final destination at nominal extra charge.

Accommodations and restaurants

Hotels are numerous and expensive in Zürich. If you don't need the five-star
    Hilton International, try the Scheuble (Mühlegasse 17, tel. 251 87 95) or
    the Limmathof (Limmatquai 142, tel. 47 42 20). The latter is just across
    the Bahnhof Bridge from the train station; not fancy but reasonable and
    convenient.
Youth Hostel Zürich, Mutschellenstrasse 114. A modern, 400-bed facility,
    run as you would expect the Swiss to run a hostel. One of the best
    hostels we have stayed in anywhere. Some distance from downtown,
    but right on the number 77 bus line.
Camping. Seebucht, Wollishofen, on the west shore of Zürichsee. Tel. (051)
    45 16 12.
Restaurants. There are plenty of expensive restaurants in Zürich, but there
    are plenty of inexpensive ones also. The Mövenpick chain has fourteen
    restaurants in Zürich, all different, but all serve good food at reasonable
    prices. If you want to try real Swiss fondue, find one of the specialty
    restaurants that are scattered around town.

Miscellaneous

American Consulate, Zollikerstrasse 141, CH-8008 Zürich. Tel. (1) 55 25 66.
Weather forecast. Tel. 162.

Rigi—
A spectacular view of three lakes

DIFFICULTY	Grade 3
DISTANCE	8 km
WALKING TIME	4 hours
MAP	K&F *Rigi Wander- und Skitourenkarte*
GUIDEBOOK	The K&F Rigi map contains trail information on the backside, in English

The Rigi is one of the most famous mountains in Switzerland, largely,
we suspect, because it is so near to Zürich. There is no doubt that the
view from the top is a fine one, actually benefiting from its relatively

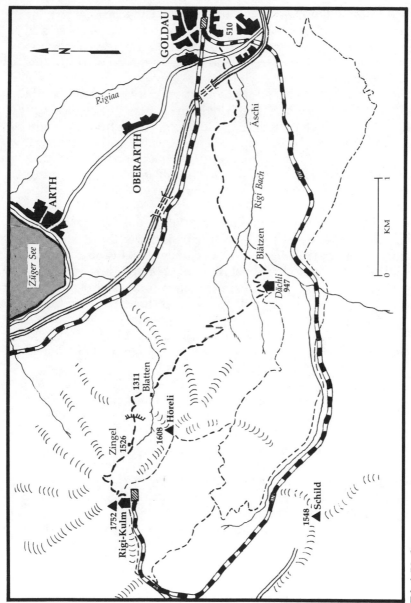

Rigi-Kulm

low elevation of 1797 meters. And the three lakes surrounding the mountain add to its scenic beauty. But all that scarcely seems to justify the two cog railways and one aerial tramway that connect top and bottom. Tradition, probably fostered by the railways and the hotels on top and slopes, has it that one should see the sunrise from the top. We can't vouch for tradition, but we can say that the view in good weather is worth the climb by shank's mare. We suggest that you make the climb on foot from Goldau, an hour from Zürich by train, and take the cog railway down (or walk the entire distance, if you have the time and inclination). Trains leave hourly for Arth/ Goldau (express trains marked "Chiasso/Milano"). At this writing, they leave at four minutes past the hour, but you should check the schedule.

At the Arth/Goldau railroad station follow the signs to the Rigi-Bahn, the cog railway to Rigi-Kulm, crossing over the tracks of the main line and into the Rigi station. Continue straight ahead through the station and out to the street. Bear right on this street and walk about 100 meters to a cross street. Here on the other side of the street there is a watering trough with good water. Just above the trough you can see the church. Look for a *Wanderweg* sign that indicates the white/red/white route "Rigi-Kulm, 4 hours." We now cross the main road and wander upward to the right. From here the route is well marked with yellow trail signs on posts.

The trail soon crosses under the autobahn. The paved road quickly becomes a single-lane gravel track that leads straight ahead up the hill, passing several large barns, and swings around to the right, more or less parallel to a high-voltage line. The route along here is marked with an occasional *Wanderweg* sign, a yellow diamond, on the electric poles. The dirt track passes first under one set, and then under a double set of steel-tower high-tension lines, crossing high pastures all the time. The cog railway, the Rigibahn, can be seen climbing up the slope to the left.

Near the edge of the meadow, just before the steep portion of the hill ahead, a trail sign indicates Goldau (whence we came), and Rigi Dächli straight ahead. This is at Blatzen, 773 meters, and we are now 275 meters higher than our starting point, but with 1000 meters yet to go. From here the way is marked with yellow paint blazes on various posts.

Just before starting up the slope the path crosses the boundary of a cantonal plant protection area, which is marked with red/white arrows. The route now becomes a footpath and enters the woods, starting to climb a steep slope by switchbacks. The way here is through a mixed forest, mostly Norway spruce and maple. The steep gorge of the Rigi Brook is on our left. We now pass through a meadow and reach a trail junction sign indicating Arth to the right, Rigi-Kulm to the left. We turn left and are soon at the Rigi Dächli, a restaurant and guest house.

The trail makes a U-turn and continues up the hill behind the building. After one switchback we reach an old cableway. Here, just under the cableway, there is a sharp switchback to the right. Trail signs on a tree, just near the house at the top end of the cableway, indicate Rigi-Kulm straight ahead. (This path also goes to the top, and is a possible part of a circle route to this point. See the map.) Our route bends to the right and in about 50 meters you will see a white/red/white trail blaze.

The trails and old logging roads in this area are somewhat confusing. However, we stay on the white/red/white-marked trail, and avoid the paths marked to Resti. We eventually head northward up a gentle grade on a somewhat narrower path than we were on lower down. We soon cross a narrow gorge on a wooden bridge and continue to climb on a gentle grade through a mixed forest of Norway spruce and European beech that has been opened up by logging. The fruits of the forester's art can be seen here: young trees growing up in the shade of the trees left after the logging.

In a short distance the trail is interrupted by a classic avalanche path. This one appears to have been followed by a rock avalanche (*Steinlawine*) when the path became wet in spring. The trail then takes one long zig, crossing the top end of the avalanche path before zagging back to our original northwestward course. In one place the trail has been blasted through a little narrow ridge, about 3 meters high, which shows the conglomerate of which the mountain is composed. This is a mixture of sand and variously sized rounded stones, obviously worn by churning waters and glued into a coarse matrix by the pressure of overlying rocks.

The trail now climbs somewhat more steeply while continuing in the same northwest direction. After a brief pitch we cross a small brook and reach a gate that leads into a high pasture at Blatten. The trail continues along the right side of the pasture, along the fence line, marked with some white/red/white metal markers and a trail sign that indicates Zingel and Rigi-Kulm straight ahead. The pasture itself is on a broad, sloping bench that lies between the summit cliffs to the west and the sharp drop-off to the valley to the east. Despite its nearness to civilization, it is surprisingly isolated by the cliffs on either side, a short vertical scarp at the upper end, and the very steep wooded slope at the lower end.

At the upper end of the pasture, we pass through another gate. Here the trail is not clearly defined because of the many cow paths. However, just beyond this gate to the left there is a trail sign on a tall Norway spruce that points right to Zingel and Rigi-Kulm. Just above this is the little scarp. Head straight up the hill and about 50 meters up from the sign find a flat rock with a white/red/white blaze on it. Stay to the right side of the pasture, following the fence line up until you encounter a clear path. This path heads leftward toward the scarp, through the center of the meadow, and directly to an easy way up.

From this point you can see the fence at the top of the Rigi-Kulm, as well as another trail that contours along the slope about halfway between our point and the top of the ridge. Our path climbs the scarp on a little ledge that has been blasted out of the rock and crosses through a gate into a upper pasture. The trail follows the fence line at the top of the scarp. Here there is a tree with a white/red/white metal blaze. Follow the fence line around to the right. Trees here do have blazes and the path is reasonably clear.

Follow the little knoll with a wood cross on top around to the left on a clearly marked path with painted blazes. Soon you will reach the farmhouse at Zingel, where you can quench your thirst with a cool drink of clear spring water. Typical of many Swiss mountain farms, this one is supplied by a cableway that runs to the valley below. We pass by the side of the building that is the upper terminus of the cableway and continue up the right side of the meadow along the fence line marking the top of the cliffs.

The views of the Züger See to the right over the cliffs are spectacular. The little lakeport of Arth and the larger town of Goldau spread out over the flat former lakebed. Farms and pastures dot the countryside. You can clearly see the Zürich Autobahn and the mainline railroad far below.

We follow the fence line as it bends leftward around toward the summit. Here again the trail is marked with white/red/white blazes on rocks. The pasture narrows at its upper end and the fence finally runs out at the rock cliff. The path crosses to the other side of the fence and heads steeply up the steep north slope, zig-zagging through grassy patches and over the rocks. This portion is steep and exposed; though the pathway is clearly marked and the footing secure, caution should be exercised. The drop off to the north side is very steep indeed.

After a short, sharp climb, the trail comes out on the flat grassy top of the Rigi. Signs of civilization are everywhere: paved paths, a television transmitting tower, lookout points with protective railings, and, of course, tourists. There are also cows at the top, at least there were on our visit. The panoramic view from the top is certainly one of the finest in central Switzerland. To the north lies the Züger See, which has been much in our view on the way up. But it pales in comparison with the Vierwaldstättersee (Lake of the Four Forest Cantons—Lake Lucerne), which occupies a half circle of foreground to the west and south. Lucerne itself is due west and seems very close; Zürich is 40 kilometers to the north.

Just below the summit lies the famed Rigi Hotel, built a hundred years ago when the cog railway was finished. (The Vitznau line was the first cog railway to be built in Switzerland and was completed in 1871. It postdates the cog railway on Mt. Washington in New Hampshire by two years; the Swiss railroad engineer Riggenbach visited Marsh's creation and returned to the Rigi to build an improved version.)

The elegance of the summit hotel certainly impressed the early visitors. The railroad terminus is a few feet below the level of the hotel and a hundred meters away. To protect the patrons from the sometimes-inclement weather on the summit, the builders blasted a tunnel from the station building to a point beneath the hotel. From that point, an elevator rises to the lobby. So it is possible to climb the Rigi, stay overnight, and watch the sunrise without ever having left the protection of man-made structures. We must admit that the weather on Alpine summits, even in midsummer, can be pretty terrible. Perhaps the tunnel was not such a bad idea.

The walk up takes about four hours; the ride down takes forty-five minutes. If you decide on the ride, you have two choices: either back to Goldau, and the train back to Zürich; or to Vitznau and a boat ride to Lucerne with train connections to Zürich. Total elapsed time for the former is about two hours; for the latter, about four hours. Connections are good, but check the timetables posted in the station at the top. Either way, the trip is scenic and rewarding.

Albishorn—
A mountain walk in the outskirts of Zürich

DIFFICULTY	Grade 2
DISTANCE	12 km
WALKING TIME	5 hours
MAP	Wanderkarte *Sihltal-Zürich*. Published by and available from SZU-Bahn ticket office
GUIDEBOOK	K&F Schweizer Wanderbuch 41, *Schweiz— die 50 schönsten Wanderungen*. Walk 21, Sihlwald–Albiswald

The Zürichsee so dominates the geography in the immediate vicinity of Zürich that few visitors realize that scarcely a kilometer from the south shore of the lake lies a pretty and very unspoiled valley— the Sihltal. Through this valley runs a remarkably clear trout-filled river, heavily wooded for nearly its entire length despite its flowing through one of the most populated districts in Switzerland. The Sihl River has its origin high in the Glarnisch Alps southeast of Zürich. After flowing north into the Sihlsee, the river turns northwestward and flows more placidly, paralleling the Zürichsee a short distance away.

Near Zürich, the river is bounded on the southwest by the long Albis Ridge. From Uetliberg, whose foot is practically in the heart of the city, to Sihlbrugg, 16 kilometers away, where the ridge meets the river, a fine trail traverses the very top of the ridge. Numerous side trails reach up from the Sihl Valley, making access easy and numerous walks possible. Access to the valley itself is made convenient by the Sihltal line of the Sihltal-Zürich-Uetliberg-Bahn, a privately owned railroad. The Zürich terminus is the Selnau railroad station, on the number 8 tram line. The tracks follow the river closely, most of the way only a few meters from the shore. (In the summer, an old-fashioned steam train makes excursion trips along the river. Check at Selnau station for details.)

With the special *Wanderkarte* that can be obtained from the ticket office at the Selnau station, you can plan any number of trips along the river or up the Albis Ridge. We have selected one such route, from Sihlwald up the ridge to Albishorn, the highest point, then down to Sihlbrugg Station and back to Sihlwald along the river.

The Sihlwald railroad station

At Sihlwald (twenty minutes from Selnau), find trail signs near the south end of the station. The route passes Forsthaus Sihlwald, crossing the road on a footbridge. Turn left, following the signs indicating Schnabel. In about 20 meters, take the gravel path up the hill, marked with a sign to Albishorn and blazed with yellow *Wanderweg* signs. The path climbs on a moderate grade through logged areas that are full of raspberry and blackberry plants. If you are here at the right season, you can have a veritable feast. The trail levels off and soon comes to a trail junction at one of the many woods roads that are used in managing the forests. Our trail to Schnabellücken (Schnabel Pass), the so-called Spinnerweg, goes straight ahead. (A shorter trail to Albishorn goes to the left.)

After walking perhaps a half kilometer more, we cross another woods road (Terrenstrasse). The Spinnerweg continues straight up the hill. After climbing steadily for another half kilometer, the path levels off and crosses another forest road. This is marked by a sign, the Waldmattstrasse. Ever since leaving the railroad station, we have been walking through a carefully managed forest. The care with which Swiss foresters manage their forests for timber production is evident everywhere, from the fenced areas to protect new seedlings from the ravages of hungry deer to the cutover areas with a few large trees left standing to provide seed and cover for the new crop. We are now passing through a mixed forest of large Norway spruce and beech trees, an open forest with a beautiful carpet of ferns on the forest floor.

A short, steep climb puts us on the ridge and the junction with the Albis Ridge trail at Schnabellücken. We have gained about 300 meters in elevation since leaving the station about an hour ago. We follow the path left along the ridgetop, here a broad gravel path marked with white stripes. We now pass through a magnificent old beech forest with trees up to 70 centimeters in diameter. About halfway up to the top of the ridge there is a developed spring with good, cold water. A few minutes after leaving the spring, the trail reaches the ridgetop at Bürglen, at 915 meters above sea level the highest point of the Albis Ridge.

Although the ridge is forested, it has a very sharp crest with

Albishorn

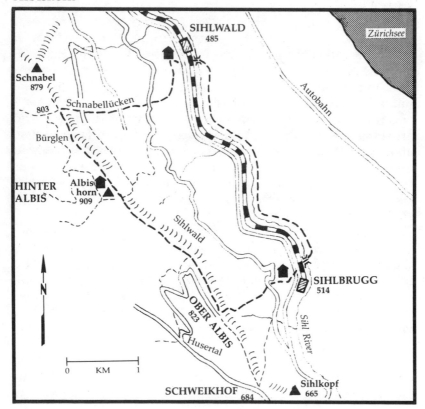

extremely steep sides, especially on the northeast side. However, there are openings from which extensive views can be enjoyed. Even on the ridge, there is evidence of logging and other forest management activities. However, the work is done so carefully that it is scarcely noticeable to the casual observer.

In about 1 kilometer, we reach the summit of Albishorn. Here there is a trail shelter with a fine view of the Zürichsee and the Sihl Valley. Nearby is the Bergrestaurant Albishorn, a fine place for lunch or a snack. (N.B.: the restaurant is closed on Friday.) The ridge path leads around the restaurant and down to a trail sign indicating "Sihlbrugg Station 1 1/2 hours" straight ahead along the ridge; and the Sihlwald station via the direct route down the ridge, about one hour.

From Albishorn south, pastures come up very nearly to the ridge, especially on the right side. Soon we see the little farming community of Ober Albis on the right, and reach a trail junction, with the right-hand branch leading to the tiny village of Husertal.

Just beyond Ober Albis, the trail enters pasture for about 100 meters before reentering the woods. The path now leaves the ridge, heading gently down the left side, passes a road that comes in from the left, and meets a signed intersection. Stay on the route marked with yellow blazes on the trees, avoiding unmarked farm roads. We are now on a somewhat broader gravel road. At a switchback in this road, note the trail junction to the right with a sign indicating Sihlbrugg Dorf and Schweikhof as well as Sihlbrugg Station. Ignore this trail and follow the road. Fifty meters farther along, the road comes to a T, with a sign indicating Sihlbrugg Station either way. Take either route, but be careful to follow the yellow diamonds indicating the marked route. Walking time to the station is about forty minutes by either route. It is, of course, possible to catch the train back to Zürich from here, but the walk along the river back to Sihlwald is so pleasant that we recommend that you take it.

From the station follow the road toward Zürich for about 200 meters, staying on the right side of the road until you come to an underpass with a *Wanderweg* sign. It goes under the railroad and crosses the river on a footbridge. Just on the other side of the river, turn left at a trail marker that indicates the path to Sihlwald. The path, paved here, passes between the river and an electric switching station. At the end of the switching station it becomes a gravel path along the river. It alternately goes through the woods and right along the river. Avoid the woods road that parallels the river and stay close to the water's edge. Finally at Schüepenloch, the track turns into a one-lane paved farm-access road. Two hundred meters past a camping area, the road bends to the left, crosses the river, and is back at the railroad station. Trains to Zürich (Selnau Bahnhof) run hourly, at fifteen minutes past the hour.

Three of Switzerland's fifty most beautiful walks

Kümmerly & Frey, Switzerland's largest publisher of hiking and climbing guides and maps, includes in its catalog *Schweiz—die 50 schönsten Wanderungen*, the fifty most beautiful walks in Switzerland. Picking the top fifty may seem like an impossible task, for almost any fifty chosen at random would qualify for someone's list. Nevertheless, we can attest from personal experience that it is a good list, one that includes rewarding walks in every area of the country, not just the spectacular Alpine region. Anyone who does all fifty will have experienced at first hand much of what makes Switzerland a unique and exciting place for the perambulating tourist.

A half dozen or so are accessible for day trips from Zürich. We have described two of them in detail: Rigi-Kulm and Albishorn. Here we describe three more in somewhat less detail for the adventurous day-hiker based in Zürich. These include Lägeren, the easternmost mountain of the Jura chain; Hohenklingen Castle above Stein-am-Rhein; and Gottschalkenberg above the Ägerisee.

A walk along the Lägeren, the eastern outpost of the Swiss Jura

DIFFICULTY	Grade 2
DISTANCE	15 km
WALKING TIME	5 hours
MAP	K&F Freizeitkarte *Kanton Zürich*
GUIDEBOOK	K&F Schweizer Wanderbuch 41, *Schweiz— die 50 schönsten Wanderungen*

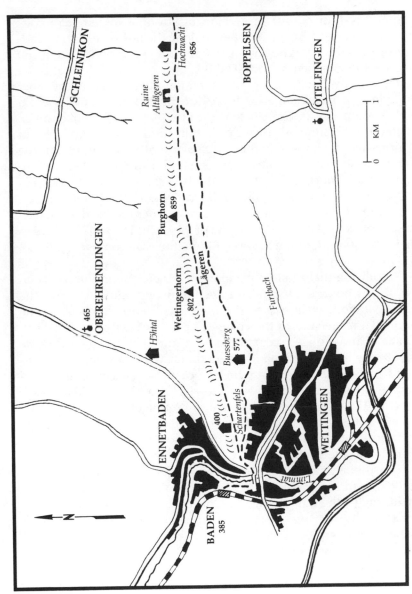

Lägeren and Burghorn

The Swiss Jura consist of a chain of strongly folded calcareous mountains stretching in a gentle arc along the northwestern boundary of the country. The southern terminus, La Dôle (1677 meters) overlooks Lake Geneva, and is the subject of one of the walks described in this book. Baden, in the canton Aargau, lies at the other end, only a few kilometers from Zürich. Baden ("baths") was a well-known spa in Roman times, called Aquae Helvetiae, much visited for the curative powers of its hot, sulfurous springs. The hot springs are still important for the life of the city and are still utilized today in the treatment of rheumatism and respiratory disorders.

There is more to Baden than the baths, however. The ruins of the Castle of Stein perch on a hill overlooking the Limmat River. And there is an interesting covered bridge across the river, which we utilize at the beginning and end of the walk. The walk itself takes us to the summit of the Lägeren Ridge, the easternmost summit of the Jura.

From the main railroad station in Zürich, trains run to Baden every half hour; the trip takes fifteen to twenty minutes. From the Baden station, walk east to the river and thence south along the Limmat Promenade to the covered bridge. Cross over to Bailiffs' Castle (Landvogteischloss), a medieval turreted and gabled castle that today houses a small museum that is worth a visit. Walk eastward and upward to Schartenfels, a castlelike structure that has a restaurant with a fine view of the city. From here, a path leads eastward along the Lägeren Ridge to Wettingerhorn (802 meters), thence to the highest point, Burghorn (859 meters). The open summit affords magnificent views of the Schwarzwald to the north and the Alps to the south.

Further along the ridge, we come to Altlägeren ruins, destroyed in 1268, and Hochwacht (856 meters), again with extensive views, including (if the day is clear) La Dôle at the other end of the Swiss Jura. Hochwacht was once a watchtower; today the watching is done by radar. The restaurant here is conveniently located, since this is the halfway point of the walk.

Retracing the route to and past the ruins, take the trail that descends the south side of the ridge to Buessberg. At this point there is a marked and signed nature trail. Near the end of the route, we pass through vineyards, thence back to the covered bridge and the Baden railroad station.

Hohenklingen Castle—
Above picturesque Stein-am-Rhein

DIFFICULTY	Grade 2
DISTANCE	10 km
WALKING TIME	2 1/2 hours
MAP	K&F Freizeitkarte *Kanton Zürich*
GUIDEBOOK	K&F Schweizer Wanderbuch 41, *Schweiz—*
	die 50 schönsten Wanderungen

In a country where superlatives are commonplace, it may seem extreme to say that Stein-am-Rhein is one of the most picturesque towns in Switzerland. Nevertheless, most tourists who have been there agree that the appellation is apt. It has kept its medieval character. Many of the houses in the Old Town sport ornate oriels—the jutting windows that permit the inhabitants a full view of the street—and are highly decorated and painted. A medieval Benedictine monastery, Kloster St. Georgen, dating from the eleventh century, has been turned into a museum and is open daily throughout the year. And there is the obligatory castle on the Rhine, Hohenklingen, accessible by road but more fun to walk to.

Stein-am-Rhein

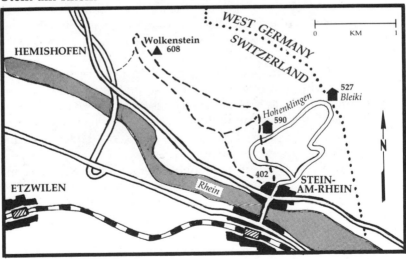

Getting to Stein-am-Rhein by train is not difficult but does require a change of trains in Schaffhausen. Trains leave Zürich hourly and the main-line (to Stuttgart) one-stop ride takes forty-two minutes. At Schaffhausen, change to the Stein-am-Rhein local for the fifteen- to twenty-minute journey. After crossing the Rhine, turn left to the dock, then follow the old city wall to the ancient tower, Untertorturm. Walk along Hemishoferstrasse to the schoolhouse, thence to the slopes of the Klingenberg, thence right at the trail arrow to three trail signs. If the nearby target range is not being used, go left and in 150 meters bear right up the slope.

If the range is being used, follow the signs to Wolkenstein through the vineyards and thence to the summit of this low hill. Either way, the elevation gain is only 200 meters, and the view from the summit is unobstructed and spectacular. It was a main observation post of the boat traffic along the Rhine and played an earlier role in the protection of the town. In recent years, the walls and battlements of the ancient castle have been excavated and can be seen along the northeast ridge.

From the top, follow the low ridge eastward to Hohenklingen. The ridge is open and affords fine views along its length. The path is a good one, not strenuous, and the walk is pleasant. The castle at Hohenklingen is one of the most frequently visited in the region. Views of the Rhine, the Rhine island Werd, and the Untersee (the lower end of Bodensee—Lake Constance) are justly famous. The area has been occupied since the time of Julius Caesar, and the view from the top indicates clearly the strategic location of the city and the surrounding hills.

From Hohenklingen to the village, the path steps its way down through the vineyards, which here face south to absorb the slanting rays of the sun. The latitude is the same as the northern tip of Maine, a place we don't associate with sun-drenched vineyards. But the Gulf Stream keeps Europe relatively warm, and the south-facing slopes make the most of what sun there is.

A suggested detour from Hohenklingen is the walk to the hill village Bleiki, right on the German border. The route traverses steep meadows, then forest to the houses of Bleiki. On the way back to Stein-am-Rhein, take the road south, utilizing a path through the vineyards at the first switchback.

Trains back to Schaffhausen run about every hour, and from Schaffhausen to Zürich somewhat more frequently.

A much-loved walk
with extensive views of the Swiss Mittelland

DIFFICULTY	Grade 2
DISTANCE	12 km
WALKING TIME	4 hours
MAP	K&F Freizeitkarte *Kanton Zürich*
GUIDEBOOK	K&F Schweizer Wanderbuch 41, *Schweiz—die 50 schönsten Wanderungen*

Between the Jura and the Alps, from Lake Geneva to Lake Constance, lies a broad, sloping surface consisting primarily of the glacial rubble from the Alps. Its lowest point is hard up against the Jura where the Aare River joins the Rhine. This is the great *Mittelland*, the agricultural heart of the country. It is an area of steep-walled valleys separating low hills that are heavily covered by field and forest. Although the hills are not high by Alpine standards, the terrain is surprisingly rugged. This is no broad German Plain. A rail trip on nearly any line involves passing through many tunnels and over many bridges.

The relatively poor drainage caused by the piling up of glacial debris has also meant that the *Mittelland* is a region of lakes that provide easy transport and communication. Although today most transport is by rail, it is not uncommon to see goods and farm animals loaded onto the many passenger boats that still ply the lakes. It is not surprising that most of the largest cities in Switzerland are located on the shores of the larger lakes: Geneva, Lausanne, Zürich.

The walk from Oberägeri affords good views of the lakes and hills of the *Mittelland*; on a clear day, the entire plateau from the Jura to the Alps can be seen. Although somewhat off the beaten track, Oberägeri can be reached readily via Zug, a twenty-five-minute train ride from Zürich. From Zug, connecting buses travel to Oberägeri, a half-hour trip. Service from Zürich is frequent, at least every hour; check the schedule for times of departure.

From the bus stop in Oberägeri, walk along Ratenstrasse to the footpath (right) to the Pfister Institute. Then follow the road toward Alosen; 200 meters beyond the switchback, pick up the trail (left) at a barn. The trail winds through the forested valley of a small brook, soon reaching the village of Alosen. Just past the post office, take the

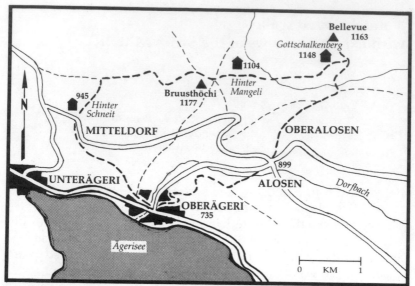

Oberägeri

steep path to Oberalosen, first through pasture, then (at a trail sign) through forest to Gottschalkenberg. This point is 300 meters above the lake level.

From Gottschalkenberg, a path leads to Bellevue, well named for its extensive views of the *Mittelland*—the Jura Mountains from La Dôle to Lägeren, Albishorn near Zürich, and the basin of the lake of Zürich—a vast panorama of Switzerland's heartland.

Returning to Gottschalkenberg, take the trail to Hinter Mangeli. Just beyond is a major trail junction; you can head directly to Oberägeri; or, as we suggest, to Bruusthöchi and Hinter Schneit, thence to Mitteldorf and back to town.

Germany

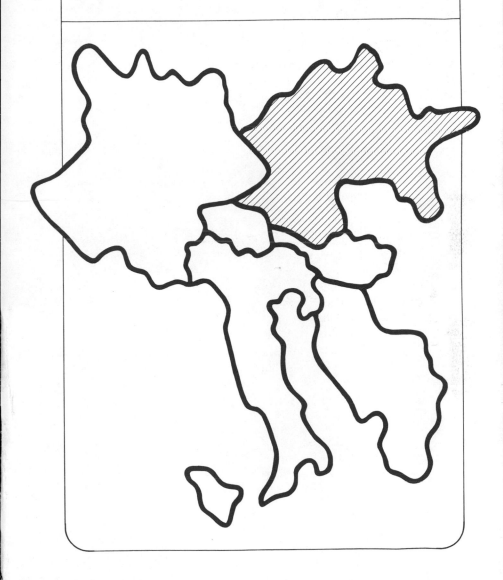

6. Munich

There are so many interesting things to do and see in Munich that you could spend days of sightseeing without leaving the city center. But Bavaria, of which Munich is the capital, is so much more than just Munich that you should get out into the countryside to see at least some of it.

Nevertheless, there are surprising places to walk right near the center of town. The Englischer Garten stretches for miles northeastward along the Isar River. Indeed, it is the largest city park in Europe. Laced with walking paths and bicycle trails, it is just right for spending a few hours in late afternoon. There is a fine beer garden at the Chinesicher Turm (Chinese Pagoda) near the downtown end of the park. The park starts at the Haus der Kunst on Prinzregentenstrasse. By subway (*U-bahn*), the park can be reached from the Giselastrasse stop on lines U3 and U6. From here, it is a short walk eastward to the park boundary, in the vicinity of the Chinese Pagoda.

The Munich Zoo (Tierpark Hellabrunn), also near the Isar River, but south of the city center, is also worth a visit. It is at the end of bus line 52, which can be boarded at Marienplatz.

TRANSPORTATION

A dozen years ago, Müncheners were upset by the disruption accompanying the construction of the subway. The city center was torn up beyond belief and it seemed as if, like Humpty-Dumpty, it could never be put together again. But it was; and the city now boasts one of the best-integrated transportation systems in all of Europe.

There are four parts to the system: the subterranean *U-bahn* (*Untergrundbahn*), which services the city center; the *S-bahn* (*Schnellbahn*), which reaches out to the suburbs; a modern street railway (*Strassenbahn*); and an extensive network of bus lines. There are few places within the city limits more than four or five blocks from a rail or bus stop. Although the network is complicated, it has been made understandable through the establishment of information boards in many places. In addition to network maps, each station on the subway has a vicinity street map showing the nearby connections with bus and tram lines. For tourists, the city publishes a brochure (in eight languages!) explaining the tariff structure and general regulations. Also available from information and ticket offices are route maps. At least one of these, *Wandern mit dem MVV*, indicates stops (mostly on the *S-bahn*) that have marked walking paths radiating out from the station.

MAPS AND GUIDEBOOKS

Two hikers' maps cover the Munich area: Fritsch Wanderkarte 7, *München*; and Mair's Freizeitkarte *München und Umgebung* ("Munich and vicinity"). They are at a scale of 1:100,000 (1 centimeter per kilometer) and include most of the area reachable in a half hour or so from the city center by rail or bus. The topographic maps of the Bavarian Land Survey, at a scale of 1:50,000, also show trails and are full of topographic and cultural detail.

Other maps are available. The best procedure to obtain one is to find a bookstore (*Buchhandlung*) that carries *Wanderkarten*—and many do—and browse through its collection.

Several good guidebooks describe walks in the Munich area. If you can read German, try to find *Mit der S-Bahn Wandern* (in two parts) or *Hundert schöne Wanderwege rund um München*, both published by Süddeutscher Verlag. Of course, you will need neither maps nor guidebooks to follow the routes we describe. But if you like maps, as we do, try to find one covering the route. It will show you many things not included on the sketch maps accompanying the route descriptions.

The most complete collection of maps and guidebooks for the Munich area, indeed for the entire Alpine region, can be found at the GEO Center. Another major publisher and distributor of hikers' maps and guidebooks is Bergverlag Rudolf Rother, which publishes the "official" guidebooks of the German Alpine Club and a series of maps, the BV Tourenblätter, for many areas in and around the Alps. The latter are half map, half guidebook, in looseleaf form, and come with a plastic case that provides a convenient weatherproof cover for trail use.

WEATHER AND CLIMATE

Summer weather in Munich can best be described as warm and humid. Rainshowers and thundershowers are common. Although the average daytime temperatures in July are moderate, about 21° C (70° F), some days may reach the low 30s, Celsius degrees (90s, Fahrenheit degrees). September and October tend to be cool and dry, with stretches of beautiful, crisp fall days interspersed with rainy periods. Winters are cold, but snowfall is comparatively rare, with cold rains predominant. The foehn, a warm, gusty south wind that blows from the Alps in the spring, sends Müncheners to their medicine cabinets for relief from "foehn sickness." Whether the origin is psychological or physiological, there is no doubt that the frequency of automobile accidents increases during periods of foehn winds.

Although weather forecasts (in German) are readily available from the Munich weather office (Wetteramt München), the only English-language forecast we know of is published in the *International Herald Tribune*.

Useful information

Tourist information

Verkehrsamt. Airport; main train station; Rindermarkt 5. Tourist information on Munich hotels, restaurants, etc.
Fremdenverkehrsverband München-Oberbayern, Sonnenstrasse 10, D-8000 München 2. Tel. (089) 59 63 51. Bavarian Tourist Association.

Maps, guidebooks, and trail information

Deutscher Alpenverein (DAV), Praterinsel 5, D-8000 München 22. Tel. (089) 29 30 86 for general information on the German Alpine Club. For information on hiking and climbing in the Alps, call (089) 29 49 40.

Bergverlag Rudolf Rother, Landshuter Allee 49, Postfach 67, D-8000 München 19. Tel. (089) 16 00 81.

Geographische Buchhandlung, Rosental 6, D-8000 München 2. Tel. (089) 260 31 80.

Local transportation

Wandern mit dem MVV—Vehrkehrslinienplan Stadt. Map of the bus lines, trams, local subway net (*U-bahn*), and the regional commuter rail lines (*S-bahn*). Contains recommendations for walks radiating from stops on the *S-bahn*. Ask for it at the city tourist office or at the information office in the main railroad station (*Hauptbahnhof*). Automats at every stop vend tickets that are valid for buses, trams, *U-bahn*, and *S-bahn*. A twenty-four-hour ticket good for unlimited use of public transportation can also be purchased through the automats at various locations around the city, including hotels. Roving inspectors check passengers' tickets. Don't lose yours!

Accommodations and restaurants

There are some 150 hotels, 100 pensions, and several motels in Munich. Despite the large number of tourist beds, they are often all filled in tourist season. Reservations are desirable anytime and a must during Oktoberfest in late September. Rates are high, even in outlying hotels and pensions.

Youth hostels. A huge (535-bed) *Jugendherberge* is located at Wendl-Dietrich Strasse 20. Tel. (089) 13 11 56. There is a student hostel, Newman Haus, at Kaulbachstrasse 29. Tel. (089) 28 50 91. The coed YMCA is at Landwehrstrasse 13. Tel. (089) 55 59 41.

Camping. There are several large, well-situated, and well-equipped campgrounds in Munich. München-Thalkirchen is near the Hellabrunn Zoo at Zentrallandstrasse 39. Tel. (089) 723 17 07. München-Obermenzig is near the entrance to the Stuttgart Autobahn.

Restaurants. There are thousands of restaurants, *Weinstuben*, pubs, and other eateries in Munich. Many of them are quite inexpensive; nearly all are good or better. All have their menus posted outside, so you will have some idea of what you're getting into. The Wienerwald chain has good broiled chicken. And even McDonald's serves beer.

Miscellaneous

American Consulate. Königinstrasse 5, 8000 München 22. Tel. (089) 2 30 21. Wetteramt München. Weather forecasts for Munich and the Bavarian Alps. Tel. (089) 53 01 77.

Along the edge
of the Ebersberger Forest

DIFFICULTY	Grade 2, mostly on forest paths
DISTANCE	10 km
WALKING TIME	3 hours
MAPS	AK 7937, *Grafing b. München*, 1:25,000
	AK 7936, *Grafing b. München*, 1:50,000
	Fritsch Wanderkarte 7, *München*, 1:100,000
	Mairs Freizeitkarte *München und Umgebung*, 1:100,000
GUIDEBOOK	Strassner, Fritz. *Hundert Schöne Wanderwege rund und München*. Süddeutscher Verlag. Walk 86 describes a parallel walk through the fields

A few miles to the east of Munich lies one of the oldest managed forests in Bavaria, the renowned Ebersberger Forest. In fact, the Bavarians were managing their forests before the Pilgrims landed on Plymouth Rock. The first forest regulations concerning their use and care were enacted in 1568! Today, the Ebersberger Forest is a carefully managed plantation of conifers, mostly Norway spruce, but with some Scotch pine mixed in.

Aside from its importance as a source of wood and wood products, it is valued by Müncheners as a pleasant place for a summer outing, a cool forest in which to escape the summer heat of the Bavarian Plain. It is easily accessible from Munich by both car and *S-bahn* and makes a fine place for a Sunday walk. Although many walks are possible, we have selected one along the southern edge, from the little town of Kirchseeon to Ebersberg, where a Benedictine monastery has existed for several hundred years.

Line 4 of the *S-bahn* leaves from the *Hauptbahnhof* (main train station) every thirty or forty minutes. (It can also be boarded at Karlplatz, Marienplatz, and Isartor in the center of town.) Make sure that the train you take is marked "Ebersberg" because some of the line 4 trains do not go all the way to Kirchseeon. Also, get on the front part of the train since at one point the rear end of the train may be decoupled to shorten its length.

At the train station in Kirchseeon, just to the left as you come up from the tunnel beneath the tracks, are a sign and map that show the *Wanderwege* in the Kirchseeon area. The path that we will take follows the southern end of the forest to the lookout tower (*Aussichtsturm*) near Ebersberg, where you can pick up the *S-bahn* for the return journey to Munich. There are several other possibilities in the Kirchseeon area, including one 6-kilometer walk to Forest House Diana, a restaurant in the heart of the forest. From there, you can loop back to the Eglharting station on the *S-bahn*. Another possibility is to take the route to Ebersberg via Forstseeon and Eggelburg. This follows back roads through open fields and is good for views but hot in the sun. This route is marked with green diamonds.

Our route is just to the north, following the forest edge. Follow Münchnerstrasse directly away from the *Bahnhof* to the Coop gro-

Ebersberger Forest

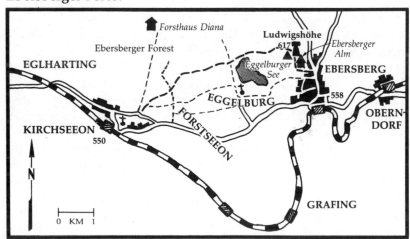

Ebersberg

cery store (a good place to obtain provisions for lunch). Along the left side of the Coop, the Kirchenweg leads straight ahead and then bends right past St. Joseph's Church. It eventually comes to a dead end as a road but continues straight ahead as a walkway uphill. Continue on this walkway, still the Kirchenweg, until it ends at the intersection of Zugspitzstrasse and Hochrigstrasse. From this point, follow white-and-red arrows left (north) down the road about 100 meters to the main highway. Just before the main highway a footway goes right, leading to a tunnel under the highway. At the end of the tunnel is a white-over-red marker that bends to the right. Immediately on leaving the tunnel, bear diagonally right onto a path in the meadow. There is a white/red marker on a post about 50 meters from the end of the tunnel. Follow along the fence line to the edge of the forest and pick up the white/red markers at this point.

The fence line eventually makes a sharp turn left. Here the white/red–marked trail heads straight ahead up a small rise, across a small opening, and back into the forest along a woods road. After crossing a small hill, the road continues straight ahead to an open field. Just before reaching the field, however, the white/red–marked trail diverges left up another small hill. The trail here winds along a ridge about 100 meters from the edge of the forest. Fields can be seen to the right. The forest here is a pure beech forest, whereas the one we just left was a pure Norway spruce stand.

Along the route there are areas of young trees enclosed by fences, indicative of the care with which German foresters tend their new tree crops. The fences are to protect the young seedlings from the ravages of the deer that abound in the area. Look for the occasional platform on stilts that hunters build for their hunting stands. You may also see the occasional cutting area, with piles of carefully peeled logs waiting to be hauled from the forest. The trail comes to a power line, and just across the fence is a main intersection of forest roads. You can cross over to this intersection through a gate to study the map posted there.

However, our trail turns sharply right here, following the white/red markers, and goes south a half kilometer to Eggelburger See. The path now leads along a woods road down a slope and soon comes to a side path, right, which leads in a few meters to the lake. The lake is a *Naturschutzgebiet*, a nature protection area of the state of Bavaria. The lake is shallow and can be relied on to be the home of large numbers of wild birds.

We now retrace our steps to the main trail, at which point the green-diamond and white-and-green-circle trails enter from the shore of the lake. The green-diamond trail is the lower trail that winds through the pastures rather than through the woods. Just after passing the north end of the lake, the way leads across an open pasture and reenters the woods. At this point the green-triangle trail continues on the woods road, whereas the white/red trail that we're taking diverges left through the woods. This is just at the edge of the pasture on the far side. The forest we now traverse is a mixed forest of beech and Norway spruce, very dense, with very little undergrowth. Since there are other paths through the forest, it is wise to follow the white/red paint marks closely. Where the trail enters the woods at the north end of Eggelburger See there is a fine view across the lake to a medieval church in the tiny village of Eggelburg.

The way soon comes to the edge of the forest with views of Eggelburg. The path joins a farm road and leads along the fence line toward the woods at the far side of the field. Shortly after entering the woods, the paths diverge. Our road goes to the right, picking up white/red markers. Just after crossing an open area with new growth, the woods road swings around to the right, but the white/ red path to the outlook tower branches left into the woods. This is well marked, but the sign to the *Aussichtsturm* and the white/red blazes at this point are partially obscured by vegetation. Partway up the hill, the trail from St. Hubertus comes in from the left. There are signs here, one pointing back to the Eggleburger See and Kirchseeon Bahnhof, 6.5 kilometers, marked white/red.

The tower is soon reached. It is a massive concrete structure, very Germanic, and was built at the beginning of World War I, in 1914. It is worth climbing the 167 steps to the top for the fine views of the forest and the town of Ebersberg.

Many of the trees surrounding the tower contain small painted memorials to German soldiers fallen in World War I. Many of the plaques contain photographs of the fallen soldiers, all of whom came from the Ebersberg area.

The path down leads directly south toward Ebersberg on a carefully constructed and stepped pathway. It is not marked with white/red marks here but is clearly the way to the town. If you are thirsty or hungry, a few steps down the path will bring you to a small restaurant. Follow the entrance road downhill to a path leading straight where the road bears left. Along the walk down there is a most felicitous view of the small villages surrounding Ebersberg. Follow the entrance road down to the main road. At the intersection, there are trail signs indicating the way right to the *Hauptbahnhof*. The path leads along Eberhardstrasse and around a small lake (Klostersee) that has a swimming area.

After 200 meters the marked route diverges left on Richardisweg up the hill. Continue straight ahead over the hill. Eventually you come to Marienplatz, the main square in town with its old *Rathaus* (town hall) and monument in the center. Turn left down the hill to the church; follow Bahnhofstrasse to the railroad station. Just past the church at the next intersection with the traffic light, turn right before going under the railroad underpass. The Ebersberg railroad station is a few meters away.

An alternative route from Marienplatz follows the upper street (Heinrich Vogelstrasse) one block and then Eichhochstrasse, which leads directly to the railroad station.

Ebersberg itself is worth a walking tour. It is an old monastery town; Benedictine monks have been here for several centuries. The church is Romanesque, but the interior is typically Baroque. There are red marble gravestones from the Gothic period, and the entrance hall has fine carved lion heads and other decorations. There are many other picturesque buildings in town; a short tour is worthwhile.

To the top of Wallberg,
high above Tegernsee

DIFFICULTY	Grade 2, dirt roads and graded paths
DISTANCE	7 km with cable car; 11 km without
WALKING TIME	2 1/2 or 4 hours
MAPS	AK Wanderkarte 2, *Tegernsee und Schliersee*
	KOMP Wanderkarte 8, *Tegernseer Tal*
	RV Wanderkarte 3, *Tegernsee–Bad Tolz*
GUIDEBOOKS	Dumler, H. F-K&F *Rundwanderungen Tegernsee*
	KOMP Wanderbuch 922, *Tegernsee–Schliersee*

Southern Bavaria is blessed with a number of attractive lakes. Some are in the lowlands around Munich, such as Starnberger See. Others are in deep clefts in the Alps, such as Königssee. Others are in the pre-Alps, surrounded by the foothills of the Alps. Tegernsee is one of these. It is a short drive or train ride from Munich and is much favored for Sunday outings.

Tegernsee, like many of its neighbors, is a product of the Pleistocene. Glaciers filled the valleys stretching north from the main massif, carving typical U-shaped valleys from the relatively soft stone. The great Tegernsee Glacier reached only as far as Gmund at the north end of the present lake. Here it dropped its rubble, damming the valley to the south, forming the lake when the ice finally melted away.

Tegernsee

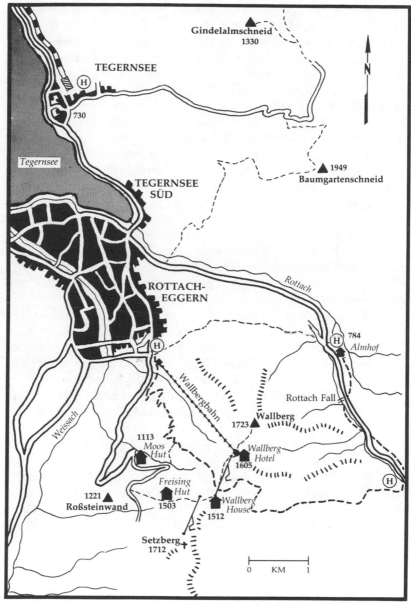

Tegernsee

The valley has been occupied for many centuries. Tradition has it that the first monastery was built on the lake in A.D. 746. By A.D. 900 the valley was the center of a thriving community of more than eleven thousand farmhouses. The Hungarian invasion changed all that, and by the end of the century the houses and fields lay in ruins; fewer than a hundred remained. But the community slowly built itself back up; today the lake is ringed with towns and villages, and the rich farming country to the north is once again the site of many prosperous *Bauernhofe* (farmsteads).

Our walk takes us up the Wallberg, a commanding presence that stands 1000 meters above the lake. The route to Tegernsee starts at the Starnberger *Bahnhof*, which adjoins the Munich *Hauptbahnhof*, to the right as you walk toward the train platforms. Through trains to Tegernsee run frequently (0756 and 0850, for example), but, curiously, the German State Railroad runs only to Schaftlach. This means that if you are traveling on a Eurailpass, you must purchase a ticket from Schaftlach to Tegernsee (which can be done on the train). No change of train is necessary, but the last few kilometers are run on a private line, rather an oddity in Germany.

The line ends in the town of Tegernsee. From the railroad station, take the number 2 bus, which goes directly to the base station of the Wallbergbahn, the cable car that runs nearly to the summit. Here you have a choice: climb the 800 meters to the top or ride the cable car. The former will take about two hours; the latter, twelve minutes. The path follows a dirt road that switchbacks its way up the mountain, more or less parallel to the cableway. From the top of the cable car, a good trail climbs the extra 100 meters to the summit. From here there are fine views of the lake to the north and the Karwendel Mountains to the south.

Returning to the top station of the cable car and the Wallberg Hotel (food and drink available), follow the path past the small chapel, close to a chair lift, to a broad saddle and trail junction. Here you have a choice of routes down, but we suggest the gravel path that leads east to Enterrottach. The upper portion is through open fields, affording fine views of the Alpine foothills to the east and south. After dropping rather sharply for the first kilometer, the path (now a paved farm road) enters the woods and drops steadily to the highway.

If time is short, you can board the bus to Enterrottach here. But a pleasant path follows the road down, first on one side, then the other, and leads past Rottach Fall, worth the short detour. At Enter-rottach, the number 1 bus for the Tegernsee railroad station can be boarded. A small inn provides refreshments for those waiting for the bus.

There are many variations to this route, depending on your time and energy. It is a well-traveled region, and the paths are numerous and well marked. Tourist boats ply the lake, and it is possible to travel between the towns of Tegernsee and Rottach near the base of the Wallberg by boat, a pleasant though short trip. Trains back to Munich are frequent (1644, 1746, 1911, for example), so it is possible to stretch the day's journey into the evening, enjoying dinner at one of the restaurants in Tegernsee.

Through field and forest
to the Andechs monastery and beer hall

DIFFICULTY	Grade 1, an easy, level walk
DISTANCE	13 km
WALKING TIME	4 hours
MAPS	AK Wanderkarte 2, *Starnberger See*
	KOMP Wanderkarte 180, *Starnberger See–Ammersee*
GUIDEBOOKS	Strassner, Fritz. *Hundert schöne Wanderwege rund um München*. Süddeutscher Verlag. Walk 33 describes part of the same walk
	F-K&F Dumler, H. *Rundwanderungen Ammersee–Starnberger See*

Many tourists and Müncheners alike make a pilgrimage to the church at Andechs, a small village southwest of Munich, to see its extraordinary rococo interior. Many more come to sample the wares of the monastic order there, the wares being what many consider to be the finest beer in Bavaria. The church sits on a little hill overlooking the Ammersee, a commanding presence that is visible from afar. At the foot of the hill is a giant parking lot, filled on a summer Sunday with cars and buses. The walk up the hill to the church is steep and, though short, is enough to arouse a powerful thirst. Perhaps that is why most of the tourists branch off to the beer hall and never do make it to the church.

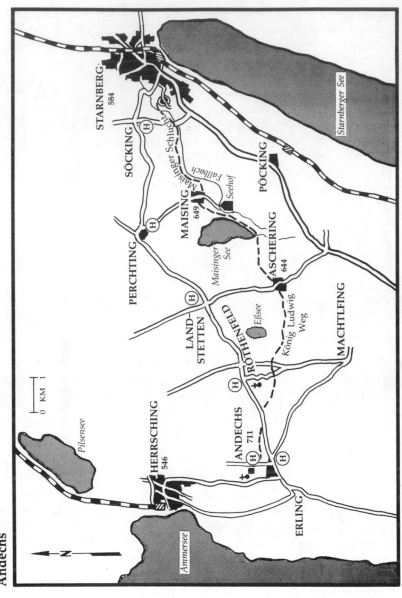

Andechs

The church and monastery at Andechs

If you visit Andechs, take time to see the church first. Although the church itself dates from the fourteenth century, the hill on which it stands was first occupied in the twelfth century by a fortress built by the Count of Andechs. The exterior is severely Gothic, but the interior is a marvel of rococo decoration and has been favorably compared with the famous Wieskirche, a few kilometers to the south. The frescoes, executed by J. B. Zimmerman, date from the 1750s. The Virgin standing above the high altar is from an earlier period, dating from 1500.

After your tour of the church, drop down to the great hall and join the line waiting to be served a liter stein of *Helles* (light) or *Dunkles* (dark). Then stop at the delicatessen counter for a chunk of cheese, a piece of wurst, and a couple of the radishes that seem to be obligatory. They do make the beer taste better, it that is possible.

Most of the visitors to Andechs come by bus or car. We suggest that you walk there, across the fields and forests that separate Ammersee and Starnberger See to the east. The walk will take you through the cool woods of the Maisinger Valley, past a small lake that is home for a multitude of birds, across the cultivated fields of the Starnberger *Bauernland*, thence to Andechs and a refreshing draught of *Andechser Bier*.

The key to this walk is the Munich *S-bahn*, the lines of which radiate from the city center like spokes on a wheel. The spokes are close enough together that you can walk from one line to another and find a convenient train back to the city. Our walk starts at Starnberg, a stop on the Tutzing (S6) line. Starnberg is an old community that has been suffering from growing pains as a result of its proximity to Munich. Now that the *S-bahn* provides frequent fast service to the city center, Starnberg has become something of a bedroom community. It is certainly in a beautiful location at the head of Starnberg Lake.

From the train station at Starnberg, head left on the plaza to Bahnhofstrasse, where a yellow sign points right to Herrsching. Turn left into a small alley next to the school, then right on Ottostrasse, still following posted signs. After crossing a small brook (Maising Brook, which we will follow for some distance), go left by a sign, *"Fussweg nach Maising"* ("Footpath to Maising"), following green triangles. Passing by the town waterworks, cross the brook at the diversion gates. Nearby is a small ski jump. At this point, the path turns left and soon enters Maising Gorge (*Schlucht*), passing under a high autobahn bridge.

Even on a sunny summer day, the gorge is filled with an eerie green light from the overarching canopy of an old beech forest. It is cool and quiet in the confines of the narrow valley. The woodland path climbs gently, finally reaching the upper end at a paved road. Turn right on the road, crossing the brook, and follow the green triangles 100 meters, then right on the road through the small village of Maising. At the far end of town, the route turns left on a gravel path (green triangles) and heads across a farmer's field. A small

Gasthaus is soon reached, where refreshments or lunch can be obtained. This is 5 kilometers from Starnberg, about a two-hour walk, or a bit less.

From the inn, follow a paved road west 100 meters (still following the green triangles) to a fork with a sign, *"Uber Aschering nach Pöcking"* ("via Aschering to Pöcking"). Follow the trail sign right to Aschering, avoiding the path left to Pöcking. The path now skirts the edge of the swampy Maisinger See, a nature preserve, and soon enters the town of Aschering. At the main street, turn right 200 meters to a sign, *"Fussweg Andechs,"* then left on a narrow paved farm road. The road soon turns to gravel as it climbs a small hill and enters a Norway spruce forest. The route here is marked with yellow 3s.

The path crosses two low heights of land, past a small pond, then reaches a paved road, which it parallels for 200 meters. It then crosses the road, right, and angles back into a field, heading toward the little village of Rothenfeld with its church spire. Before reaching Rothenfeld, the path turns left across fields (following markers on concrete posts) to a paved road. Follow this road left to a parking area (marked with a blue P). At the end of the parking place, a sign indicates König Ludwig Weg, which we follow through the forest for a short distance to fields on the other side. The church at Andechs is visible from this point, and the path, now paved, leads directly to the parking lot and bus stop just below the hill on which the church and monastery stand.

The number 351 bus goes to Herrsching, where you can board the *S-bahn* for the return journey to Munich. If the timing is more convenient, you can take the number 351 bus in the other direction, back to Starnberg, a somewhat longer ride. Either way, the *S-bahn* trains to the city run frequently.

Through the valley of the Mangfall

DIFFICULTY	Grade 2, on roads and paths
DISTANCE	20 km, with possibility of 5 km shortcut
WALKING TIME	6 hours (5 hours with shortcut)
MAP	KOMP Wanderkarte 181, *Rosenheim–Bad Aibling*
GUIDEBOOK	Strassner, Fritz. *Hundert schöne Wanderwege rund um München.* Süddeutscher Verlag. Walk 1

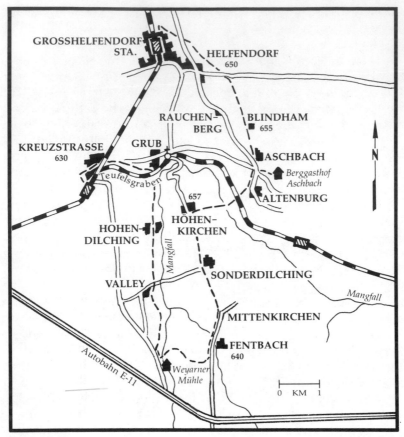

Mangfall

Forty kilometers southeast of Munich, near the end of the Kreuzstrasse (S1) line of the *S-bahn*, two Roman roads cross at the village
of Helfendorf. Nearby you can find evidence of Roman civilization,
and everywhere is evidence of the long-continued human occupa-
tion of this area. Remains of old fortresses and medieval castles
abound, and there are many beautiful Baroque churches with ornate
decorations.

If there were only ruins and old churches to visit, this area
would be high on anyone's list. But there is much in the natural
scene to tempt the walk-minded tourist. Ice Age glaciers terminated

here, leaving their record in the form of glacial moraines. And the Mangfall River, which drains Tegernsee, cut a narrow trench in the moraine country as it made a U-turn to the south before heading eastward to its confluence with the Inn River at Rosenheim. This pretty little valley with its steep, wooded slopes provides excellent walking for one who wants to get away from Munich for a day.

The region is reached easily via the Salzburg Autobahn (Weyarn exit) or the S1 line of the Munich *S-bahn*. The trip we describe starts at the Grosshelfendorf station. This is a three-quarter-hour ride from the Munich main station. Trains run every twenty minutes, but only a few of them proceed to the end of the line. Make sure the train is marked "Kreuzstrasse." There is probably one leaving the main station at 0820, but check the schedule.

Although we have not walked the route ourselves, it is easy to follow. Much of it is along country roads, past small villages, and through a felicitous mosaic of field and forest. Several shortcuts are possible, if time does not permit walking the entire 20-kilometer route.

From the Grosshelfendorf station, walk north a few hundred meters parallel to the railroad to the old Roman road (Römerstrasse). Turn right and proceed along the road, watching for the trail left to Kleinhelfendorf. (If you miss this, continue to the center of town and pick up the road east to Kleinhelfendorf.) Here there is a fine church, worth a visit. From the center of the village, follow the road south through Blindham to Aschbach. The last 300 meters are along Rosenheimerstrasse. In Aschbach, a fine view can be had from the hotel-restaurant that bears the town's name.

Proceed southwestward toward Altenburg with its castle. A short distance south of town, remains of medieval Altenburg can be found, with ruins of the castle wall in evidence. Our route proceeds toward Nieder Altenburg, over the Mangfall River, thence to Klein-hohenkirchen. At the center of town, turn south and follow the road to Sonderdilching, site of an early fortress and castle. (For a short-cut, take the road to Valley from here.) Fentbach, 2 kilometers south, is also the site of medieval ruins. South of the town, take the road west to Weyarn Mill at the crossing of the Mangfall. Here a path heads northward along the west slope to the town of Valley, with its large castle and brewery. Roman stonework can be seen in the garden of the castle.

The route continues northward through Hohendilching to the

mouth of Devil's Valley (Teufelsgraben), which during the Ice Age was the outlet of the Isar Glacier. In Grub, take the road west to Kreuzstrasse and the *S-bahn* station. Note that trains back to Munich run about once per hour on a rather irregular schedule.

A walk along the beautiful Ammersee to the St. Ottilien monastery

DIFFICULTY	Grade 1, parts may be boggy
DISTANCE	20 km
WALKING TIME	5 hours
MAPS	AK Wanderkarte *Ammersee und Umgebung*
	KOMP Wanderkarte 180, *Starnberger See–Ammersee*
GUIDEBOOK	F–K&F Dumler, H. *Rundwanderungen Ammersee–Starnberger See.*

The Kloster St. Ottilien is only about a kilometer from the Geltendorf stop on the *S-bahn*. We suggest you go the long way around, from Türkenfeld via Ammersee. It will take you a lot longer, but you will see much, much more on the way, including the beautiful Ammersee and fine views of the distant Alps. So, if you have only a few hours, visit just the monastery; but if you have a day to spend, follow our route along trails and back roads. There is much to be seen, a *Mischmasch* of Bavarian countryside scenery.

The region is readily accessible via the Munich *S-bahn* line 4, westbound to Geltendorf. Trains run about every half hour. Make certain that the one you take goes to Geltendorf; some go only as far as Pasing. The trip takes about forty minutes.

Our walk starts in Türkenfeld, the next-to-the-last station. Walk east parallel to the tracks about a half kilometer to the road to Beuern. Take this road south (right) about 200 meters to the path branching left to Burgholz. Shortly after entering the forest, near the confluence of two small brooks, you may find the traces of a medieval fortress, in the form of the remnants of the excavation.

After leaving the forest, the path soon reaches the road south to Eching. In the north part of the village, remains of an ancient wall can be seen. The road through town passes under Route 12 toward Ammersee and soon picks up the shoreline path to Unterschondorf.

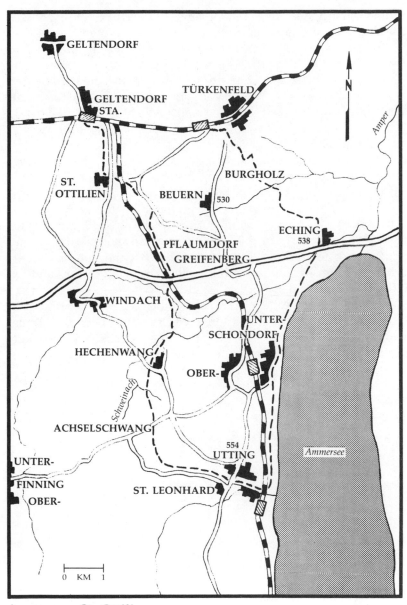

Ammersee–St. Ottilien

From the path there are excellent views of the church at Andechs, a commanding presence on its hill overlooking Ammersee.

In Utting, about 2 kilometers south of Unterschondorf, stand two churches worth a visit. The path along the shore is between the railroad and the lake; take the first road crossing the rail line and head toward the churches. Follow past the second church, St. Leonhard's, to the road (right) to Achselschwang. In a little over 1 kilometer, a path heads right across fields, regaining the road at Achselschwang. Turn right along this road (toward Oberschondorf) for 200 meters, then left (north) along a farm road to Hechenwang. Here there is a fine church dating from 1714. Follow the road east through the village, taking the branch north (left) to Neugreifenburg.

At Neugreifenburg, walk through the railroad underpass, then north along the tracks 1 kilometer to the farm road that branches right to Pflaumdorf. Turn left along the road through the village, past a Baroque church. Follow the road north to the monastery of St. Ottilien. From here, it is a short walk to the *S-bahn* tracks and the Geltendorf railroad station.

If you do not have a full day to devote to this walk, it is possible to cut it in half by taking the train from Utting to Geltendorf. Trains run rather infrequently, probably at 1322 and 1502; check the schedule at the Utting railroad station.

7. Garmisch-Partenkirchen

Old photographs of the Loisach Valley show Garmisch and Partenkirchen as two separate towns with a substantial distance between them. The Winter Olympics of 1936 changed all that, catapulting the two villages to an international ski resort. Today the villages are one, and only the Partnach River marks the old separation.

The big tourist attraction is the cog railway up the Zugspitze, the highest mountain in Germany (and one Germany shares with Austria). That journey is something of a thrill, but when you get to the top, there's nothing much to do but look around a bit, then take the train back down. It is much more rewarding to get out and walk the trails and really see something of the high mountains. There is plenty of opportunity for mountain walking in the surrounding countryside.

There are numerous sights in town that are worth a visit between mountain walks, or on a day not suited for high-country excursions. The complex of buildings that Hitler built to show off his winter athletes is certainly impressive. The Eisstadion contains three indoor ice-skating rinks with room for 12,000 seated spectators. Nearby are five indoor swimming pools and one outdoor pool. The Skistadion faces the massive ski-jumping structures. Several of the racing trails end at the stadium, where 80,000 spectators can watch the skiers finish their downhill runs. The facilities are very much in use today; more than seventy-five competitions, ranging from curling to tobogganing and, of course, ice-skating and skiing, are held every winter.

In the summer, the stadiums are empty and the twin towns quiet. This is a time for wandering the slopes or relaxing in the warm sunshine. The Philosophenweg is a gentle path at the foot of the Wank that connects St. Anthony's Church in Partenkirchen (a gracious building dating from 1708) with the village of Farchant. In the other direction, a trail only slightly more demanding leads to Gamshütte, a pleasant place for refreshment and relaxation after the short but steep pitch from the Fauken-schlucht. Both of these walks are possible most of the year, certainly anytime the ground is free of snow.

TRANSPORTATION

Because of its location on a direct rail link between Munich and Innsbruck, Garmisch-Partenkirchen is readily accessible from either, though somewhat closer to the latter. Nevertheless, travel times are nearly equal, about one and a half hours. The most convenient train leaves either the Innsbruck or Munich *Hauptbahnhof* about 0730 and arrives in Garmisch about 0900. But check the exact times, and be sure not to take the faster trains that follow the water-level route through Kufstein.

Transportation within the twin cities is by bus lines that connect the major recreation areas and facilities. Service is frequent, every fifteen minutes most of the day.

MAPS AND GUIDEBOOKS

An excellent guidebook, albeit in German, is *Die schönsten Wanderungen rund um Garmisch-Partenkirchen, Mittenwald, Murnau, Oberammergau, Bad Kohlgrub und Umgebung*. Even if you can't read German, the sketch maps are good and much of the trail information is self-explanatory. The pocket-size book is published in Garmisch and can be obtained locally. The best map for wandering is the RV Wanderkarte 11453, *Garmisch-Partenkirchen Mittenwald*, at the scale of 1:30,000.

WEATHER AND CLIMATE

The topographic situation of Garmisch-Partenkirchen that brings lots of snow in the winter also brings lots of rain and cloudiness in the summer. Rainshowers are frequent; about half of summer days have them. Thunderstorms occur on about six days per month in the late spring and summer. They become much less frequent in the fall; and September and October are ideal months for hiking. A caution, though: snow can occur any time of year above timberline, even in summer. Hikers must be alert to the possibility of bad weather and be prepared to change plans if a summer storm brings snow.

Temperatures are relatively cool. This is partly because of the elevation (700 meters) and partly because of the topographic situation of the town in a broad valley, which forms a natural cold-pocket. So nights may be quite cool even though daytime temperatures in the valley are quite pleasant.

Useful information

Tourist information

Verkehrsamt, *Bahnhof.*
Amtliches Bayerisches Reisebüro (ABR). Official Bavarian Travel Bureau. *Bahnhof.* Tel. 5 51 25. Inquire about guided hikes in the summer.

Maps, guidebooks, and trail information

Verkehrsamt der Kurverwaltung (Information bureau of the Spa Administration), Bahnhofstrasse 34. Tel. 25 70. Conducts guided hikes in the summer. Sells trail maps and guidebooks.
Bergsteigerschule Zugspitze, Rathausplatz 14 (in Sport Kratzmair). Tel. 30 40.
Wander- und Kletterschule Sport Wipfelder, Klammstrasse 3. Tel. 48 05.
Buchsdruckerei und Verlag A. Adam (Adam Publishers), Druckergasse 3. Tel. 29 35. Publishes a local guidebook.
Deutscher Alpenverein (DAV), Bahnhofstrasse 13. Tel. 27 01.

Local transportation

Town bus. Several lines connect the various ski lifts with the *Bahnhof*. Lines also connect with outlying settlements. Main terminal and transfer point is at the *Bahnhof*.

Accommodations

Garmisch-Partenkirchen is considered to be a health resort and has hundreds of hotels and other accommodations. There are so many that it is usually not difficult to find suitable accommodations in all price ranges during summer months. Booking office is the Verkerhrsamt der Kurverwaltung listed above.

Youth Hostel, Jochstrasse 10. Tel. 29 80. Bus F from *Bahnhof* to Burgrain. Two hundred ninety-six beds.

Naturfreundeheim des TVDN, Schalmeiweg 21 (Partenkirchen). Tel. 43 22. Friendly, comfortable accommodations.

Miscellaneous

Weather forecast. Tel. 5 20 20.

An easy walk
to the famous Partnachklamm

DIFFICULTY	Grade 2, rain gear appropriate for the walk
DISTANCE	7 km maximum, less with ski lifts
WALKING TIME	2–4 hours, depending on route
MAPS	F&B Wanderkarte 322, *Garmisch-Partenkirchen*
	RV Wanderkarte 11453, *Garmisch-Partenkirchen*
	Mittenwald, 1:30,000
GUIDEBOOK	*Die schönsten Wanderungen rund um*
	Garmisch-Partenkirchen, Mittenwald, Murnau,
	Oberammergau, Bad Kohlgrub und Umgebung.
	Garmisch-Partenkirchen: ADAM-Verlag. Good
	maps and color photos; available locally

The 100-meter-deep Partnachklamm is scarcely 3 kilometers from the main railroad station, as the crow flies. You might expect that a famous tourist attraction so close to town might be somewhat overrated. But not so with this one. The Partnach River has carved out a narrow gorge with vertical sides. In turn, the local stoneworkers have carved a trail out of these sheer walls. The result is a spectacular walk, accessible in just a few minutes from the center of town.

There are many possibilities for walks in the area. It is possible to see the gorge with a minimum of walking, utilizing horse-drawn taxis and cable cars. But good paths criss-crossing the area provide opportunity for numerous walks, including one to the top of Eckbauer that can be done in a half day. We describe several routes; we suggest you obtain a copy of a trail map, from which you can plan a dozen walks.

All of the routes described start at the Olympic ski stadium, reachable by city bus (any bus marked "Skistadion-Kainzenbad" and marked 1, 2, 3, or 4 will get you there in ten minutes from the *Hauptbahnhof*). From the bus stop near the stadium, take the road that heads south along the river. Although this road is closed to public traffic, it is possible (but not recommended) to take a horse-drawn taxi to the gorge. First stop (in fifteen minutes) is the little restaurant Lenz'n-Hütte.

The path immediately crosses the Partnach on a bridge and continues left up the valley to Wildenau, a tiny settlement with several inns as well as the valley station of the Graseckbahn cable car. Here the trail leaves the road and heads for the gorge. It soon reaches the entrance station, where a nominal fee is collected (free for members of the Alpine Club!). The path through the gorge was built in 1910–1912 to bring wood from the upper reaches of the Partnach. One is filled with wonder at the determination of the townspeople to construct this access route to the upper pastures and forests. For most of the way, the path has been carved out of solid rock. Caution is advised, for the footing may be wet and slippery.

At the upper end of the gorge, take the path to the left, to the imposing Forsthaus Graseck, another hostelry for food, drink, and overnight accommodations. Turn right and follow the farm road south a few hundred meters to the trail junction at the point where the road bends sharply to the left. The route up Eckbauer leaves the road left at this point, but take a few minutes to walk to Mittergras-

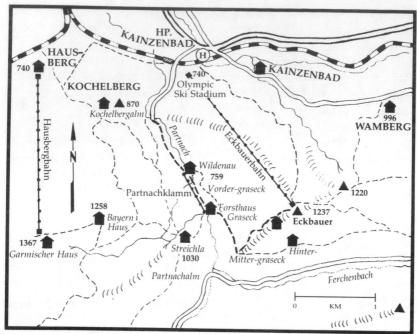

Partnachklamm

eck. The views of the Alpspitze from the farm meadows will cause a heavy drain on your film supply!

But back to the Eckbauer trail junction. The path (P6) quickly enters the woods and climbs steeply, switchbacking up the south-westerly ridge. If the climb (nearly 300 meters of elevation gain) generates a powerful thirst, there is, of course, another restaurant near the top. And if you have stopped at each one of the *Hütte*, you may not have time to walk down and so will have to ride the cable car. But the walk back to the Olympic stadium along P6 is an easy and attractive one, with views of Garmisch-Partenkirchen along the way.

There are so many paths along these slopes that you can arrange a walk of almost any distance and duration. At the top of the Klamm, for example, you can go right instead of left, to Streichla. From here, a farm road heads back to the starting point at Lenz'n-Hütte. Alternatively, after walking the farm road for a kilometer, you can take a path (P3) diverging left to Kochelberg-Alm and down to town, not far from the *Bahnhof*. Whichever way you take, you will not be disappointed with the paths and scenery in and around the Partnachklamm.

A high Alpine walk
to the spectacular gorge of the Höllental

DIFFICULTY	Grade 4, well-graded paths, but slippery in places
DISTANCE	10 km
WALKING TIME	4–5 hours
MAPS	F&B Wanderkarte 322, *Garmisch-Partenkirchen* *RV Wanderkarte 11453; Garmisch-Partenkirchen Mittenwald*, 1:30,000
GUIDEBOOK	*Die schönsten Wanderungen rund um Garmisch-Partenkirchen, Mittenwald, Murnau, Oberammergau, Bad Kohlgrub und Umgebung.* Garmisch-Partenkirchen: ADAM-Verlag. Good maps and color photos; available locally

The Germanic passion for reaching the top somehow, whatever the cost, seems to have reached a zenith in the Garmisch region. The Zugspitze, highest peak in Germany, boasts not one but two incredible cable cars to the summit, one from the German side, the other from the Austrian side. (Indeed, there is a customs house at the very summit!) For those who prefer mine tunnels to cable cars suspended high above the rocky cliffs, the Germans have provided the Zugspitzbahn, a cog railroad that tunnels its way to the top, or near it. The Garmisch-Partenkirchen section of the German Alpine Club contributed its share of difficult feats of construction by building the "trail" through the Höllentalklamm in the first years of this century.

Trail it scarcely is. For much of the way through this incredibly narrow cleft in the rocks, it is more like a mine tunnel. The way is lit by dim electric lights and an occasional window cut in the rock wall of the gorge. When the trail does come out into the open, the view of the gorge is spectacular, to say the least. The river rushes and pounds its way between vertical walls. At times, you are walking *over* the river, where the footway has been cantilevered over the rushing water.

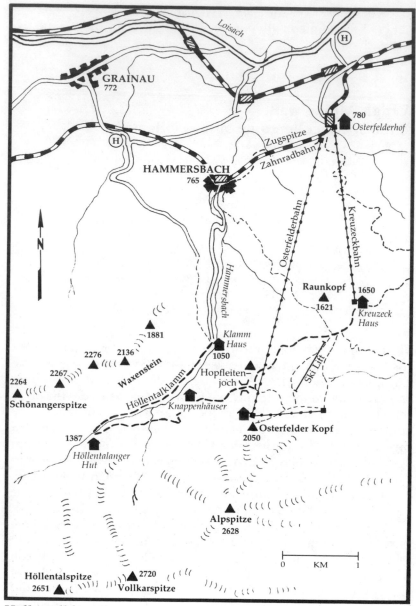

Höllentalklamm

If you continue up the Höllental, you eventually come to a great glacial basin that sweeps down from the very summit of the Zugspitze. There is a way to the summit through the Höllentalkar, but it is only for *geubte Bergsteiger*, experienced mountain climbers. Ordinary walkers can work their way well up the valley, far enough to sample the majestic beauty of the Zugspitze and its neighbors of the Wetterstein Mountains. You can walk up from Hammersbach and down the same way; but we suggest that a round trip utilizing the height-conquering cables of the Kreuzeckbahn will give you more of the flavor of this rugged high country. Besides, the cable car eliminates nearly 1000 meters of tedious climbing through relatively uninteresting heavily forested slopes.

Starting point for the trip is the base station of the Kreuzeckbahn. City buses 1, 2, 3, and 4 shuttle between the Olympic stadium and the Osterfelder and Kreuzeck cable-car stations, right next to each other. There is also a stop on the Zugspitze cog railway right at the cable cars, so getting there presents no difficulty. Getting to the top via cable is no problem either: pay the fee and enjoy the quick ride to the Kreuzeck. There is, of course, a restaurant at the top cable station, in case you missed breakfast. Our trail starts at a sign indicating the route to the Höllentalklamm and Hammersbach, marked KK1 and KE3. (We stay on KK1.) The broad path leads left through a gate, shortly reaching a trail junction, where our route proceeds right on the less steep trail. Leaving the service road, the trail contours the slope just at timberline, with extensive views of the Loisach Valley and the mountains around it.

In a few hundred meters from the top of the lift there is a trail junction; we take the right-hand bend, which is not the steepest trail. Here it is very broad and well graded. The trail climbs gently and soon passes the base station of a T-bar ski lift. After we pass the base station, our trail to Höllental and Hupfleitenjoch diverges right, whereas the broad road we've been on keeps going up the hill to Kreuzeck. The path, now narrow, contours the slope, climbing very gently. This is just about at timberline, and the views to the right down to the Loisach Valley are extensive.

The trail now passes through a conifer forest of larch and Norway spruce and underneath the cables of the Osterfelder *Seilbahn* high above. We climb up a long switchback and just before reaching a pass come to a trail junction. A signpost indicates the way ahead to the Knappenhäuser and Höllental. The trail designation is H5. In just a few minutes we reach the pass, about forty-five minutes from the top of the Kreuzeckbahn. A short trail climbs the Schwarzenkopf (a 60-meter vertical rise) for a fine panoramic view.

From the pass down into the Höllentalklamm, the trail is steep and zig-zags down a broad gully. The Höllentalanger Hut is visible far below. Along this stretch, the footway is primarily on limestone, which can be very slippery in wet weather. However, the path, which at places is cut into the rock face, is broad and well graded and not particularly dangerous, although caution is advised, especially on the wood steps. At any rate, fixed cables have been installed on the more exposed locations. After the steep portion, the trail contours around the slope, through tunnels blasted out from the cliff, and eventually reaches the Knappenhäuser, a hut with food, drink, and overnight accommodations. Beyond the hut, the trail heads downward toward the Höllentalanger Hut.

On the opposite wall of the valley, a spectacular waterfall, the Mariensprung, can be seen. The waterfall springs full force from an opening high on the cliff and plunges in a great cascade to the valley floor. Upon reaching the hut, we find that this cascade forms the principal tributary of the Höllental River. Although the main stream drains a vast glacial cirque, the stream bed is dry at the site of the hut, the water flowing beneath the gravelly surface and reappearing downstream.

The hut is a typical full-service Alpenverein hut. Here our route turns downstream, meets and crosses the river, then proceeds along the north bank to the entrance of the Höllentalklamm, about a half hour from the hut. Although there is a charge for the walk through the gorge, it is nominal and certainly a small price to pay for the upkeep of the spectacular trail. However, it is possible to avoid the gorge by taking the trail that goes up the southeast wall of the canyon.

The Höllentalklamm is one of the famous sights of the Garmisch area. The trail through the gorge was built by the Garmisch-Partenkirchen section of the German Alpine Club just after the beginning of the century. It was largely blasted out of solid rock, passing through dimly lighted tunnels, opening onto galleries that provide a view of the rushing cascade and a tiny strip of blue sky above, occasionally cantilevered on ironworks suspended over the river, and passing under the famous iron bridge. The walls stretch vertically upward as much as 120 meters, yet the width at the bottom is

Trail cut in rock face at Höllentalklamm

frequently less than 5 meters. In its 1-kilometer length, the stream drops 146 meters.

It is a most spectacular walk, albeit a wet one even in dry weather. A raincoat and nonslip shoes are appropriate. At the bottom end of the gorge, the entrance hut bars the way. Here the gatekeeper exacts his tribute, but only a couple of deutschmarks. Refreshments are available here. Below the entrance, the trail drops down quickly to a gravel road, which it follows to Hammersbach.

The gravel road finally reaches a paved village road, which you should follow right about 100 meters to a sign indicating the way to the Zugspitzbahn railroad station. Here you can hop the train back to Garmisch; the trains come every half hour.

Austria & Liechtenstein

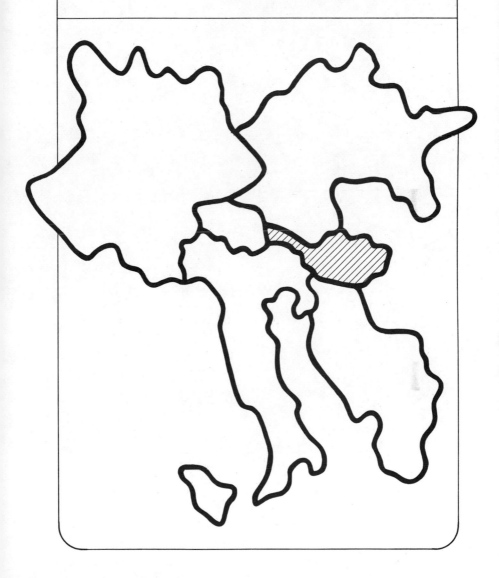

8. Innsbruck

Innsbruck is something of a hiker's paradise. The east-west valley of the Inn River is very narrow, and the high mountains rise precipitously both north and south. Hiking trails start at the very edge of town, and in a few minutes you can be far from the city bustle. Base stations of two aerial tramways—one up Hafelekar, the other up the Patscherkofel—are close to the center of town.

More than any other Alpine city we know of, Innsbruck caters to hikers and climbers. Several years ago, the Innsbruck Tourist Office established Club Innsbruck, which provides free guided mountain walks and climbs to tourists who remain in the city for three nights during the summer season. Brochures are widely available at city hotels and at the hotel reservation office in the main railroad station. You must sign up the day before; and you won't know where you are going until the group gathers in the morning. But the tours are guided by experts from the Innsbruck Alpine School and are geared to the experience level of each day's group.

If you don't want to join a group, or won't be in Innsbruck for the required three nights, strike out on your own. There are many possibilities for walks of all difficulties. We describe two rather easy ones, both above timberline. We also describe two fairly strenuous walks, one of them leading to the summit of a 3000-meter peak.

TRANSPORTATION

As in most European cities, the *Hauptbahnhof* is the hub of the local and long-distance transportation network. Although a relatively small city, Innsbruck has three tramway and twenty-five bus lines fanning out from the *Bahnhof Platz*. It is also on the main line from Munich to Italy over the Brenner Pass, and has good train service east and west as well.

MAPS AND GUIDEBOOKS

The place to go for maps and guidebooks is the Freytag-Berndt und Artaria bookstore on Wilhelm-Greil Strasse 15, two blocks from the *Hauptbahnhof*. The collection is immense. Just behind the bookstore is the headquarters of the Innsbruck section of the Austrian Alpine Club. They, too, have maps and guidebooks and are very helpful with information for the visiting hiker. A very useful map, full of information on the local transportation network, cable cars, and ski areas, as well as being a street map, is the *Innsbruck Stadtplan*, published by the city and widely available.

WEATHER AND CLIMATE

To a considerable extent, Innsbruck is shielded from winter storms by the surrounding mountains. Thus precipitation in the fall, winter, and spring accounts for about sixty percent of the annual total, or about 56 centimeters. Forty percent, or about 36 centimeters, falls in the three summer months, mostly in showers and thundershowers. Higher up, precipitation amounts increase dramatically. On the Patscherkofel, 1200 meters above the valley, annual precipitation amounts to 120 centimeters.

Lightning and thunderstorms are frequent in the mountains, especially in early summer. The average number of days with a thunderstorm is five in June, eight in July, five in August, and two in September. Although summer precipitation is in the form of rain in the lower valleys, snowfall is not uncommon above timberline any time of the year.

Summer temperatures are mild in the valley, but substantially cooler at timberline. Typically, the temperature falls about six Celsius degrees for every 1000 meters of increased elevation.

The four walks described in this chapter all involve walking above timberline. Although the walks are easy in good weather, remember that conditions can deteriorate rapidly in summer storms. In case the weather appears unsettled, inquire at the Innsbruck Tourist Office (Städtisches Verkehrsbüro) for the day's forecast.

Useful information

Tourist information

Städtisches Verkehrsbüro, Burggraben 3, 6020 Innsbruck. Tel. (05222) 25 7 15.
Tiroler Fremdenverkehrswerbung, Boznerplatz 6, A-6100 Innsbruck. Tel. (05222) 20 7 77.

Maps, guidebooks, and trail information

Alpine Auskunft (Alpine information), Tiroler Landesreisebüro, Boznerplatz 7, A-6010 Innsbruck. Tel. (05222) 34 9 85. Information on walking and climbing in the Tyrol.
Österreichischen Alpenverein (ÖAV), Wilhelm-Greil Strasse 15, A-6200 Innsbruck (off rear courtyard). Tel. (05222) 24 1 06. A major section of the ÖAV, very helpful even to nonmembers.
Freytag-Berndt und Artaria KG, Wilhelm-Greil Strasse 15, A-6200 Innsbruck. Fantastic assortment of trail maps, guidebooks, and other publications on the mountains of the world.
Club Innsbruck, a city-run tourist program, conducts free daily guided hikes in the summer for tourists who stay at least three nights. Inquire at the Städtisches Verkehrsbüro, Burggraben 3. Tel. (05222) 25 7 15.

Local transportation

Innsbrucker Verkehrsbetriebe operates three tram lines and twenty-five bus lines in and around Innsbruck. Network map included on the *Innsbruck Stadtplan Information Panorama.*
Austrian postal buses extend the bus network farther out. Buses leave from the central bus station next to the *Hauptbahnhof.* Free schedules are available.

Accommodations

Hotel Information Office, *Hauptbahnhof*. Tel. (05222) 23 7 66.
Youth hostels. Youth Hostel Innsbruck, Reichenauerstrasse 147, A-6020
    Innsbruck. Tel. (05222) 46 1 79. One hundred ninety beds. Open all
    year. Youth Hostel Schwedenhaus, Rennweg 17b, A-6020 Innsbruck.
    Tel. (05222) 25 8 14. One hundred beds. Summer only.
Camping. Campingplatz Innsbruck-west, Kranebitter Allee 214. Tel. (05222)
    84 1 80. Campingplatz Reichenau, Reichenauerstrasse. Tel. (05222) 46 2
    52. Bus connection to city center.

Miscellaneous

Weather forecast. Given in English every morning at 0805 over the Austrian
    state radio and television (ÖRF). Tel. 16 for a German-language forecast.

Along the Goetheweg
to Pfeishütte

DIFFICULTY	Grade 4, mostly above timberline
DISTANCE	10 km
WALKING TIME	6 hours
MAPS	F&B Wanderkarte 322, *Wetterstein, Karwendel, Seefeld*
	KOMP Wanderkarte 26, *Karwendelgebirge*
GUIDEBOOK	Schiechtl, H.M. *Tiroler Wanderbuch 2.* Innsbruck: Tyrolia Verlag, 1977

It is easy to understand why Innsbruck has been so thoroughly
identified with Austrian mountain climbing. The Inn River Valley is
just wide enough to support a good-sized city. And the mountains
rise up from that valley in one grand sweep. The Nordkette (North
Chain) of the Karwendel Mountains is an almost overwhelming
presence, shining in the summer sun, glistening white when fresh
snow mantles the ridge in fall and winter.

   It is not surprising, either, that the Hafelekar, the nearest peak
on the ridge, should be one of the first Austrian peaks to be climb-
able by cable car. The cable, built in 1927, runs nearly to the top of
Hafelekarspitz, nearly 1800 meters above the Inn River. Even

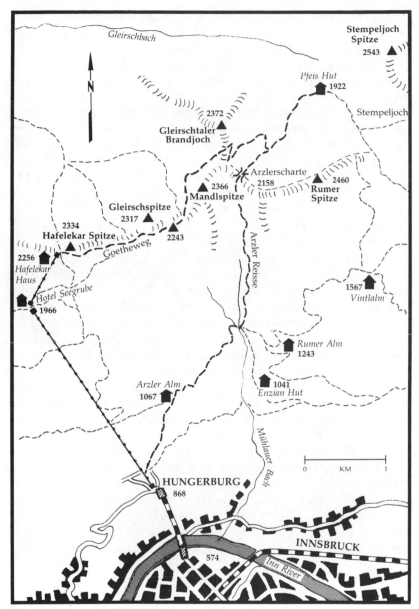

Hafelekar and Pfeishütte

though it is only 100 meters higher than the Patscherkofel, Innsbruck's southern sentinel, it is a much more rugged peak of true Alpine character. A walk along the Goetheweg, a well-graded path that traverses the very crest of the ridge, will reward the hiker with an Alpine experience just a few minutes away from downtown Innsbruck.

The southern slope of the Nordkette is laced with trails of great variety. We have selected a route from the top of the cable car to the mountain hut, the Pfeishütte, run by the Innsbruck section of the Austrian Alpine Club. Although it is above timberline, the path is nearly level for most of the way. Indeed, the total climb is only 120 meters, with a 470-meter drop to the hut. Many hikers do the easy round trip; we suggest riding the cable car up and walking down. But the variety of trails will enable you to select a route of almost any difficulty.

The first portion of the journey is via the Hungerburgbahn, a funicular railway that starts in the city, on the south side of the river, a fifteen-minute walk from the city center. The base station can also be reached by the number 1 tram from Maria-Theresien-Strasse or the C bus from the main railroad station, to the Hungerburg Talstation. From the top of the Hungerburgbahn, follow signs to the base station of the Nordkettenbahn. This is a two-section lift; transfer at Seegrube to the Hafelekar section.

The upper station of the lift is at 2269 meters, only 65 meters lower than the summit of Hafelekar. The Goetheweg, our trail, avoids the summit, but a good trail makes the detour and rejoins the main trail on the other side. Take your choice. The Goetheweg, marked 219, must have been laid out with a surveyor's level. It winds around the ridge, first south, then north. The side slopes are extremely steep and the path is secured with cables in places. The views of the Inn River Valley, with its mosaic of farms and woods and small towns, are nothing short of extraordinary. Across the valley to the south, you can make out the Europabrücke, the highest automobile bridge in Europe, standing tall on its slender stilts. Here also, you can see the substantial snow fences just below the trail, in reality sturdy avalanche-protection devices.

As the trail passes to the north side of the ridge, the wild and uninhabited upper reaches of the Gleirschbach and the Gleirsch-Halltal range come into view. Eventually, the trail drops down to a broad saddle to the left and contours around the giant scree slope of the Mühlkar. At the north end of the cirque, the trail climbs sharply

On the trail to Pfeishütte

on zig-zags to the pass at Mandlscharte (2277 meters). The Goethe-weg then angles down to the broad floor of the Pfeis. This broad morainal valley is dotted with the sinkholes so characteristic of these limestone mountains. The limestone produces an interesting Alpine flora. Colorful flowers alternate with the sturdy krummholz. To the north, the barren slopes of the Gleirsch chain reveal steeply tilted bedding planes—evidence of the vigorous crustal deformations that are still going on. The trail continues its gentle descent, a minor ridge is rounded, and the Pfeishütte (1922 meters) comes into view, 250 meters down and three-quarters of an hour from the pass. (Along one stretch, where the valley narrows, give a shout. You'll be answered with a loud and clear echo!)

On the way to the hut, you may have noticed a sturdy sign that obviously had something to say, albeit in German. Ominously it tells the tale of a party of four strong hikers who were caught by an October snowstorm. Though near the safety of the hut, they never reached it, and perished here. The lesson is clear. Even though this terrain may seem friendly and benign on a mild summer or autumn day, it is above timberline, where snowstorms can occur *any* month of the year. So check the forecast before leaving for the day, keep an eye on the clouds, and carry clothing to keep you warm and dry in case of a sudden storm. And, most importantly, be prepared to turn back if a storm threatens.

After lunch at the hut, retrace your steps past the warning sign to a trail junction. The branch to the right is the one we came down; now proceed toward Arzlerscharte, the low pass visible straight ahead. The trail number on this stretch is 217, and is well marked with red/white/red paint blazes. At the pass, a marked route leads left up the ridge to the Rumer Spitze (2460 meters). The route is well marked, but is not for inexperienced climbers. From the pass, it is also possible to take a path back to Mandlscharte, if you want to return to the cable car.

This you might want to do after looking at the trail ahead. It goes straight down the rubble- and scree-filled Arzler Reisse (gulley). The stones are at the angle of repose so that footing is tricky if you are not accustomed to such scree slopes. But if you are, and have sturdy knees, it makes for a quick descent. A trail down is more or less visible, but it is mostly a matter of heading down the gully, following the line of least resistance.

Eventually we reach a forest road. For the return to Hungerburg, follow the road right past the Innsbruck water tunnel to Arzler Alm, where refreshments can be obtained. (There is a good spring here also.) Here the trail diverges left from the road (sign) and follows a dirt road to Hungerburg and the funicular to Innsbruck.

A slightly longer, but easier, route from the Pfeishütte follows trail 221 toward Stempeljoch but takes the branch to Kreuzjochl about 1 kilometer from the hut. At the next junction, follow the path right (west) toward the Rumer Spitze for a few hundred meters, then the path left (south) to Vintlalm and Rumer Alm. This latter is on the road intersected by the direct descent from Arzlerscharte and is about 1 kilometer from that point.

On the Patscherkofel, Innsbruck's favorite mountain

DIFFICULTY	Grade 3–4
DISTANCE	10 km
WALKING TIME	4–5 hours
MAPS	F&B Wanderkarte 241, *Innsbruck–Stubai–Sellrain–Brenner*
	KOMP Wanderkarte 036, *Innsbruck–Igls–Hall i. Tirol*, 1:30,000
GUIDEBOOK	Schiechtl, H. M. *Tiroler Wanderbuch 2.* Innsbruck: Tyrolia Verlag, 1977

Innsbruck and Hafelekar from Patscherkofel

Few walks in the Innsbruck area are as scenic and pleasant on a mild summer day as the walk along the Zirbenweg, high on the north slopes of the Patscherkofel. The path, nearly level for its 7-kilometer length, is just at timberline and wanders in and out of the trees and krummholz, the scrubby and twisted mats of timberline trees. It connects the upper stations of two cable cars and thus makes possible an easy walk when the weather is mild. The walk is an educational one, too, since it has been supplied with some forty-four signs describing the trees and flowers and other natural phenomena that can be observed along the trail. Although the text is in German, the scientific names are in standard Latin and therefore accessible to the amateur or professional botanist or zoologist. Since the path is on the north side of the mountain, exceptional views of Innsbruck and the towns and farms of the Inn Valley are with you the whole way. It is a marvelous way to spend a sunny Sunday.

The trip begins with a bus ride to Igls from the *Hauptbahnhof* in Innsbruck, line J. The bus is marked Igls–Patscherkofelbahn. The bus leaves half-hourly, on the hour and half hour. Take the bus to the end of the line, which is right at the cable-car station. Cable-car departures are frequent during the summer season, about every six minutes *nach Bedarf*, "according to demand." The trip to the upper

Patscherkofel

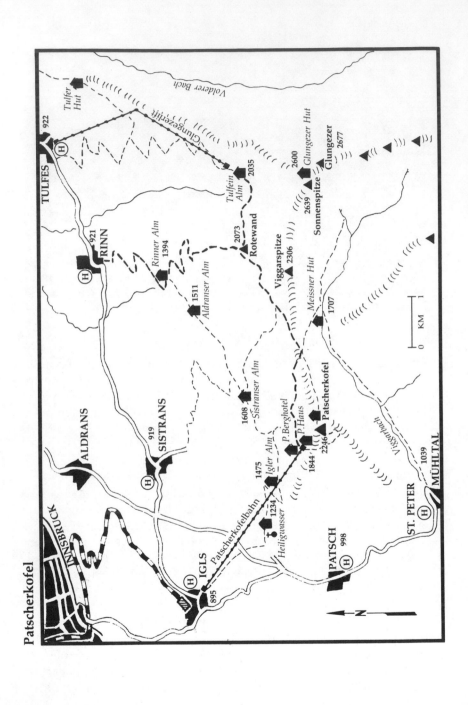

station takes approximately fifteen minutes. On leaving the upper station, walk north along a well-trod path along the rampart. Here you will have a magnificent view of the city and the mountains to the north across the Inn River Valley.

At the end of this rampart, a trail switches back to the right, toward the hotel just behind the upper station of the cable car. In about 100 meters, find the signpost that indicates the beginning of the Zirbenweg. The path leads left around the shoulder of the Patscherkofel. In a few meters there is the first of the nature-path signs explaining the genesis of the Zirbenweg. The path is named after the local name for *Pinus cembra*, Arolla pine, here the common timberline tree. The path also marks the approximate northern extension of the extensive Tyrolean pine forest.

(If you want to go over the summit of the Patscherkofel, a trail leads from here off to the right, and climbs the summit, which is only a few hundred meters above. This may not be a particularly interesting climb since the summit is covered with television antennas and microwave dishes, a weather station, and a restaurant, as well as the upper station of the chair lift that runs from the upper station of the Patscherkofelbahn.)

The signposts along the Zirbenweg describe a number of interesting local phenomena, including the location of avalanche paths and starting zones. It is likely that timberline has been lowered nearly 200 meters in elevation in the past several hundred years as a result of cattle and sheep grazing at high elevations above timberline. This grazing has increased the danger of snow avalanches because the trees were removed in areas where avalanches typically start. You can also see evidence of rock and mud avalanches that have occurred as a result of heavy rainfall subsequent to the destruction of the deep-rooted vegetation by snow avalanches.

Along here you will find larch trees, a deciduous conifer tree, the beautiful and ubiquitous alpenrose, and the pine for which the trail is named. The typical habitat for this hardy tree is the high-altitude region from 1500 to 2400 meters above sea level. Some reach a ripe old age, as indicated by a sign next to a 250-year-old tree. The pine is tough and elastic and well suited to withstand the rigors of high wind and cold that buffet these trees all year long. Finally the trail meets the path that traverses the summit at Boscheben, a little mountain restaurant where food and drink can be obtained. This is the first time we have been on the ridge, and we can now see into the valley of the Viggarbach to the south. The upper reaches of this valley, a wild and rocky cirque, are ringed about by an imposing chain of peaks: Glungezer (2600 meters), Kreuzspitz (2746 meters) with its summit cross, Rosenjoch (2796 meters), and Grünbergspitze (2790 meters).

From this point, an alternate route leads down to the Viggarbach Valley and Meissner Hut (indicated by signs at the junction), and the trail to St. Peter in the Wipptal, where the bus to Innsbruck can be boarded.

The Zirbenweg continues along the ridge, toward Rote Wand and Tulfein Alp. The trail wanders back and forth from one side to the other, eventually reaching a very steep south-facing forested slope that appears never to have been logged or heavily grazed. Here the timberline is about 2000 meters. On the north-facing slope, which is gentler, there is a much lower timberline, apparently having been abnormally lowered by heavy grazing and logging.

Within a few minutes another trail junction is reached with the route straight ahead going over Viggarspitze to Glungezerhütte. The Zirbenweg branches left, passing through a stand of Norway spruce occupying its ecological niche below the larch and Alpine pine. Soon we walk through a curious mixture of krummholz, typical of timberline, but with an unusual twist: occasional trees of tall and erect larch and pine poke through. Since the krummholz is supposed to exist where large trees cannot withstand the severe timberline weather, something unusual must be going on here. It appears that when the heavy grazing pressure that led to a lowered timberline was reduced, krummholz developed, but at an atypically low elevation. This in turn produced conditions favorable for full-size trees to poke their way through the krummholz mat.

Soon the trail to Sistranser Alm branches left. (It is marked with blue paint blazes and leads in less than an hour to the restaurant at Sistranser Alm, where food and drink can be obtained. From this point, the trail continues down to Sistrans, where the bus back to Innsbruck can be boarded.)

However, we stay on the Zirbenweg to Rote Wand. The trail works its way across the talus slope beneath the cliffs of the Neunerspitze. Huge blocks of rock lie in jumbled profusion. Somewhat incongruously, trash containers have been placed along this section of trail, a mistake, for they do not seem to be emptied and indeed are an invitation for walkers to discard their trash rather than packing it out. But ignore the trash containers and look carefully at the rocks. Water collects in the cracks, then freezes, exerting primal forces to split asunder massive blocks. Sometimes the blocks remain close together, perhaps to catch a pine seed that germinates, grows, and exerts further pressure. Other blocks, poised on a steep slope, may find their centers of gravity pushed far enough away from the slope to enable them to start a crashing journey to the slopes below.

We pass one great red block, the Rote Wand, and in 200 meters reach a trail junction. Here we have a choice. Straight ahead on the Zirbenweg, we reach Tulfein and the cable car to Tulfes and the bus back to Innsbruck. The distance is about 2 kilometers along a level path. If you prefer some downhill walking, take trail 45 to the left to Rinn, as we will do. The trail drops immediately into the krummholz, then soon into the timber. The footway is narrow and steep, but clear, and is marked with frequent red or red-and-white paint blazes and the occasional tin number 45 sign, black numbers on yellow background, nailed on the trees.

The trail soon enters a logging road. Some care is required along this stretch, since logging activities have obscured the footway in places. However, the route is well marked with red-and-white paint blazes. On one of the roads, a sign points left (west) to a tiny chapel, the Kriegerkapel. It is a worthwhile five-minute detour on a level road, for it sits on a little promontory and has a beautiful view of the Inn River Valley below.

Retracing our steps eastward along the logging road, we soon come to a junction: straight ahead (trail 42) for the ski lift; or switchback left and down the hill for Rinneralm and Rinn. We take the low road.

Having left the pine forest, we are now in a dense Norway spruce forest. We see lessons in good forestry: carefully logged areas thick with vigorous new growth; well-tended old stands with carefully pruned boles, standing straight and tall; logging roads with little or no erosion. It is obvious that the Austrians value their forests highly, not only for recreation but also for the wood that they produce.

After several switchbacks along the road, watch for a sign indicating the trail diverging left to Rinneralm and Rinn. In a few minutes you will reach the little restaurant at Rinneralm, where you can obtain food and drink, a pleasant stop on the way down. The road follows the woods road on down, marked with number 45 signs. When you meet a gravel road that continues up the mountain, keep to the left, heading downhill.

At an intersection just before reaching town, the trail heads straight down to town. However, a sign indicates that the way right leads to the bus station. Take this route to a fence gate. Keep left, and head straight down to town. This will take you directly to the bus station at the Gasthaus Post. Innsbruck buses leave approximately hourly, at 1512, 1620, and 1805.

Climb the Rinnenspitze, a 3000-meter peak

DIFFICULTY	Grade 5
DISTANCE	12 km
WALKING TIME	7–8 hours
MAPS	F&B Wanderkarte 241, *Innsbruck–Stubai–Sellrain–Brenner*
	KOMP Wanderkarte 36, *Innsbruck–Brenner*
GUIDEBOOKS	Reifsnyder, W. E. *Hut Hopping in the Austrian Alps*. San Francisco: Sierra Club Books, 1973
	Schiechtl, H. M. *Tiroler Wanderbuch 2*. Innsbruck: Tyrolia Verlag, 1977

It is possible to get to the glacier country in a one-day trip from Innsbruck. Possible, but a long, hard day indeed. The trip we describe takes you to the top of a 3000-meter peak high above a half dozen glaciers in the Stubai Alps. From the Rinnenspitze, a vast panorama of craggy peaks and glistening glaciers is spread at your feet. It is perhaps the most spectacular view of the Stubai from a peak that is accessible to the non-rock-climbing hiker.

Not that the climb is completely benign. Although the trail to the top is well marked, and the scariest parts are secured by steel cables pinned to the rock, it is not a trip for the acrophobic. But if a little rock scrambling doesn't faze you, you will find this a most exciting and rewarding climb.

Although the trip can be made in one day, if you can spare a weekend, you can overnight at Franz Senn Hut and make the climb easily the following day. The hut has excellent accommodations, both in private rooms and in the more crowded mattress rooms. Blankets are provided, and all you have to bring is clothing and shoes suitable for an above-timberline scramble. Whether you stay overnight or not, you will wish you had more time to explore this spectacular and inspiring Alpine wonderland.

An Innsbruck city bus (the Stubai line) runs from the *Hauptbahnhof* directly to Neustift in the Stubaital. From here, take the Jeep-bus to Oberriss, at the end of the road in Oberbergtal. The supply cable lift to Franz Senn starts at Oberriss; if you desire, you can have your pack cabled to the hut for a nominal fee.

From the hut (refreshments) at Oberriss, the trail leads westward across a meadow and then climbs sharply on a series of switchbacks, staying on the north side of the brook. (Just below the switchbacks, avoid paths to the left that dead-end at the brook.) After a climb of about a kilometer, the way becomes less steep, and the hut soon comes into view. Views are extensive on this stretch, which is above

Franz Senn Hut and the Rinnenspitze

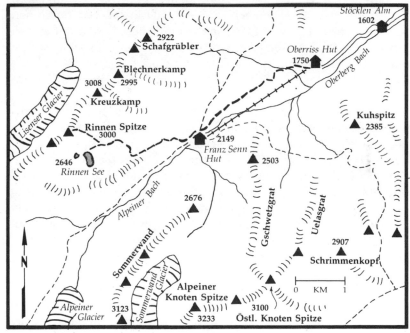

timberline. Behind us lies the Oberbergtal, with the pastures at Oberriss and Stocklenalm, closed at the far end by the twin peaks of the Schlicker See Spitze and the Hohen Burgstall. Just to the right of Burgstall, down the rocky rib, you can make out the Starkenburger Hut.

And ahead of us a short distance lies Franz Senn Hut, set in the great glacial valley of the Alpeiner Bach. This is a typical glacier-sculpted valley, rounded, with a rather swampy river draining the glacier at the head end. We cross the nearly level meadow to the hut, after spending an hour and a half climbing the 400-meter rise from Oberriss. "Hut" is perhaps a misnomer for this rather imposing structure, which has accommodations for 250 and boasts hot showers and flush toilets. Nevertheless, it is very reasonable, the food is good, and it is a fine place to spend a couple of days exploring the meadows and peaks of the Alpeiner Bach.

But if we want to make the top of the Rinnenspitze, we must not tarry too long. The trail from the hut leads northward over a bridge, bears sharply right, and leads in about ten minutes to a trail junction. The trail angles sharply to the left, following the sign to the Rinnen See, and climbs the valley wall in a southwesterly direction. In a short while, a flat bench is reached and the outlet of the Rinnen See is crossed. The trail then climbs more steeply to another trail junction, just below the lake, which, though not yet visible, can be reached in five minutes. The lake is a glacial tarn set in a cirque reminiscent of many of the small high-altitude lakes of the Sierra Nevada.

From the junction (sign), the trail to the peak branches northward and climbs the southeast ridge in a series of switchbacks. The peak is clearly visible from this stretch. The summit ridge is attained about 200 meters east of the summit. Although the ridge is sharp and rocky, the way is clearly marked with paint blazes. Some rock scrambling is necessary, and in a few places cables are placed to assist the climber. *Trittsicherheit*, the ability to place your feet safely and securely, is required on this stretch, but the scramble is not difficult. From the top, peaks and glaciers in profusion greet the eye. To the west, the Lisenser Glacier seems to reach up nearly to the summit. Due south lies the Alpeiner Glacier; and in between, the smaller but nearer Berglas lies under our feet. Because the Rinnenspitze is lower than many of the surrounding peaks, yet has an unobstructed view, the panorama from the summit is truly spectacular.

The climb from the hut takes about three hours, a vertical ascent of 860 meters. The return to the valley follows the same route, takes about a half hour less to Franz Senn, and a half hour less from there to Oberriss. Incidentally, you can call the Jeep-bus from the hut (226-218) to arrange for transportation back to Neustift and the Innsbruck bus.

Along the ski tracks of the Olympians

DIFFICULTY	Various, generally Grade 4
DISTANCE	Various, 6–12 km
WALKING TIME	2–6 hours, depending on route
MAPS	F&B Wanderkarte 241, *Innsbruck–Stubai–Sellrain–Brenner*
	KOMP Wanderkarte 36, *Innsbruck–Brenner*
GUIDEBOOK	Schiechtl, H. M. *Tiroler Wanderbuch 2*. Innsbruck: Tyrolia Verlag, 1977

At the head of the Lizum Valley, at an elevation of 1600 meters, lies the ski resort Axamer Lizum, site of the 1964 Winter Olympics. High Alpine meadows combine with moderate slopes served by long lifts to make one of the finest ski areas in the Innsbruck area. This ready access to the high country also makes for good summertime walking. Views from the bare ridges are extensive in all directions, but the scenery is dominated by the massive spires of the Kalkkogel to the south. As the name implies and their bright beauty attests, these mountains are formed from limestone. One of the most beautiful walks in the area skirts the north face of the range, nearly on the level, and is reachable at both ends by ski lifts.

Despite its apparent remoteness at the upper end of the narrow, heavily wooded Lizum Valley, Axamer Lizum is surprisingly easy to reach. Postal buses make the trip from the main railway station in Innsbruck to Axamer Lizum in forty-five minutes. And they run approximately hourly throughout the day. Morning buses leave at 0800, 0900, and 1000.

The route starts at the top of the Birgitzkopfl chair lift, heads south on trail 111, essentially on the contour, to the saddle at Halsl. Trail 111 continues southwestward, climbing gently through Lizumer Kar, the glacial cirque on the north side of Marchreisen

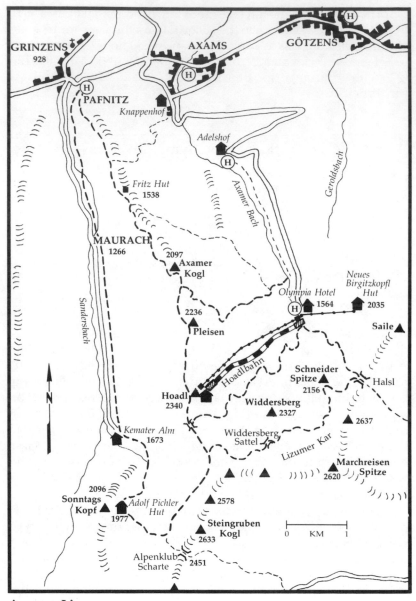

Axamer Lizum

Spitz, to Widdersberg Sattel. This is the highest point of the walk, at 2262 meters just over 200 meters higher than the starting point at the top of the chair lift. We now drop to the junction of the trail coming from Hoadl, mountain station of the other lifts from Axamer Lizum. We can, of course, go to Hoadl and take the lift back to our starting point.

But to continue the walk along the Kalkkogel, continue south along trail 111 to Adolf Pichler Hütte, a suitable lunch stop. The hut has food, drink, and overnight accommodations. This is a major trail junction; here we follow trail 117 north down the Griesbach to Kemater Alm (another mountain inn), thence down Sandersbach to Grinzens. The postal bus from here to Innsbruck runs approximately every hour (at 1545, 1655, 1745, and 1920), and the trip takes forty-five minutes. The distance for this walk is 15 kilometers and the walking time about five hours. The latter half of the walk from Kemater Alm to Grinzens is along a dead-end road. It is possible to hire a taxi for this part of the journey; you should inquire at the restaurant at Kemater Alm.

The ski lifts from Axamer Lizum open up a large area for walks of various durations, most of the walks rather gentle, considering the fact that the area is above timberline and the nearby Kalkkogel so rugged. Alternatives to the route described above include taking the cable car or funicular to Hoadl, then walking south to join trail 111 and the described route in either direction, or walking to Hoadl and making one of the circuits back to Axamer Lizum, as indicated on the map. Any way you take it, you will be making "one of the most rewarding and felicitous walks in the Innsbruck region," according to *Tiroler Wanderbuch 2*.

9. Salzburg

Salzburg always seems to be larger than life. Overshadowed in terms of size more than tenfold by Munich to the west and Vienna to the east, it still has a great cosmopolitan air. After all, it is the birthplace of Mozart and the home of one of the great music festivals of Europe—the Salzburg Festival. There is much to see and savor in this city of a hundred thousand. Salzburg is dominated by the great Hohensalzburg Castle, which sits on a dolomite block 120 meters above the river. It dates from the eleventh century and is the largest preserved fortress in Europe. A funicular railway runs from the main square near the cathedral to the top of the hill, a journey worth taking not only for the tour of the fortress, but also for the fine views of Salzburg and the surrounding countryside.

There is much to see in the countryside. The rolling hills and lakes of the Salzkammergut stretch eastward from the Salzach Valley. To the south lie the high peaks of the Berchtesgaden Alps. Curiously, if you travel due south from Salzburg, you run into the German border. A small piece of Bavaria juts southeastward into Austria. This little intrusion contains some of the most spectacular scenery in Bavaria—the fabled Königssee, a narrow fjordlike lake in the heart of Berchtesgaden National Park.

For close-in walking, try Kapuzinerberg, a hill in the very center of town. A clearly marked nature path starts near the north end of the Staats Brücke over the Salzach River. A bit farther out, Gaisberg (1288 meters), 850 meters above river level, has a network of trails.

To be sure, it has a road to the top—and a restaurant—and can be reached by bus. Nevertheless, many trails criss-cross the mountain and provide pleasant walking despite nearness to the city. The number 4 trolley-bus to Obergnigl will take you to the base of the mountain near the point where European Long-distance Footpath E4 enters the city. The numerous paths on the mountain are well marked and a map is scarcely necessary. If you wish to have a trail map, the area is covered on Kompass Wanderkarte 17, *Salzburger Seengebiet*.

TRANSPORTATION

Hub of the Salzburg transportation network is the *Hauptbahnhof*, from which all but one of the tram lines fan out. Mirabellplatz, about 1 kilometer south of the station on Rainerstrasse, is another hub for bus and tram transportation. Salzburg is on the main line between Munich and Vienna, about two hours by fast train from Munich and three hours from Vienna. The city is served by a close-in airport, reachable by autobus S from the *Hauptbahnhof*. From North America, the usual route is to fly to Zürich, then transfer to Austrian Airlines or Swissair for the short flight to Salzburg.

MAPS AND GUIDEBOOKS

For the immediate vicinity of Salzburg, Kompass Wanderbuch *Salzburg Tennengau* is the guidebook of choice. It describes seventy mountain walks within 20 kilometers of the city in words, maps, and profiles. Even if you don't read German, you will find the important information readily accessible. Numerous maps of the city and environs are available; one catalog lists twenty-five. Rather than look for a specific one, we suggest that you browse a local bookstore. Most carry a good line of maps and guidebooks.

WEATHER AND CLIMATE

Salzburg lies on the very northern edge of the Alps. It might be expected to have a climate similar to that of Munich, which is about 100 kilometers west but at about the same elevation and in a rather similar geographic location. Climatic charts show that Salzburg is just a bit wetter and cloudier than Munich. Annual precipitation at Salzburg is about 1300 millimeters as compared with 1100 millimeters at Munich. But temperatures are very similar: a degree warmer in the summer, a degree colder in the winter (indicative of Salzburg's slightly more continental climate), but averaging about the same for the year.

Salzburg averages about 31 days a year with thunderstorms and 160 days with measurable precipitation. Average cloudiness is high, about sixty-five percent for the year, with only slightly lower values for the two least cloudy months, August and September. These are the best months for hiking, with September having the edge since it has fewer thunderstorms and rainy days than does August.

It is interesting to compare the climate of Salzburg with that of the summit of Sonnblick, a 3100-meter peak about 80 kilometers due south. In July, the average temperature on Sonnblick is only 1.6° C (35° F) compared to 17.8° C (63° F) at Salzburg, a 16.2°-Celsius-degree difference. Since Sonnblick is nearly 2600 meters higher, this makes the temperature decrease just 0.6 Celsius degrees per hundred meters of elevation increase, typical of mountain climates everywhere. In other respects, however, the climate of the two locations is not too different. Sonnblick is somewhat wetter, with 1500 millimeters annual precipitation, about twenty percent more than Salzburg, and a little more humid, but with only two-thirds the number of thunderstorms. One big difference: Sonnblick is in the clouds most of the time, with 277 days reporting fog each year.

The lesson of these figures is clear: the mountains are much colder than the lowlands nearby. The prudent hiker carries warm clothing and protection against rain and snow when venturing into the high country. Even in July, temperatures can reach the freezing mark; and the precipitation, when it comes, is as likely to be snow as it is rain at elevations above timberline.

Useful information

Tourist information

City Tourist Offices. Main office, Auerspergstrasse 7, A-5024 Salzburg. Tel. (06222) 74 6 20. Hauptbahnhof. Tel. (06222) 71 7 12. Salzburg center, Münchner Bundesstrasse 1. Tel. (06222) 32 2 28.

Landesverkehrsamt (Salzburg Provincial Tourist Office), Mozartplatz 1. Tel. (06222) 43 2 64.

Maps, guidebooks, and trail information

Österreichischen Alpenverein (Austrian Alpine Club), Sektion Salzburg. Nonntaler Hauptstrasse 86. Tel. (06222) 46 6 44.
Salzburger Bergsteiger- und Wanderschule. Neutorstrasse 55. Tel. 44 1 29.

Local transportation

Six tram lines and seven bus lines link the *Hauptbahnhof* and bus terminal at Mirabellplatz with city locations and neighboring communities.

Accommodations

City Tourist Office (tel. 74 6 20) can help with hotel accommodations. Salzburg's hotels are not quite as expensive as those of its larger neighbors. Try the Europa, 31 Rainerstrasse (tel. 73 2 93) near the *Hauptbahnhof*, for modern but not too expensive accommodations. The Hohenstauffen, 19 Elisabethstrasse (tel. 72 1 93), is somewhat less expensive.
Youth hostels. Salzburg has five. Jugendgastehaus, Josef-Preis Allee 18, A-5020 Salzburg-Nonntal. Tel. (06222) 4 26 70. Three hundred sixty beds. Jugendherberge Salzburg, Glockengasse 8, A-5020 Salzburg. Tel. (06222) 7 62 41. One hundred eighty beds. Haus der Jugend, Franz Hinterholzer Kai 8, A-5020 Salzburg. Eduard-Heinrich-Haus, Eduard-Heinrich-Strasse 2, A-5020 Salzburg-Josefiau. Tel. (06222) 2 59 76. One hundred fifty-two beds. Jugendherberge, Aignerstrasse 34, A-5020 Salzburg. Tel. (06222) 2 32 48. Eighty beds.
Camping. Camping Salzburg, near Haus der Jurgend (see above). Tel. (06222) 8 11 35. Camping Salzburg-West, near Salzburg-West autobahn exit. Tel. (06222) 8 56 02.

Miscellaneous

American Consulate, Gaisbergstrasse 67. Tel. (06222) 22 9 05.
Weather forecast. Tel. 16.
Avalanche warning (Lawinenwarndienst Zentrale). Recorded message: 196; answered phone: 43 4 35.

Over the Salzburger Hochthron
to the Schellenberger ice caves

DIFFICULTY	Grade 4, rough mountain path, partly above timberline
DISTANCE	11 km, not including tour of the cave
WALKING TIME	5 hours
MAP	RV Wanderkarte, *Berchtesgadener Land*, 1:30,000
GUIDEBOOKS	AV-Führer *Berchtesgadener Alpen* (includes trail map)
	KOMP Wanderführer *Berchtesgadener Land*

High above the border town of Markt-Schellenberg lie the fascinating ice caves that bear the town's name. Carved out of the soft limestone of the Berchtesgadener Kalkalpen, they were formed primarily as the result of the sinking of great blocks of stone underneath the surface of the earth. Although partially filled with ice, there is little running water, except for icemelt. Indeed, most of the ice in the caves was formed during the last Ice Age; pollen dating has put the age at least three thousand years before the present. When the caves were first discovered is not known, but their location is marked on an 1826 map. Since that time they have been the object of much research and visitation.

Our route approaches the caves from above, from the ridge of the Salzburger Hochthron. Most of our climbing will be done by cable car from the tiny village of Sankt Leonhard, on the Austrian side of the border. From Salzburg, the village is reached by the number 9540 bus in about twenty-five minutes. (Buses leave the main railroad station approximately hourly in the morning at 0700, 0800, and 0920, but check the schedule for exact times. Also, make sure that you have your passport.) From the bus stop, it is a short walk to the base station of the Untersberg cable car. A short ride brings us to the ridge at 1776 meters, a little bit below the summit of Geiereck at 1805 meters. There is a restaurant at the mountain station of the lift, but it may not be open during the week if it is not the high season of July and August.

From the cable-car station, follow trail 410, blazed with red/white/red paint stripes and occasional red-and-blue blazes. Our trail keeps to the ridge while a broad (unmarked) ski trail follows the contour more or less parallel to the hiking trail. We are above timberline, and views are extensive in all directions. After about 1.5 kilometers of ridge running, the trail drops steeply down the side of the ridge, reaching a trail junction in a narrow gorge. Signs indicate the route right to Störhaus (a mountain hut providing food and overnight accommodations); a few yards in this direction there is a small hut that may provide shelter in a storm. We take the left branch to Toni Lenz Haus, our next destination.

From the pass, the trail drops down a sheer slope on wooden steps, enters a series of tunnels blasted out of the rock by the miners of Schellenberg, and finally levels off in a glacial cirque on the south-

Salzburger Hochthron and the Schellenberger ice caves

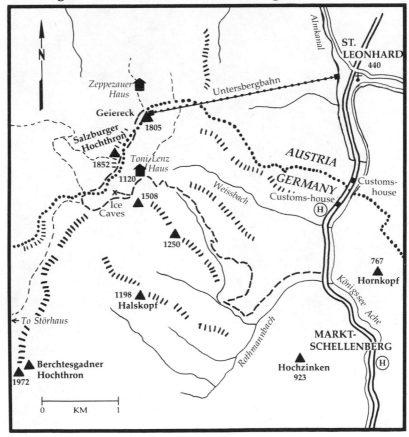

east side of the ridge. The steep part of the trail has rather rough footing in places and caution should be observed, especially in wet weather when the limestone rocks may be slippery.

The trail now contours around the cirque to the junction of the

Ice stalagmite in Schellenberger ice cave

spur trail to the ice caves. You may find one of the guides here, waiting for customers for the trip through the caves. The trip takes about an hour and is certainly worth it, if you have the time. But be warned: the caves are cold; in summer, the temperature is at the freezing point. A warm jacket is a necessity. Use of the guide is obligatory, but the fee is nominal. When one of us took the tour, there was no one else; but this didn't stop the guide from giving his entire "canned" spiel (in German), just as if he had a group of twenty!

From the junction of the spur trail, it is but a few hundred meters to Toni Lenz Haus, a good place for rest and refreshment (and rewarming, if you have just come from the caves). This is a privately run hut, open to the public, with overnight accommodations, if you desire.

From the hut, the trail drops straight down steeply, staying close to the bottom of a small valley, staying on the northeast side of the brook. It soon enters a beech forest, switchbacks steeply down to the brook, then leaves the brook on a wide arc to avoid the cascades, eventually reaching the Bachgraben. Here the trail stays above the brook and its cascades, although it can be seen and heard below most of the way. The trail then swings northward away from the brook and drops gently through heavy forest to the road. From here it is about a half kilometer north to the German customs station and the bus stop, where the bus back to Salzburg can be boarded at 1625, 1735, or 1900.

The Königssee—
Germany's most spectacular Alpine lake

DIFFICULTY	Grade 2, a moderate walk on graded paths and back roads
DISTANCE	8 km if the Jennerbahn is taken for the downward portion; 10 km if the entire route is walked
WALKING TIME	4–5 hours
MAP	RV Wanderkarte 1, *Berchtesgadener Land*, 1:30,000
GUIDEBOOK	Meister, Georg. *Nationalpark Berchtesgaden.* Kindler Verlag. This beautiful book on the national park describes our route in the reverse direction

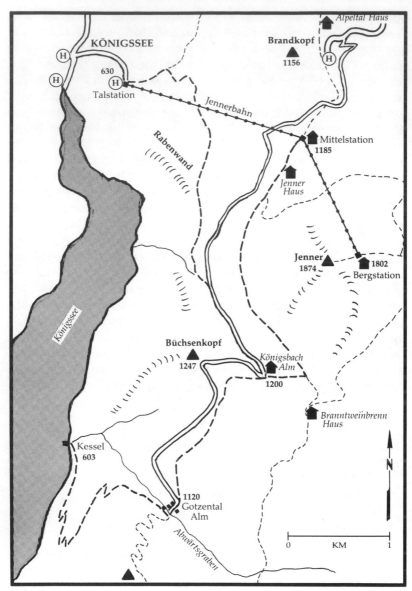

Königssee

Riding the tour boat down the narrow cleft of the Königssee, you can easily imagine that you are gliding along a Norwegian fjord. But the water is fresh, and the sheer walls that plunge into the water are Bavarian. The Königssee is famous for having the most romantic scenery in Upper Bavaria, and we won't quarrel with that description. The limestone walls above shine brightly in the sun, contrasting with water made dark by its 300-meter depth. The waters of the lake are protected from the winds by the steep walls of the cleft and often make a giant reflecting pool. The lake extends 8 kilometers south from the town of Königssee, threading its way between the rock walls. It averages less than a kilometer in width; at one location, St. Bartholomä, it is scarcely 200 meters wide.

St. Bartholomä itself is worth a visit. The twin Moorish turrets of the lakeside chapel are a landmark visible from most of the lake. This chapel was built in 1724, although a chapel has stood on the site since 1134. The inn nearby was originally built as a hunting lodge for the rulers of the principality of Berchtesgaden. A good path leads westward up the glacial valley, past the tiny forest chapel of Sts. Johann and Paul to the "ice chapel," a glacial cirque cut deeply into the south wall of the Watzmann. This is a beautiful walk, but is often crowded with tourists who take the motor launch to St. Bartholomä for a stroll and picnic. If you want to get away from the crowds, try the walk from Kessel on the lake, up to the high plateau on the east side, and back to the town of Königssee along the "high route."

But you have to get to Königssee first. This is not difficult from Salzburg, for there are frequent (hourly) direct buses from the main railroad station, a ride of less than an hour. (Remember to take your passport, for Berchtesgaden is in Germany.) After leaving the bus in Königssee, follow the crowds south toward the docks. In the height of the summer season, boats leave every ten minutes. You must purchase your ticket at the kiosk before boarding the boat, and make sure you get a one-way ticket to Kessel. Since the boat does not normally stop at this lonely dock, tell the ticket-taker on the boat that you wish to get off there. And try to get a seat near the gangway.

The sheer rock walls produce an echo, the clarity and strength of which must be heard to be believed. So, the boat will stop in front of the rock face of the Brentenwand. Here the ticket-taker/tour-guide takes out his trumpet and sounds the clarion notes of a traditional Bavarian song. And back they come, so clear that you start to look for the trumpeter on the shore! This performance is followed by the

Dock at Kessel, Königssee

inevitable passing of the hat, but one really doesn't mind; it is a special experience.

Once the captain has restarted the boat, make yourself ready, for Kessel is just a few hundred meters away. There is nothing there but a tiny dock, a primitive shelter hut, and the beginning of our trail, marked 494 to Gotzental Alm. It angles southward up the steep but wooded slope. The climb is moderate, but the path is graded and well maintained. It suffers a number of switchbacks before turning eastward and climbing steeply through a narrow gorge to the meadows and farmhouses at Gotzental Alm. The climb to this point takes about two hours.

The path follows a farm road across the brook by the cluster of farmhouses, to a farm road that diverges right at a signpost, "Königsbach 3/4 St." The trail is marked 493 and 497. It climbs gently through field and forest (some good examples of German forestry here), then crosses a flat pass before dropping down to the group of houses (and small restaurant) at Königsbach. Here you have a choice: either follow the road (eventually a trail) to the base station of the Jennerbahn; or walk to the midstation and take the cable car down.

To take the cable car, head up the valley at Königsbach to the junction of trail 497. Turn left and follow the trail, which contours around the Jenner to the midstation. Just before reaching the cableway, you will pass a mountain hut (Dr. Hugo Beck Haus) with food and overnight accommodations. The midstation is reached in 200 meters; the ride down to the village takes but a few minutes.

The alternative route from Königsbach Alm follows the farm road (marked 493) downhill 1 kilometer, at which point a trail branches left from the road, continuing down the Königsbach for a short distance before swinging right, away from the brook, and heading due north. The path here is a broad and graded gravel walk. After passing under the cables of the Jennerbahn, it soon turns into a paved street that continues downhill to the base station. Buses leave the Jennerbahn base station for Berchtesgaden at 1534, 1635, and 1728, connecting with buses to Salzburg at 1600, 1710, and 1835, respectively.

Eisriesenwelt—
The world of the ice giants

DIFFICULTY	Grade 2, walking shoes, warm clothing
DISTANCE	4 km (5 km if cable car is bypassed) plus 2 km inside cave
WALKING TIME	2 hours plus 2 hours in cave
MAPS	F&B Wanderkarte 102, *Untersberg, Eisriesenwelt, Königssee* KOMP Wanderkarte 15, *Tennengebirge*
GUIDEBOOKS	AV-Führer *Tennengebirge* (includes map) Steinbicker, Earl. *Great Trips/Europe: Eisriesenwelt.* Available from Euro-File, 2406 18th Ave. NW, Olympia, WA 98502

High above the Salzach Valley, an hour's rail journey from Salzburg, lies the Eisriesenwelt, a spectacular cave with more than 40 kilometers of galleries. The galleries near the main entrance are laced with fascinating formations of frozen water, rivers, and walls of ice that have built up over many thousands of years. In the winter, natural ventilation brings in frigid air, keeping the interior below freezing. Spring snowmelt trickles into the cave, freezing onto the existing ice surfaces. The ice does not melt in the summer because the drainage of cold interior air toward the main opening keeps the warm air out. Thousands of years of this annual cycle have built up thick layers of clear ice, accessible in parts of the cave where some space remains.

A tour through the cave is thus a tour through an icy wonderland. Guide service is available from May through September; use

Eisriesenwelt ice caves

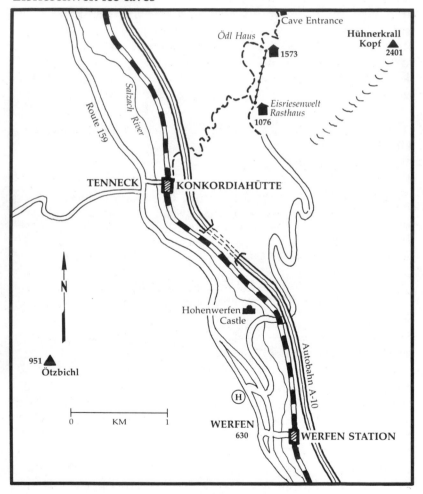

of the service is obligatory but inexpensive. Carbide lamps are provided by the guide; it is not necessary to have your own flashlight. At strategic locations, the guide will light magnesium strips to illuminate some especially noteworthy sight.

We are indebted to Earl Steinbicker for much of the information in this section. He describes this tour in his *Great Trips/Europe* brochure *Eisriesenwelt*.

The trip starts at Werfen, 45 kilometers south of Salzburg in the Salzach Valley. Trains leave from the *Hauptbahnhof*. A local that stops at Werfen leaves at 0853; check the schedule to be sure. The rail line follows the broad valley of the Salzach, gradually climbing to more wooded and rolling country south of Hallein. The valley constricts markedly at Golling and curves sharply as it enters the narrow and steep Werfen-Golling cleft. Here the Salzach cut one of the deepest north-south valleys in the Alps as it pushed its way northward to the Danube.

If you want to walk both ways to the caves, debark at the Konkordiahütte station, the station for the village of Tenneck. From here a marked trail leads to Dr. Friedrich Ödl Haus and the ice caves. For the more conventional and somewhat easier route, continue four minutes more to the Werfen station. Cross the river in front of the station, through a tunnel under the highway, and follow the street north to the center of town and the Eisriesenwelt *Auskunftstelle* (information bureau), where you can get information on the taxibus that goes part of the way to the caves. When you reserve your seat on the taxibus, make arrangements for the return trip unless you plan to walk down.

The gravel road is steep and narrow, a good introduction to a typical Alpine mountain road. We can be thankful that the Austrian bus and taxi drivers are an experienced lot! The road trip ends at a parking lot, the beginning of a pleasant path to the base station of a cable car. The path continues up to the Ödl Haus, where food, drink, and lodgings can be obtained. If time is short, ride the cable car to the hut, a four-minute swoop up a nearly vertical slope.

After lunch or a snack at the hut, join the group being organized for the fifteen-minute walk to the cave entrance. Here the guide will provide lanterns for all and lead the group through the entrance to the cave. The temperature inside is near freezing, so you will want to put on warm clothing as you enter. Just beyond the entrance hall, stairs lead to the upward-inclined Posselt Hall, named after its discoverer more than a century ago. The guide leads the way with a magnesium flare, which casts eerie shadows on the frozen walls. Over the Great Ice Wall, through Hymir and Thrym into an icy rendition of Middle Earth, stairs and walkways lead to the Cathedral of Alexander von Mork, cave explorer of an earlier age. He never really left the cave: his ashes rest in an urn in the hall named after him.

The tour soon reaches the farthest recess open to the public, and the return journey is begun. Soon the entrance hall is regained, and the group comes out into the blinding light of day. The tour through this icy kingdom is one that will not soon be forgotten.

It is all downhill to Ödl Haus, where you can get a hot drink or a cold one to fortify yourself for the trip down to the valley. There is a good trail that leads to the railroad station at Tenneck. Trains from Werfen to Salzburg stop at the Konkordiahütte station. There are several late afternoon and evening trains (probably 1614, 1714, and 1844), but you should check the timetable. (There is usually one posted at the Ödl Haus.)

Up the Kehlstein
to Hitler's Eagle's Nest

DIFFICULTY	Grade 4
DISTANCE	13 km
WALKING TIME	5 hours
MAPS	F&B Wanderkarte 10, *Berchtesgadener Land*
	RV Wanderkarte 1, *Berchtesgadener Land*, 1:30,000
	KOMP Wanderkarte 14, *Berchtesgadener Land*
GUIDEBOOKS	KOMP Wanderbuch 900, *Berchtesgadener Land*
	KOMP Wanderführer 920, *Berchtesgadener Land*

When Adolf Hitler was released from jail after the abortive putsch of 1923, he settled in Obersalzberg, a tiny mountain community near Berchtesgaden. After he seized power in 1934, he embarked on a frenzied building program in an attempt to make this residence the symbol of his power. His villa lay on the north slopes of the Kehlstein, an impressive 1800-meter mountain, and on a perverse whim, he had a sanctuary and lookout built on the very top of the moun-

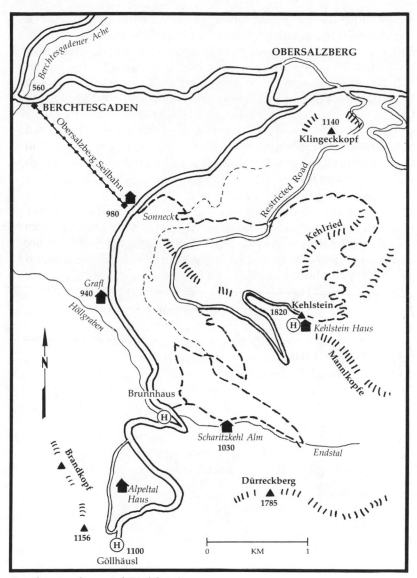

Berchtesgaden and Kehlstein

tain. The project involved carving a twisting road up the mountain and blasting a shaft the last 120 meters to the summit. This was Hitler's Eagle's Nest, the site of a number of infamous meetings.

Contrary to legend, however, the Eagle's Nest was never a military installation, and not much used by Hitler. It is reported that he visited the summit only a half-dozen times. Nevertheless, it has become a popular place for Americans to visit and ponder the strange story of Hitler's infamy. It is easily visited, since every half hour a bus runs up and down the spectacular access road from Obersalzberg to a parking place just below the summit. From there you can take the lift to the Eagle's Nest, now a mountain inn, the Kehlstein Haus (no overnight accommodations).

But if you prefer to walk either or both ways, that has also been made somewhat easier by the construction of a ski lift from Berchtesgaden to Sonneck, partway up the mountain. From the upper station, follow the road north about 200 meters to the point where a trail takes off right. The trail climbs steeply at first, joins a mountain track that angles up the north slope, crosses the bus road, then curves southward around a spur of the mountain. It climbs through a narrow valley, zig-zagging its way up to the top.

For the route down, you can take the trail marked KS, which follows the bus road for a ways, then diverges left on a narrow track and works its way down to a paved road at Brunnhaus. This road can be followed north to the ski lift. A local bus also runs along this road to Berchtesgaden, but we do not know how frequently it runs.

Buses from Salzburg to Berchtesgaden leave the bus station at the *Hauptbahnhof* at 0700, 0800, and 0920 for the fifty-minute journey. (Remember to take your passport, for Berchtesgaden is in Germany.) Return buses leave Berchtesgaden at 1600, 1710, and 1835.

10. Vienna

Vienna may be the music capital of the world. But it is probably true that the Viennese spend more time walking in the Prater and the Wienerwald than attending concerts in the Opera House or in the Konzerthaus. Indeed, the Vienna Woods offer an embarrassment of riches to the weekend walker and Sunday-afternoon stroller. What better way to spend a sunny afternoon than to take a walk along Beethovengasse to the vineyards on the slopes of the Kahlenberg, then down to Grinzing for a glass or two of fruity *Heuriger* (new wine) in the garden of a *Weinhauerhaus*?

You do not even have to get out of the city to enjoy a country walk. The Prater is a large wooded park that stretches southward from the center of the city along the Danube. The north end can be reached by *U-bahn* (line 1, Praterstern station), while the Stadt Brücke Lusthaus station on the *Schnellbahn* will put you off near the middle. The north end is the home of the famous Prater amusement park, complete with roller coasters and giant ferris wheel. But the rest of the park is laced with paths suitable for walking, jogging, cycling, and riding.

TRANSPORTATION

Getting around Vienna and its environs is easy, the result of an extensive network of streetcars, buses, subways, and surface rail lines. A good city map showing all of the transportation lines is published by Vienna Public Transport and is available at a nominal charge from ticket offices. It is in three languages, including English, and is one of the first things you should obtain if you plan to use public transportation.

MAPS AND GUIDEBOOKS

By far the best guidebook for the Wienerwald wanderer is the *Wander Atlas Wienerwald*, published by Freytag-Berndt und Artaria in Vienna. It contains twenty-two trail maps that cover the entire area at the scale of 1:50,000. It lists over six hundred noteworthy destinations in the Wienerwald, enough to keep the most ardent walker busy for several years. Although the text is in German, the map legends are in English; and even the descriptions of the sights to see are in uncomplicated German.

WEATHER AND CLIMATE

Vienna is the easternmost city covered in this guidebook, the farthest from the Atlantic Ocean, and thus has the driest, most continental climate. Annual precipitation is about 70 centimeters, with a summer maximum and winter minimum. Maximum temperatures in the summer months rarely exceed 27° C (80° F), while winter temperatures hover close to the freezing point. At the low elevation of Vienna (at this point, the Danube is about 150 meters above sea level), snow lasts only during the midwinter months, and hiking in the Wienerwald is normally possible from April through November. At higher elevations (such as the Schneeberg, described herein), hiking is confined to the summer months of July through September.

Useful information

Tourist information

Tourist-Information Opernpassage, Karlsplatz, 1010 Wien. Tel. (0222) 43 16 08. In the pedestrian underpass near the Opera. Also at the airport and along the autobahns.

Austria Information Office, Margaretenstrasse 1, 1040 Wien. Tel. (0222) 57 57 14.
Niederösterreichische Fremdenverkehrswerbung (Lower Austria Tourist Office), Paulanergasse 11, A-1041 Wien 4. Tel. (0222) 57 67 18. Information on the region outside Vienna.

Maps, guidebooks, and trail information

Österreichischer Alpenverein, Sektion Wien, Mitisgasse 5, A-1140, Wien. (Call Walter Miedler, local section head.)
Freytag-Berndt und Artaria KG, Kohlmarkt 9, 1010 Wien. Best store for hikers' maps and guidebooks.

Local transportation

Wiener Stadtwerke-Verkehrsbetriebe (WSB) operates the buses, subways, and trams in Vienna. Tickets, which are good on any unit of the system, can be purchased from ticket offices at major stops and from news-stands, or from conductors or machines on trams. Three-day passes available from WSB ticket offices. Excellent map, *Öffentliche Verkehrs-mittel in Wien*, available from ticket offices.
Airport bus service. Buses run half-hourly between the airport and the City Air Terminal at the Hilton. There is also service between the airport and the Westbahnhof and Südbahnhof.

Accommodations

Hotel accommodations can be booked through any of the official tourist information offices (see above).
Youth hostels. Jugendherberge der Stadt Wien (Hütteldorf), Schlossberg-gasse 8, 1130 Wien 13. Tel. (0222) 82 15 01. Three hundred beds. Near the Hütteldorf station of the *U-bahn*. Ruthensteiner Youth Hostel, Robert Hamerling-Gasse 24, 1150 Wien 15. Tel. (0222) 83 46 93. Seventy-seven beds. Convenient to the Westbahnhof, but often filled up.
Camping. Camping Wien-West I, Hüttelbergstrasse 40. Tel. (0222) 94 14 49. Camping Wien-West II, Hüttelbergstrasse 80. Tel. (0222) 94 23 14. Camping Wien-Süd, Breitenfurter Strasse 269. Tel. (0222) 86 92 18. Camping Strandbad Rodaun, near Perchtoldsdorf, south of Vienna. Tel. (0222) 86 01 34. Open all year.

Miscellaneous

American Embassy, Boltzmangasse 16, A-1091 Wien. Consular offices, Friedrich Schmidt Platz 2. Tel. (0222) 31 55 11.
Canadian Embassy, Dr. Karl Luger-Ring, A-1010 Wien. Tel. (0222) 63 66 26.
Weather forecast. Tel. (0222) 15 66. (Also on radio and television at 0805, in English.)

The Lainzer Tiergarten—
A royal hunting preserve in the Vienna Woods

DIFFICULTY	Grade 1, carefully graded or paved paths
DISTANCE	Various, described route about 9 km
WALKING TIME	Various, described route about 2 hours
MAPS	F&B *Wander Atlas Wienerwald*, map 12
	Lainzer Tiergarten brochure (park office)
GUIDEBOOK	Lainzer Tiergarten brochure, available from entrance gate kiosks, although in German, has useful pictures and descriptions of the park and its history

More than four hundred years ago, the royal foresters—really gamekeepers—first administered what is now the Lainzer Tiergarten as the Kaiser's game preserve. The Auhof, their headquarters, still stands at the northern end of the preserve. In 1772, Empress Maria Theresia ordered a wall to be built around the entire preserve, all 2200 hectares of it. When completed, the wall stretched for 24 kilometers. The preserve was large enough, it would seem, to satisfy the hunting whims of any consort. After World War I, it was gradually opened up for public use; but it was not until 1937, when the city of Vienna purchased the park, that it was fully opened to the public.

Today, the Lainzer Tiergarten is one of the finest and largest enclosed recreation areas and nature preserves in Europe. Here wild pigs and wild sheep wander at will. Several hundred deer roam the forests and fields; and in July and August, the famous Lipizzaner horses are put to pasture in the Hermesvilla section for "summer freshening."

The main portion of the park is open from Palm Sunday until the first of November, although a small portion near the Lainzer

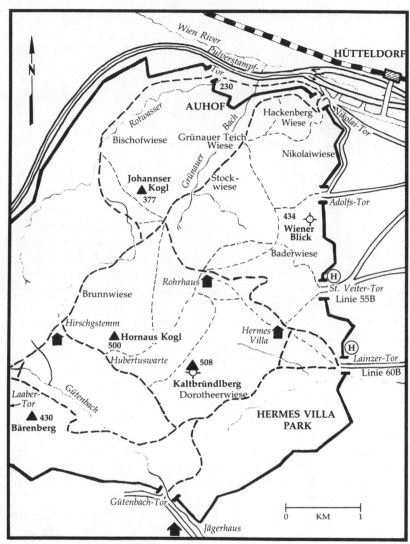

Lainzer Tiergarten

gate is open year-round. Visiting hours are from 0800 until dusk, Wednesday through Sunday, and entry is free. The Tiergarten is readily accessible by several public transportation routes. We describe one walk, but there are paths throughout the park and you can scarcely get lost, especially if you have the park map, which can be obtained at any of the park entrances. Many of the paths are park service roads (not open to public motor vehicles); others are well-graded dirt paths marked with red paint blazes. There are a number of shelter huts (no facilities) in the park and three restaurants accessible only to walkers.

It is, in short, a marvelous introduction to the Wienerwald, a fine place for an afternoon walk. Our route takes us from the Nikolai gate to the restaurant Rohrhaus, thence to the Pulverstampf gate.

Take the U-bahn, line U4, to Hütteldorf, the end of the line. After leaving the train, head south and cross the canal on a pedestrian bridge. (Note the signs here for the city youth hostel, a few blocks away.) Go straight ahead a short block to Auhofstrasse, turn right several blocks to Niklausgasse and a sign pointing left to Lainzer Tiergarten. Follow along a short distance to Nikolai-Tor, one of the park entrances. Just inside the entrance, there is a kiosk where you can obtain light refreshments and a park map.

From here, a woods path leads straight ahead to Nikolaiwiese (meadow) and to Hackenbergwiese. The trail meets the road from Nikolai-Tor. Here turn left, cross the brook, and take the trail leading left, marked Adolfs-Tor and Rohrhaus. The trail leads up a small valley, through a beautiful beech forest. Near the top, the trail branches, left to Adolfs-Tor, right to Rohrhaus, our route. In a few minutes, the trail enters a meadow and a short branch leads left to Wiener Blick, with its impressive views of the city. Regaining the main trail, keep straight ahead to Rohrhaus, a pleasant place for lunch or a snack.

From Rohrhaus, a trail leads south to Kaltenbründlberg, the highest point in the park at just over 500 meters above sea level. However, this is only 100 meters above Rohrhaus, an easy climb. There is a lookout tower here, the Hubertuswarte. The route back follows a woods path north to Laurenzer Wald. From here, you can walk back to Nikolai-Tor along the paved service road, or left along the road to Pulverstampf-Tor.

The walk to Pulverstampf-Tor is a pleasant one, through meadows and hayfields, along the Rotwasser Brook. Although this is a nature preserve, there is active logging and haying in the park, and you may well see a tractor tedding the new-mown hay. To Europeans, conservation means wise *use*, and they see no conflict between the recreational use of a preserve such as the Tiergarten and the harvesting of the resources that can be provided by the area. Of course, they log carefully, stack the logs neatly, and make very little fuss over "despoiling the wilderness." At any rate, the Viennese love their Lainzer Tiergarten, and we can easily see why.

At Pulverstampf-Tor, the walk back to the Hütteldorf station follows the stone wall that surrounds the park. The path is a city sidewalk, within sight and sound of city traffic. It is a twenty-minute walk to the bridge over the canalized river to the station.

Through the vineyards
to Kahlenberg and Grinzing

DIFFICULTY	Grade 1, mostly on paved paths and walks
DISTANCE	10 km, can be lengthened or shortened
WALKING TIME	3 hours for described route
MAPS	Falk Verlag, *Falk Plan Wien* (widely available in the U.S.) shows many paths and streets in the area, but does not show which ones are marked paths. F&B *Wander Atlas Wienerwald* shows the marked paths but not all the others
GUIDEBOOK	None necessary

If you are a Beethoven fan, this walk is for you. Take the tram to Nussdorf, cross Eroicagasse, and walk along Beethovengang to Beethovenruhe, where there is a bust and monument. Follow up the Schreiberbach through the Muckental. Then climb through the vineyards while the strains of the *Pastoral* symphony hum through your head. Then back to Grinzing for a pitcher of new wine, *Heuriger,* in one of the outdoor wine gardens the town is famous for. It is not difficult to absorb the atmosphere that must have prevailed when the composer was wandering through the same vineyards, perhaps humming the same melody as the *Pastoral* took shape in his mind.

But even if you're not a Beethoven fan, the paths around the Kahlenberg make for a most pleasant walk on a sunny afternoon.

Grinzing

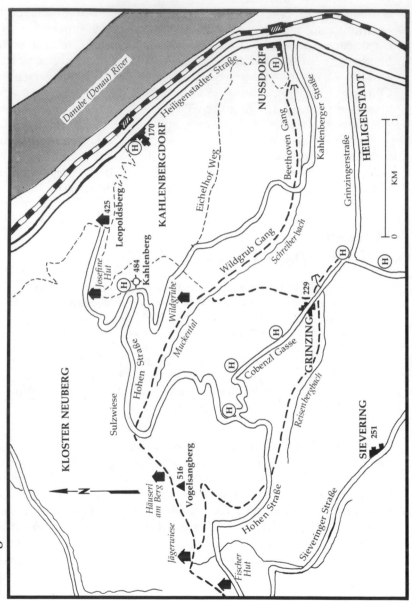

Danube (Donau) River

Heiligenstadter Straße

KAHLENBERGDORF

NUSSDORF

HEILIGENSTADT

Leopoldsberg

425

170

Josefine Hut

484 Kahlenberg

Eichelhof Weg

Beethoven Gang

Kahlenberger Straße

Grinzingerstraße

Wildgrub Gang

Schreiberbach

Wildgrube

Muckental

Hohen Straße

Sulzwiese

Cobenzl Gasse

GRINZING

229

Reisenbergbach

KLOSTER NEUBERG

N

Häuserl am Berg

516 Vogelsangberg

Jägerwiese

Hohen Straße

SIEVERING

251

Sieveringer Straße

Fischer Hut

KM

1

0

Several of Vienna's tram and bus lines make the region a few minutes away from downtown. And the paths are numerous and good. Indeed, one of the European Long-distance Footpaths runs through the area; and the northern terminus of the Wienerwald-weitwanderweg (WWWWW for short!) is in Grinzing. No need to pack a lunch; there are numerous trailside inns. But a canteen of water may be useful on a hot, sultry day.

So, take the D tram from downtown Vienna to the end of the line in Nussdorf. This leaves you on Zahnradbahnstrasse, literally Cog-wheel Railway Street, which is followed a short block to a trail sign, "Stadt Wanderweg 1" (City Trail 1). Follow along the creek, crossing Eroicagasse, to Beethovengang. Although the path is paved along the creek, motor vehicles are not permitted. At the next bridge, cross over the creek to Beethovenruhe, a tiny park with an impressive bust of the composer.

Typical of many European brooks, this one (the Schreiberbach) is carefully confined between stone walls, occasionally disappearing into a tunnel only to reappear a few meters away. Land is so valuable in the cities that there seems to be a great pressure to keep wild things like a brook carefully tamed. Anyway, it is not long before the brook is "unconfined," about where Beethovengang changes to Wildgrubgasse, still following the brook.

After the path passes a graveyard and a small chapel, a bridge left leads to Grinzinger Steig (a shortcut to Grinzing and the bus). Here we bear right and follow the right side of the valley along the vineyards. At the next bridge, you have a choice. Either follow the yellow-blazed path straight up the Schreiberbach to the ridge; or climb the steep path through the vineyards to the summit of Kahlenberg. If you choose the latter, the path branches right a few meters upstream from the bridge (trail sign) and climbs steeply to Kahlenberger Strasse, a paved road. Turn left and follow the twisty road to the top and the Kahlenberg Inn. There is a fine view of Vienna from the terrace or from the lookout tower nearby. (Just to break the Beethoven spell, let it be noted that Mozart wrote the *Magic Flute* while staying at the inn.)

From the Kahlenberg, follow the ridge westward, paralleling the road on European Long-distance Footpath E4, staying on the ridge after the road swings leftward down the hill. (At this point, the yellow-blazed trail along the Schreiberbach comes in. If you are in a hurry to get back, you can follow this path back down to the junction

Bust of Beethoven in Beethovenruhe park

at Muckentaler Weg. Either follow this path to Grinzing, or continue straight ahead to Nussdorf and the D tram.) Continuing along the ridge, you will soon reach a camping place and mountain inn (Häuserl am Berg). Just beyond this, a path leads left down the slope to Bei der Kreuz Ecke, a major junction, where the Wienerwald connecting trail (444) leads down to Grinzing.

Grinzing is still a village, despite its proximity to Vienna, and is much the same as it was in Beethoven's day (except for the autos!). The streets are crowded on a warm summer evening; sounds of

music—perhaps from a harmonium or other rare instrument—
come from the hidden courtyards of the inns. Avoid the temptation
to stop in the first *Heuriger* you come to. Find one that appeals to
you, order a pitcher of the new wine, and sample the wares of the
traditional *Heurigen Proviant*, a self-service counter loaded with
spicy meats, fragrant cheeses, and slabs of good bread. We guarantee that it will be dark before you can tear yourself away to board the
38 bus back to town.

Through a forest of giant beech trees to Greifenstein Castle

DIFFICULTY	Grade 2, an easy walk through the forest
DISTANCE	10 km
WALKING TIME	2½ hours, not including tour of castle
MAP	F&B *Wander Atlas Wienerwald*, map 2
GUIDEBOOK	None necessary

Greifenstein Burg—one of the castles on the Danube—may not be
one of the most spectacular castles in Austria, but it is rich in history
and well worth a visit. First built in 1135 by the Passauer bishops, it
was partially destroyed by the Hungarians in 1447 and then again by
the Turks in 1529. It has since been rebuilt and restored and today
houses a museum and a restaurant. There are guided tours, but, so
far as we know, they are all conducted in German. (Incidentally, the
restaurant is closed on Tuesday, the day we visited!) The castle can
be reached by a twenty-minute walk from the Greifenstein railroad
station, but it is much more fun to come by the back door, as it were,
from Höflein-an-der-Donau via Hadersfeld, a tiny village on the
edge of the Wienerwald.

It is possible to combine this trip with a boat ride up the Donau
from Vienna, although this requires an early start. You can obtain a
combined boat-rail ticket at the DDSG (Donau-Dampfschiffahrts-
Gesellschaft) office at the Reichsbrücke, near the Vorgartenstrasse
station on the U1 line of the subway. The boat leaves at 0800 (but
check current schedules!) and arrives in Greifenstein at 0945. Taking
the boat would require making the trip in the reverse direction,
visiting the castle first. Trains back to the city leave hourly from the

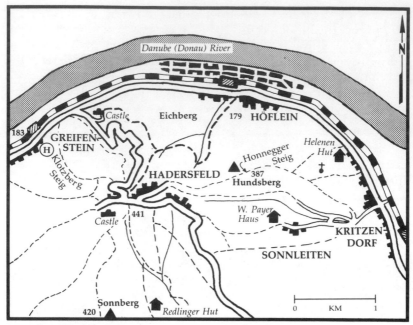

Greifenstein Castle

Greifenstein station. Unfortunately, the boat does not stop at Greifenstein on its return trip, so it is not possible to combine a rail trip there with a boat ride back.

However, we think it better to visit the castle at the end of the walk rather than at the beginning, so we will describe a walk starting at Höflein.

Trains leave hourly from Franz-Josefs-Bahnhof (reached by the U4 subway line). The local train (*Regional Zug*) takes about twenty-five minutes for the trip to Hoflein. The trail leaves from the east side of the station. On that side of the railroad station building is a chart showing the trails in the vicinity. The trail to Hadersfeld (marked white/red/white) starts immediately across the road from this point and heads directly south along a small creek for about 100 meters. It then switches back to the left up a dirt path to an upper road that leads right, along the line of the stream.

In a few minutes this road changes to a dirt track at a cemetery. It is well marked with red paint and signposts. The path, now a woods road, leads up through a fine beech forest on the east side of a small brook that occupies a very steep sided and narrow valley. Soon our path comes to an intersection of a number of woods roads, but continues straight across, following the red markers. Care must be taken in following the path through these woods, for there is a profusion of woods roads. The path alternately follows, crosses, and diverges from them. All the way, however, the path is well marked by the red blazes.

Just after passing a hunter's outlook, the trail takes a sharp bend to the right and follows a woods road without markers for about 200 meters before the red blazes start again. The trail, now a woods road, passes through a magnificent beech forest with trees that are up to a meter in diameter at breast height. If there ever was a cathedral-like forest, this is it. The smooth, straight, gray trunks stretch upward to the overarching canopy of light green beech leaves. The forest floor is carpeted with lush surface vegetation, forming a green mantle over the damp earth. On the day we were there, a light mist swirled through the trees, softening the outlines of the trunks and producing an eerie, mystical scene.

Just after reaching a level spot, the green trail from Greifenstein to Hadersfeld comes in from the right. A short distance farther along, a red trail branches sharply right, leading to Greifenstein via the Fleischhackergraben. In 50 meters more the trail comes out on a street in Hadersfeld, at a trail sign. Hadersfeld is a tiny village, but it does have a *Gasthaus* where you can obtain food and drink (except on Tuesdays!).To get there, follow Alois Aigner Gasse to the main road. Turn left and walk about 100 meters to the inn on the left side of the road.

Retracing your steps now to the trail junction, follow the main path down, avoiding the red trail that diverges left and continuing straight ahead on the main (green) trail. Two hundred meters farther on, after crossing a slight rise, the trail to Greifenstein Castle diverges left, while the trail back to Höflein diverges right. There are signs and liberal paint splotches at this intersection. After passing through woods on a broad, nearly level path, the trail heads down rather steeply on an old cobbled way and shortly comes out on a parking lot by the castle.

The green trail follows the road on down to the parking lot, then swings around to the left, following white/green/white blazes. It soon comes to a paved crossroad, where the lower trail from Haderfeld comes in. The way from here to town is marked with red-and-green stripes, interspersed with white. This road (which is the road from Hadersfeld to Greifenstein) leads down to the main highway along the Donau. Here there are trail signs with red-and-green markers. You should turn left to walk to the railroad station or ship landing. Trains leave hourly at twenty minutes past the hour for Franz-Josefs-Bahnhof in Vienna.

A ride to timberline
on a clanking cog railway

DIFFICULTY	Grade 3–4, easy walking along graded paths, but above timberline
DISTANCE	7 km
WALKING TIME	3 hours
MAP	F&B Wanderkarte 22, *Semmering-Rax-Schneeberg*
GUIDEBOOK	None

The high Alps seem too far away from Vienna to be experienced on a one-day trip. But there is an exception, and this one provides an exciting ride on a cog railway and a chance to take a walk above timberline on easy trails. Schneeberg—Snow Mountain—is visible from the higher elevations of the Vienna Woods. Although rather low by Alpine standards—2076 meters, the elevation of Mt. Mitchell in North Carolina—its summit is well above timberline and covered with true Alpine tundra. Early in the summer season, Alpine flowers bloom in profusion.

The trip to Hochschneeberg violates our constraint of keeping trips within an hour's train ride from the city. But it is such a fascinating trip, one that can be done in a long day, that we have included it. If the day is sunny and warm, it will be a trip you will not forget. Be warned, though, that the walking portion of the trip is above timberline; what may be a warm day in Vienna will be cool above timberline. And the weather can turn bad rather suddenly when a cold cloud envelops the mountaintop. So, take warm clothing and some rain protection. Hiking shoes are not really necessary, so long as you stay on graded paths. But if you want to wander through the tundra, sturdier walking shoes are in order.

Trains to Puchberg-am-Schneeberg, where the cog railway

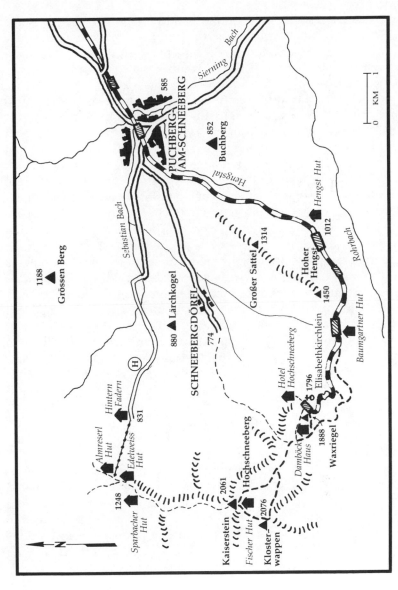

Hochschneeberg

starts, leave from the Südbahnhof (South Station) in Vienna, some distance from the Westbahnhof, the usual arrival point for travelers from the west. Tram number 18 runs between the two stations, a fifteen-minute journey. The Südbahnhof is also a stop on the subway (line U2) and on the *Schnellbahn*.

The best train to take from the Südbahnhof leaves about 0700 (but check current schedules). This will get you to Puchberg about 0845. A later train, at 1000, gets you to Puchberg at 1130. Both require *Umsteigen* (changing trains) in Wiener Neustadt. (Note that the connection is tight. Upon alighting in Wiener Neustadt, walk through the pedestrian tunnel to the platform farthest away from the station house, where the Puchberg train is boarded.) The seven-o'clock train may have direct cars to Puchberg; check with the conductor in the Südbahnhof in Vienna. The ride to Puchberg from Wiener Neustadt is a pleasant one as the train winds through the Austrian countryside, making frequent stops for local passengers and to load and unload boxes and bicycles, mailbags, and miscellany, the hundreds of things that keep the rural economy going.

While on the train to Puchberg, you can purchase the special ticket for the mountain railway (if you did not do so in Vienna). Also, you should obtain from the conductor a *Platzkarte* that will guarantee you a seat on a particular train. You should ask the conductor for one even if you are traveling on a Eurailpass, which is good for the entire journey, including the mountain portion. If you do not obtain one from the conductor, make sure you obtain one from the ticket agent in Puchberg. The trains, which run more frequently as the demand increases, are boarded by the colors on the seat cards.

Now the fun really begins, for here we take the *Schmalspurigedampfbetriebenezahnradbahn*—narrow-gauge, steam-operated cog-wheeled railroad—for the chugging, clanking ride up the mountain. Before you board, take a few minutes to study the engine. The boiler slopes down in front so that on the steep portions of the track it will be level for maximum efficiency. A third, toothed rail is centered between the regular tracks. A driving wheel, difficult to see because it is underneath the low-slung engine, engages the teeth and drives the engine forward. The engine always stays on the downhill end of the train, pushing the cars up, holding them back on the way down. This is for safety reasons; no worries about broken couplings. If you have ridden the cog railway on Mt. Washing-

Cog railway, Hochschneeberg

ton in New Hampshire, this will all be familiar to you. The Mt. Washington railway was built before this one; the original engines and cars are still in use and look their age. Even though the engines on the Schneebergbahn were also built a century ago, they look sturdy and serviceable and are obviously kept in good repair.

Now it is time to board the cars for the journey. Although the cars are old, they, too, are well maintained. The wooden seats are not the most comfortable in the world, especially if you are facing downhill when the train is on a steep slope!

The train climbs through meadows at first, then through woods, mostly Norway spruce and occasional larch. Eventually the larch wins out, then finally is replaced by timberline pine. A fifteen-minute rest stop is made at Baumgartner Haus, providing an opportunity to walk around a bit, enjoy the view, and perhaps purchase refreshments. Try the homemade steamed fruit buns. They are delicious! Far above, a chapel, the Elizabethkirchlein, can be seen.

After leaving the station, the train enters the first of two tunnels. Close the windows! Because the air flow is up the tunnel, the smoke from the engine in the rear travels forward over the cars. Even with the windows closed, some of the smoke seeps in. But soon the train comes to the end of the tunnel, pushing the smoke ahead of it.

At this point the train crosses timberline and enters the Alpine tundra. After passing through the second tunnel, it works its way around to a broad plateau and the *Bahnhof*. Upon arriving at this point and debarking, you should obtain another seat ticket for the return journey. Times of the return journeys are posted on a chalkboard at the station and also at the ticket office inside, indicating hours of departure and noting the ones that are sold out (*Ausverkauft*).

From the upper terminus, it is a five-minute walk to the Berghaus Hochschneeberg, where food and lodging can be obtained. The trail map listed at the beginning of this walk can also be purchased there. Damböck Haus is only fifteen minutes away, in the direction our trail takes. The trail, really a cart track, is marked with green paint blazes. It contours around the southwest side of the Waxriegel, a rounded hump to the right. In about a half kilometer, a yellow-blazed trail branches left through the meadow to Baumgartner Haus. Stay on the broad path, which leads in a few hundred yards to Damböck Haus. This mountain hut is operated by the Austrian Tourist Club (Österreichischen Touring Klub, ÖTK) and is open to the public. Good food, overnight accommodations in the *Matratzenlager*, and mountain *Gemütlichkeit* are available in abundance here.

(If you are ready to head back, a red-blazed trail takes off behind the hut and goes over the low summit of the Waxriegel. This is a good place to explore the krummholz, the low, almost impenetrable thicket of pines characteristic of timberline here. It is almost like a Chinese maze. Openings work their way through the maze, only to end a few meters from the other side. But the krummholz itself is so thick that it is almost impossible to get through.)

Our path continues past Damböck Haus to a trail junction, where a trail diverges right to Schneidergraben, a steep mountain trail back to Puchberg. (Note: this route is not recommended, for it may not be passable in early summer because of snowdrifts in the steep sections.) Our path climbs gently to a saddle where a trail, marked yellow/white (sign to Klosterwappen), diverges left. From here, the main summit ridge of the Hochschneeberg is clearly visible, with its collection of buildings. Klosterwappen on the left is the highest peak (2076 meters); Kaiserstein on the right is only slightly lower (2061 meters). It is possible to make a circuit over the ridge from this trail junction.

The main trail proceeds straight ahead. The switchbacks up to Kaiserstein and Fischerhütte are plainly visible. The climb from this point takes about an hour. From the top of Kaiserstein, views are extensive in all directions. The low hills of the Wienerwald are visible beyond the limestone ridges of the pre-Alps. The massif of Raxalpe is to the southwest, with the main Alpine ranges beyond.

From this summit, a ridge trail (marked red) proceeds to the main summit and a transmitting tower. From here you can follow the yellow trail down to the trail junction. However, we did not take that route. The easiest way is to retrace your steps back to the *Bahnhof*.

If you have time before the return trip, visit the imposing chapel of the Elizabethkirchlein ("Elizabeth's little church"). It is a curious structure, sitting all alone out on the tundra. The devout Austrians have managed to build such religious structures in what may seem rather odd places. Nevertheless, there is a quiet austerity to this chapel, a suitable place for a few minutes' contemplation of the wonder of the mountains.

The last regularly scheduled train leaves the station at 1735, although there are later trains if the number of passengers warrants. The 1735 arrives in Puchberg at 1900, in time for the 1920 to Wiener Neustadt and the 2020 from there to Vienna. It makes for a long day, but one that will be treasured for a long time.

Höher Lindkogel—
The highest peak in the southern Vienna Woods

DIFFICULTY	Grade 2
DISTANCE	12–18 km, depending on route
WALKING TIME	4–6 hours, depending on route
MAPS	F&B *Wander Atlas Wienerwald* (maps and text)
	F&B Wanderkarte *Wienerwald*
GUIDEBOOKS	F-K&F *Rundwanderungen Wienerwald*
	KOMP Wanderführer *Wanderregion Wien*

A few miles south of Vienna, the Höher Lindkogel guards the Wienerwald from its 850-meter height. It is the highest peak in the southern part of the forest, some 500 meters above the level of Baden, the nearest town and railroad station. Although the top is, of course, well below timberline and quite heavily wooded, a lookout tower provides extensive views of the Vienna basin and the pre-

Höher Lindkogel

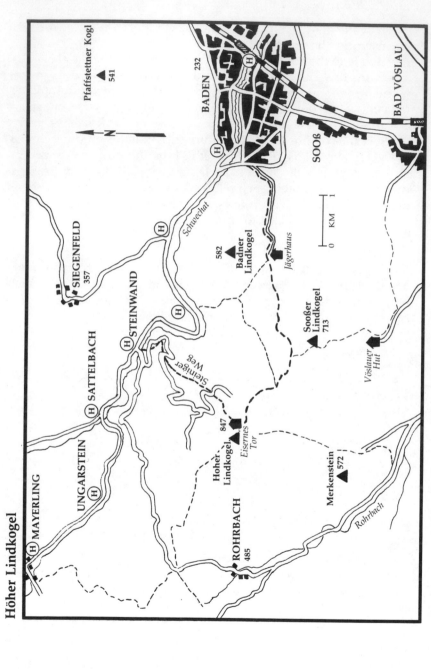

Alps to the west. The mountain is covered with trails, and there are many possibilities for walks.

Baden itself is famous for its hot springs and therapeutic baths. Mozart and Beethoven both lived there at various periods of their lives. Indeed, parts of the Ninth Symphony were composed there. The springs are sulfurous and smelly and, when mixed with the local mud, are supposed to do wonders for you, especially if you are Viennese. The surrounding countryside is noted for its vineyards; they smell better and their products taste better than the hot springs.

Baden is the first main stop on the rail line south from the Südbahnhof in Vienna, which itself can be reached by *U-bahn* or *S-bahn* from the city center. Trains for Baden leave every hour on the hour, returning at hourly intervals in the afternoon. The trip is about twenty minutes. From the Baden *Bahnhof*, either walk westward along the main street north of the river, or take the bus to the second bridge. Cross the river (the Schwechat), bear right, and walk several blocks to the road that leads to Restaurant Jägerhaus. (It is possible to drive or take a taxi to this point.)

The trail, number 42, follows up the Weichseltal, eventually leaving the valley to climb the ridge, where it joins the ridge trail from Soosser Lindkogel. It follows an up-and-down course, reaching the summit of the Höher Lindkogel about 4 kilometers and two hours from the Jägerhaus. At the top is a lookout constructed in 1865 by order of Archduke Albert that affords fine views of the southern Wienerwald, the Vienna basin, and the foothills of the Alps to the west. Nearby is a mountain hut, Eisernes Tor (an earlier name of the mountain), maintained by the Austrian Tourist Club, with food, drink, and overnight accommodations. A transmitting facility for the local television network is also located on the top.

There are several possibilities for the return journey, depending on your time and inclination. The shortest is to retrace your steps to the Steiniges Weg, which descends steeply northward to the Helenental. Here you can take the bus back to the Baden railroad station. A longer alternative follows the ridge westward (trail 404) to the junction with trail 42 north to Mayerling and the bus to Baden. The path to Soosser Lindkogel leads eventually to Vöslauer Hütte, thence by road or trail to Bad Vöslau and the train back to Vienna. Trains depart Bad Vöslau at 1557, 1601, 1707, 1743, 1814, and 1842. These local trains stop at Baden five minutes later, but there are express trains from Baden at 1644, 1738, and 1904.

11. Vaduz

If you drive the autobahn north from Sargans, toward Bregenz and Munich, you may notice a storybook castle high above the Rhine just before reaching Buchs. If you do, you are looking at the home of a real prince, the ruler of the Principality of Liechtenstein, Franz Joseph II. You must look sharp, though, else you will whiz right by the 25-kilometer border.

A better plan, one followed by increasing numbers of tourists, is to make the detour to the east side of the Rhine and drive north through Liechtenstein to Vaduz, the capital and home of a fourth of the country's 24,000 residents. And if you do, you might consider taking a half day to explore the hill country east of Vaduz. You will thus have explored at least part of the smallest Alpine country.

Liechtenstein is not the smallest country in Europe. That honor goes to Vatican City; and Andorra and Luxembourg are smaller. But in Liechtenstein's 160 square kilometers lies a surprising variety of landscape, from the broad flood plain of the Rhine to the towering peaks of the Vorarlberg, along the border with Austria. Indeed, the principality once was part of Austria; that ended in 1719 when the Austrian emperor proclaimed the "Imperial Principality of Liechtenstein," part of the Holy Roman Empire. When that empire collapsed, Liechtenstein became a free state, though it maintained its ties with Austria.

Perhaps because its front door faces Switzerland, Liechtenstein developed closer and closer ties with that country. Two hundred years after its founding as an independent state, it entered into a formal arrangement with Switzerland, which ultimately led to its becoming part of the Swiss Customs Union. Today, Switzerland manages its postal service; and Swiss currency is the medium of exchange. Although maintaining a fierce independence in political matters, it is in many respects part of the Swiss hegemony.

At any rate, it is a delightful country to visit. Vaduz has the National Gallery, housing much of the prince's art collection. And there is a worthwhile stamp museum, if you are a philatelist. Vaduz is in the geographic center of the country and is a good place from which to explore the countryside.

TRANSPORTATION

Although the main-line trains between Zürich and Innsbruck pass through Liechtenstein, few of them stop. It is necessary to change to a bus at Sargans for the half-hour ride to Vaduz. Sargans, in turn, is an hour by fast train from Zürich; and trains run nearly hourly. Check the schedules. If you are coming from the east or north, it is possible to get to Vaduz by bus from Feldkirch or by train from Buchs. Within Liechtenstein, bus transportation is by Swiss postal bus since the Swiss run the mail service there.

The autobahn bypasses Liechtenstein, traversing the west bank of the Rhine. However, just north of Sargans, a local road crosses the river and proceeds to Vaduz.

MAPS AND GUIDEBOOKS

Kümmerly & Frey publishes a guidebook in its International series, Wanderbuch 5, *Fürstentum Liechtenstein*. The guidebook, in German, describes one hundred walks and climbs in Liechtenstein. Two maps are available: the *Touristenkarte Fürstentum Liechtenstein*, which may be obtainable locally; and Kompass Wanderkarte 21, *Feldkirch–Vaduz*. The latter has trail information (in German) on the back side.

WEATHER AND CLIMATE

The weather of Vaduz is typical of that of the Swiss *Mittelland* as typified by Zürich. A comparison of the data for Feldkirch, just outside the boundary, with that for Zürich, shows few differences. Feldkirch has about twenty percent fewer days with rain, and fewer thunderstorms. Temperatures are nearly identical.

It is interesting to compare the data for both locations with that for Santis, a 2500-meter peak located on a direct line between the two cities. Temperatures are about 12 Celsius degrees (22 Fahrenheit degrees) colder at the top of the mountain, a decrease with height of six-tenths of a Celsius degree per 100 meters. Cloudiness is somewhat greater on the summit, but rainy days and thunderstorms are about the same. However, precipitation is much greater, about 2.5 meters of water collecting on the summit, compared with 1.1 meters in Zürich. Of course, much of the precipitation on the summit is in the form of snow.

So, the weather from May through September should be suitable for the walk to be described. Masescha is well below timberline and so not likely to experience snow in the summer months. Nevertheless, you should remember that the weather can turn nasty at upper elevations and should be prepared for this possibility.

Useful information

Tourist information

Verkehrsbüro Vaduz, Englanderbau, Städtle 37, FL-9490 Vaduz. Tel. (075) 2
  14 43.
Liechtensteinische Fremdenverkehrszentrale, Box 139, FL-9490 Vaduz. Tel.
  (075) 2 14 43.

Maps, guidebooks, and trail information

Liechtensteiner Alpenverein (LAV), Ramschwagweg, FL-9496 Balzers. Tel.
  (075) 4 12 49.
Buchhandlung und Souvenirs Haas, Vaduz. Maps and guidebooks can also
  be purchased from Verkehrsbüro Vaduz.

Local transportation

Liechtenstein has bus service connecting all communities. Schedule available from the tourist office or post office.

Accommodations

Hotel Real, FL-9490 Vaduz (on the main street). Tel. (075) 2 22 22. Reasonable rooms, good restaurant.

Park-Hotel Sonnenhof, FL-9490 Vaduz. Tel. (075) 2 11 92. More expensive, but off the main street.

Youth Hostel Schaan-Vaduz, Untere Ruttigasse 6, FL-9494 Schaan. Tel. (075) 2 50 22. One hundred four beds.

Camping. Camping Bendern, Gasthof "Zum Löwen" in Bendern (7 kilometers north of Vaduz). Tel. (075) 3 14 65. Open all year. Camping Vaduz-Süd, near Gasthof "Meierhof," 3 kilometers south of Vaduz on Triesen Road. Tel. (075) 2 18 36. Open all year. Camping Mittagspitze, between Vaduz and Balzers.

Miscellaneous

Weather forecast. Tel. 162.

Exploring the alps and castles of Liechtenstein

DIFFICULTY	Grade 2
DISTANCE	7 1/2 km
WALKING TIME	3 hours
MAP	KOMP Wanderkarte 21, *Feldkirch–Vaduz*
GUIDEBOOK	K&F Wanderbuch Internationale Reihe 5, *Fürstentum Liechtenstein*

This delightful walk, which is described by Earl Steinbicker in his *Great Trips/Europe* pamphlet *A Mountain Walk near Vaduz*, will take you through the forests and meadows near Vaduz, past the ruins of an ancient fortress, and past the "modern" thirteenth-century castle

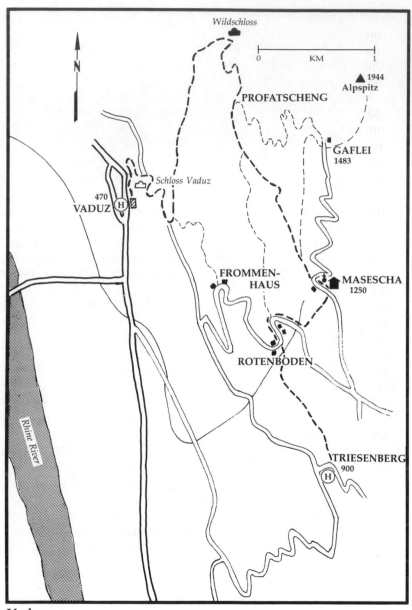

Wildschloss

PROFATSCHENG

▲ 1944
Alpspitz

KM

GAFLEI
1483

Schloss Vaduz

470
VADUZ Ⓗ

**FROMMEN-
HAUS**

MASESCHA
1250

ROTENBODEN

Rhine River

TRIESENBERG
900

Vaduz

that is the home of the ruling prince. You will visit several tiny farm communities; on the entire trip you will be treated to expansive views of the Rhine Valley to the west and the Vorarlberg Mountains to the east. And you can reach the starting point by bus, eliminating most of the climb.

At the bus terminal across the street from the tourist office in the middle of Vaduz, take the bus to Triesenberg, a resort village 7 kilometers away. From the bus stop, follow the road left (north) to Rotenboden, along a mostly level ridge. The road leads through pastures and there are extensive views of the Rhine Valley below. At Rotenboden, the road bends right (east), soon passing a waterfall to the left. Just beyond, pick up a farm road and footpath on the left, marked "Masescha." In a half kilometer, the path reenters the road at that small settlement. This is nearly 800 meters above Vaduz and the highest point on the walk.

Masescha boasts an interesting fourteenth-century church and a restaurant, both worth a visit. It is the oldest Walser settlement in the region. A few yards north of Masescha, at a bend in the road, a trail marked "Vaduz über Wildschloss" takes off to the left. It passes through thick woods to the tiny settlement at Profatscheng. Just beyond, the trail forks and our route follows the path marked "Ruine Wildschloss und Vaduz." Descending rapidly, we soon come to a logging road, which we follow to the ruins of an ancient fortress, Wildschloss.

Beyond the ruins, the path heads southward along a dirt road toward Vaduz. At an intersection, take the left fork marked "Schloss Vaduz" and follow it to the paved road, then right a few meters to the royal castle. It is a fine old castle and houses the magnificent art collection of the reigning prince. Unfortunately, it is not open to the public, but many of the paintings in the collection can be seen in the National Gallery in town.

Beyond the castle, a path leads left down to town. Here there are several restaurants for relaxation and libation before continuing your journey to wherever.

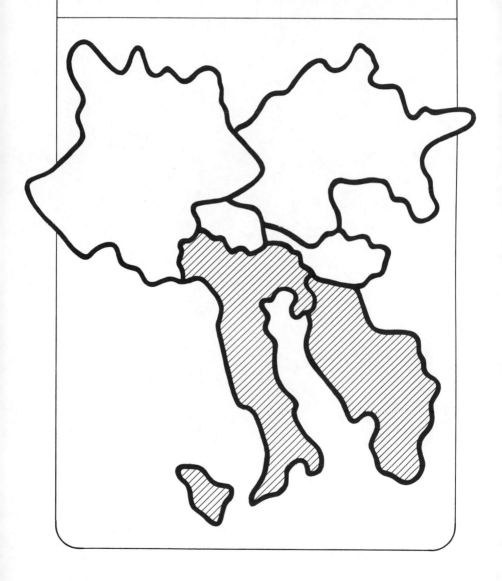

Italy & Yugoslavia

12. Verona and Bolzano

Some of the most spectacular mountain scenery in the Alps is in the Dolomites, in the northernmost part of Italy, hard up against the Austrian border. It is a remote region, difficult of access. The nearest cities of any size are Innsbruck to the north and Verona to the south. Although the main rail line between Rome and Munich passes through the region (via the Brenner Pass), distances are great enough to preclude day hikes in the region from either Innsbruck or Verona. The best trains take two hours to travel from either Verona or Innsbruck to Bolzano in the heart of the region. From there, most of the travel to trailheads must be by bus, a slow process on the twisty mountain roads.

Nevertheless, the mountain scenery is spectacular enough to warrant special efforts to see it. The Drei Zinnen (Three Pinnacles), perhaps the most extraordinary limestone monoliths in the Alps, should be on any mountain lover's list. But without an automobile at one's disposal, they are almost impossible to get to. Almost impossible, but not quite. A solution, if you have two days to devote to the trip, is to stay in or near Bolzano, Brixen, Cortina d'Ampezzo, or Misurina overnight. This will allow a full day for a mountain walk, albeit with a rather late return to Verona or Innsbruck. But more about this later.

Bolzano, a small city of a hundred thousand inhabitants, is the capital of the autonomous Italian province of Bolzano and the center of tourism in the Dolomite Alps. If you are an Austrian, you think of this region as the South Tirol; if you are an Italian, you probably think of it as Upper Adige (Alto Adige). But whichever, Bolzano is the gateway to the numerous valleys and villages that comprise the Dolomites. To the east lies the world-famous ski resort, Cortina d'Ampezzo, site of the 1956 Winter Olympics, connected to Bolzano by the Dolomite Road. Although the road is only 109 kilometers long, its twists and turns and climbs preclude a rapid trip and insist that one take a slower, more scenic journey. Indeed, the road is justly famous as a superb example of the road builder's art.

The city of Bolzano has its own attractions for wanderers. Its *Hausberg* is Ritten, a 2259-meter peak overlooking the town and providing a pleasant day's hike and climb, to which several ski lifts provide partial access. The first of these, the Oberbozen lift, starts just 100 meters from the railroad station, on Rittnerstrasse. From the top of the lift, an old-fashioned trolley will take you to Klobenstein (Collabo), a fine old village. A series of remarkable earth pyramids can be reached in a half hour from the village. From Klobenstein, the summit of Ritten can be reached in about four hours, although an hour and a half can be lopped off by taking an upper chair lift. Several mountain huts and inns along the way provide an excuse for stopping and enjoying the spectacular views.

TRANSPORTATION

Verona is at the crossroads of a main east-west rail line linking Milan and Venice, and the north-south line over the Brenner Pass. By fast train, Verona is less than two hours from Milan, Venice, and Bolzano. Trains leave for Bolzano about every two hours. Verona is also at the crossroads of the north-south and east-west superhighways, so no matter how you come, Verona will be easy to get to.

Bolzano is a transportation hub for the Dolomite region and has numerous bus lines fanning out in all directions. The main bus company is the Südtiroler Autobus Dienst (SAD). The station is a block from the railroad station, to the left as you leave the main door. A timetable is available at the bus depot. Although the buses seem to go everywhere, service is not frequent and you must pay attention to the schedules to avoid being stranded.

MAPS AND GUIDEBOOKS

The Bolzano Tourist Office publishes a brief brochure, *Wandern um Bozen*, describing several walks in the area. It is in German. An excellent guidebook, if you can read even a little German, is the Kompass Wanderführer *Dolomiten Bozen/Meran*. It describes a hundred walks of varying lengths and difficulties. The major map publishers all have maps covering the Dolomites, and local newsstands and bookstores carry a good selection.

WEATHER AND CLIMATE

Bolzano's climate is relatively benign, considering its location in the heart of the Dolomite Alps. But on the southern flank of the Alps, sunshine is greater and temperatures higher than at similar elevations on the north side, just a few miles away. In the summer, the persistent presence of the Azores high-pressure area means predominantly sunny skies, although afternoon clouds and showers are common. In the summer period (June, July, and August), thunderstorms occur on about fifteen days.

Winter snowfall is relatively light in the immediate area around Bolzano, although the higher elevations of the Dolomites have as much as 5 or 6 meters. Total precipitation for the year averages less than 1 meter in the valley, but more than twice that in the nearby mountains. Low-elevation walks in the immediate vicinity of Bolzano may be possible even in the wintertime, although higher elevations will be snow covered. Consult the climate tables on pages 8 and 9 for more information.

Verona has a milder climate yet, but not nearly so pleasant. Fog is frequent in the Po Valley. Indeed, it is so frequent and pervasive that it has been the subject of much scientific study. However, Verona has fewer foggy days than does Milan—which has more than half its days foggy in the fall and winter months. Visibility is also restricted in the Po Valley; in December, more than half the days have visibility less than 1 kilometer. The higher elevations to the north are above all this, and have much clearer weather. So if the weather is poor in Verona, head for the hills!

Useful information

Tourist information

Ente Provinciale Turismo (EPT), Via C. Montanari 14, I-37100 Verona. Tel. (045) 2 50 65.
Azienda Soggiorno e Turismo, Piazza Walther 28, I-39100 Bolzano. Tel. (0471) 2 56 56.
Landesverkehrsamt für Südtirol, Waltherplatz 22, I-39100 Bolzano. Tel. (0471) 2 69 91.

Maps, guidebooks, and trail information

Alpine Auskunftstelle, Waltherplatz 8, I-39100 Bolzano. Tel. (0471) 2 18 67. Conducts guided hikes in summer.
Club Alpino Italiano (CAI), Obstmarkt 45/2, I-39100 Bolzano. Tel. (0471) 2 11 72.
Südtiroler Alpenverein (AVS), Sernesiplatz 34/2, I-39100 Bolzano. Tel. (0471) 2 11 41.

Local transportation

Südtiroler Autobus Dienst (SAD), Bolzano. Tel. (0471) 97 12 59. Extensive bus routes in the Dolomites. Bus terminal in Bolzano is across from the railroad station.

Accommodations

Hotel Unterhofer, Piazza del Grano (Kornplatz) 5, I-39100 Bolzano. Tel. (0471) 2 78 80. A pleasant hotel near the railroad station.
Youth Hostel Riva del Garda, Piazza Cavour 10, Riva del Garda (Trento). Tel. (0464) 51 22 94. Halfway between Verona and Bolzano, this is the only youth hostel in the area.
Haus der Naturfreunde-Internationale, Gneidweg 5, I-39019 Dorf Tirol bei Meran. Tel. (0473) 9 34 12.
Camping. Camping Romeo e Giulietta, 5 kilometers west of Verona on route 11. Tel. (045) 4 00 05. One of many camping sites on the shores of Lake Garda. Camping Bozen, Sankt-Heinrich-Strasse, Bolzano. Tel. (0471) 2 47 66. On the Brenner Pass road, near Weinstube "Schlechtleitner." Open March–October.

In the shadow of the Geislerspitz

DIFFICULTY	Grade 3–4
DISTANCE	11 km
WALKING TIME	4 hours
MAP	F&B Wanderkarte WKS 5, *Cortina d'Ampezzo*
GUIDEBOOKS	F&B Wanderatlas *Dolomiten* (with trail maps), 1:75,000
	Haydn, A. *Führer darch das Grödner Tal*. München: Bergverlag Rudolf Rother, 1977. Includes trail map
	KOMP Wanderführer *Dolomiten Bozen/Meran*. Walk 48

Val Gardena—Grödner Tal to the Germans—is a celebrated international ski area, with its Sella Ronda, an extraordinary complex of linked lifts accessible with a single lift pass. In the heart of the Dolomites, it is also a center for rock climbing and mountaineering, with 3181-meter Langkofel on the south and the Geisler group on the north. At the head of the valley, the Sella group dominates with its sheer walls of bright limestone. It is this profusion of light-colored rock that gives the Dolomites their distinctive appearance, that appearance changing dramatically as the sun- and skylight change. When the high sun glints off the rock, the light may be almost blinding. Yet as the sun sets and the sun's rays are filtered through ever-thicker layers of the atmosphere, the color changes to yellow, orange, and deepening reds. Alpenglow on a Dolomite peak is something to behold!

The Geisler group in the Dolomites

But the Dolomites of northern Italy are almost unknown to many of the tourists and would-be mountaineers who flock to the northern slopes of the Alps. The Italian Dolomites are surely in this position primarily for reasons of access, or rather, lack of it. They are rather far from the major Alpine and cisalpine cities. Bolzano is an hour and a half by fastest train from Verona, and three hours from Milan. Neither is the region more accessible from the north. Access is via the Brenner Pass on the main line from Munich to Rome, but even the fastest trains labor on the steep grades and sharp curves: at least a two-and-a-half-hour ride. So an excursion to the heart of the Dolomites requires an early arising and late return or, preferably, a two-day excursion.

Ortisei (St. Ulrich) is perhaps best known (at least amongst those of us for whom toys are important) as the site of the Sevi factory, famous throughout the world for its handcrafted wooden toys. It is also the gateway to the Val Gardena of the skier. Ortisei sports one of the longest chair lifts that we have ever been on. The Raschötz chair lift is nearly 3 kilometers long and takes the pain out of the 900-meter ascent to the beginning of our high-country walk.

St. Ulrich

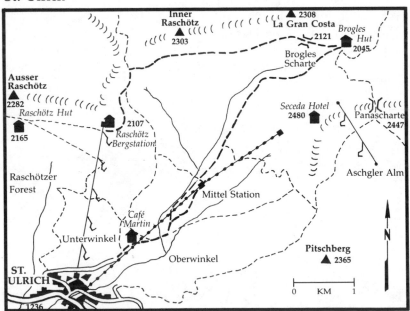

But first we have to reach Ortisei, simple enough if you catch the 0810 bus from Bolzano. Beware: the next bus is not until 1110 (check the schedule for current times of departure). We missed the bus, took the train to Waidbruck, and started to walk the winding and steep road up the Grödner Bach. Fortunately, an auto traveler took pity on us and gave us a ride to Ortisei.

Ortisei, in common with most of the towns in this region, is still very much an "old" town. Despite its commitment to serving the wintertime skier with a variety of mechanical lifts and comfortable accommodations, it has maintained much of its rural charm. Wood-carving, especially of religious figures, is a major activity of the local artisans; and the shops are full of fine specimens. So take a few minutes before or after your walk to at least window-shop, if not to buy a memento or two of this delightful town.

Our journey begins at the Raschötz chair lift, reached by following signs from the bus depot. The long ride passes through beautiful open stands of Arolla pine, reaching the summit station (2107 meters) just below timberline. After alighting from the lift, take trail 35, marked with red/white paint blazes, to the right, climbing gently through patchy woods to a small knoll with a spectacular view of the bright spires of the Sella group. Shortly beyond the knoll, the trail breaks out of the woods into open tundra and contours the south side of the Raschötz Ridge. Views to the east and south are extensive along this open stretch. The trail is nearly level and well constructed, and the walk is delightful.

Straight ahead, Brogles Scharte remains in view, and is soon reached. It is a broad, open, lumpy pass, with the lowest point rather poorly defined. From the pass, you can see Brogles Hütte just below, a five-minute walk to refreshment and overnight accommodations. From the lowest point of the pass, rather much on the far side, trails lead back to Ortisei.

Our route heads southwestward down the slope and quickly enters the timber. (Another, slightly longer route, heads south to Panascharte, thence southeastward to Ortisei—see accompanying map.) The clumps of Arolla pine are interspersed with meadows that sport a profusion of wildflowers. The path then descends into the woods rather sharply for a distance, finally coming out in a meadow and crossing a heavily eroded river valley. Here it crosses the river and continues its descent through open meadows. The path may become indistinct, but the way is clear. The trail to this point, coming down the valley, is somewhat rough because it has been heavily eroded and there are multiple pathways. Following it is not difficult, but the footing is tricky at times. Soon we reach a service road for the middle station of a gondola lift; the road diverges left and climbs a little hill to a fence, thence to the terminal. If the hour is late and you are tired, you can take the gondola down to St. Ulrich. For the best trail down, go straight ahead at this point—just where you meet the road to the midstation—into the woods. The way is marked by trail signs. Just beyond a gate, a sign indicates "St. Ulrich, 45 minutes."

The trail keeps to the north side of and essentially parallel to the cable-car line, which can occasionally be seen through the woods. (The accompanying map shows a trail crossing to the south of the line. This is the service road, a possible but less pleasant route.) Soon you see houses, ski lodges, and farms to the left, along the route of the *Seilbahn*. Now the vegetation is largely Norway spruce and larch, with a few hardwoods mixed in. Shortly after the second crossing under the cables near Café Martin, the path meets a paved road, which it follows on down to St. Ulrich. It then crosses over the brook, which cascades into a spectacular waterfall directly beneath the bridge.

Bus service back to Bolzano is infrequent, to say the least. However, there is (or was; check the schedule) a bus leaving for Bolzano at 1800. The ride takes an hour. If you follow the trail to St. Christina via Panascharte, the same bus leaves there fifteen minutes earlier. Trains leave Bolzano at 1905 and 1936 for the two-hour ride to Verona.

Around the Drei Zinnen, the quintessential Dolomite peaks

DIFFICULTY	Grade 3
DISTANCE	7 1/2–15 km, depending on route
WALKING TIME	3 1/2–6 1/2 hours, depending on route
MAPS	F&B Wanderkarte WKS 10, *Sextener Dolomiten*
	KOMP Wanderkarte 58, *Sextener Dolomiten*
GUIDEBOOKS	F&B Wanderatlas *Dolomiten* (with trail maps), 1:75,000
	KOMP Wanderführer *Dolomiten Bozen/Meran*. Walk 91

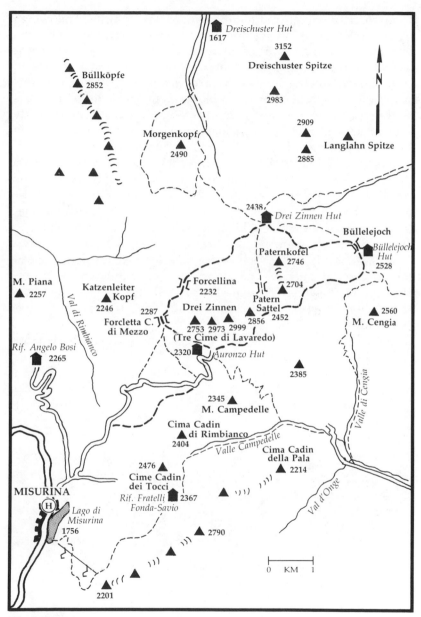

Drei Zinnen

More than any other peaks in the Dolomites, the Drei Zinnen—Tre Cime di Lavaredo in Italian and Three Pinnacles in English—symbolize the rugged and austere beauty of the Dolomites. Three giant rocks rise straight up out of the wide Pian da Rin, ensuring an untrammeled view. The sheer rock faces themselves face the northwest so that they will catch the reddening rays of the setting sun, setting the rocks on fire with vivid alpenglow. And they are readily accessible. The walk from Lake Misurina is not arduous; and now there is a road a good part of the way, one that will take you by bus, if you desire, to a nearly level trail that encircles the mountains. As a result, the Drei Zinnen are probably the most visited, certainly the most photographed, peaks in all the Dolomites. But don't let the threat of crowded trails deter you: the Drei Zinnen are magnificent, a sight to see, even though other tourists will most certainly be seeing them with you.

Like Ortisei, the area is not very close to major tourist centers or transportation routes. So getting there takes a little doing. Nevertheless, there is bus service to Misurina; and even a bus that climbs the road from Misurina to Auronzohütte, the start of the walk. It is possible to do the "short route" in one long day, but if you can, take a weekend for the trip. Summertime accommodations in Misurina

Lake Misurina

Büllelejochhütte

are plentiful and inexpensive. And there are several Alpine huts with overnight possibilities, including the famous Drei-Zinnen-Hütte. Other possibilities are Auronzohütte at the end of the road, more a hotel than a hut; Büllelejochhütte, more typical of the small backcountry hut; and Rifugio Lavaredo, a small but friendly hut. But if you stay at Drei-Zinnen-Hütte, you may have the opportunity to see the glory of alpenglow on the peaks at sunset. It is worth the chance.

The best way to get to Misurina from Bolzano is by SAD (Südtiroler Autobus Dienst) bus. A bus leaves Bolzano at 0715 and travels direct to Cortina d'Ampezzo, stopping at Schluderbach at 1000. Although this is 5 kilometers from Misurina (some of the buses do go via Misurina, but not this one), it should be possible to hire a taxi and arrive at the bus stop in Misurina in time for the 1025 bus to Auronzohütte, arriving there at 1055. The last bus down from Auronzohütte leaves at 1700, so you will have a full six hours for exploring.

From the bus stop, follow the wide, graded, and quite level path to Rifugio Lavaredo. A curious kind of Alpine graffiti decorates the Alpine meadows below the trail. Hikers with nothing better to do gather the white limestone rocks and line them up to form their names or those of their friends—not really a pretty sight, but better than some defacing, since it is possible to spread the rocks around to some semblance of their original state. Painted graffiti are harder to destroy. If you have a few minutes to spare, bring a bit of the Alps back to its natural state!

At Lavaredo, you have a choice. Either cross Paternsattel direct to Drei-Zinnen-Hütte, a walk of about an hour; or continue on to Büllelejochhütte, thence to Drei-Zinnen-Hütte, a walk of two and a half to three hours' duration. The heavy traffic goes over Paternsattel; the trip via Büllelejoch is less traveled and more interesting, yet level most of the way. Once you are over the pass, a short, steep drop brings you to the contour trail that crosses the giant scree slope below Bodenknoten Ridge and leads directly to the hut.

From the hut, the trail takes off toward Paternsattel but quickly diverges right (west) across the Pian da Rin, right in front of the sheer walls of the Drei Zinnen. The trail passes a tiny pond, then climbs gently to the Forcletta C. di Mezzo and the broad, level path back to Auronzohütte. Although you can take the bus back to Misurina, the walk downhill is pleasant and not so steep as to strain knees unaccustomed to downhill pounding. The route more or less follows the road, eventually joining it about halfway down. From the pass, it is also possible to take a rougher trail south to the road. This is shorter than the way via Auronzohütte.

If you take the 1700 bus down the mountain road, you will have a half hour to see the sights in Misurina before catching the 1800 bus to Toblach; thence you go by SAD bus to Fortezza and take the train back to Bolzano, arriving there just before 2200, in time for the 2216 train to Verona. It is a full day, but one you will remember a long time.

13. Milan

Milan, the second largest city in Italy, is the industrial heart of the country. It lies in the upper end of the Po Valley, the broad, flat plain that separates the Alps from the Apennines. The plains around the city are crowded with factories and commercial establishments, but the city itself has much to offer as a tourist attraction. The cathedral, started in 1386, is a marvel of white marble, adorned with spires, pinnacles, gables, and statues. A walk on the roof to observe the pinnacles and statues at close hand is one of the highlights of any sightseeing tour of the city.

At the same time, it must be admitted that there are few places for woodland walkers in or near the city. Nevertheless, the foothills of the Alps are surprisingly close. Chiasso, at the southern end of Lake Como and the first Swiss city that the traveler heading north reaches, is fifty minutes from Milan by fast train. One can be in the heart of the Swiss pre-Alps in an hour and a half. Train service is good and it is possible to make a one-day walking excursion to very pleasant terrain.

TRANSPORTATION

The transportation hub in Milan is the Stazione Centrale. Trains north to Switzerland via the Simplon Tunnel depart approximately every hour. The one leaving Milan at 0710 (check current schedule!) arrives in Lugano at 0840 and in Bellinzona at 0916. The next good train leaves two hours later, arriving too late for starting a day hike. Returning trains leave Bellinzona at 1745 and 1945 for the two-hour trip to Milan.

MAPS AND GUIDEBOOKS

A section of European Long-distance Footpath E1, which goes from the North Sea to the Mediterranean, passes through Milan. However, the section from Chiasso to Gavi south of Milan is not marked and passes through largely industrialized country on the Lombardy Plain. Indeed, Craig Evans, in his *Trail Guide to Europe's Long-distance Footpaths*, states, "To walk this section of E-1 takes a lot of daring and endurance. The route is completely unmarked. No maps are available on a scale large enough to be useful to walkers. Also, since almost all side roads and paths are either on private property, and therefore inaccessible to the public, or end abruptly, the walker has no choice but to follow paved roads. Hence, it is recommended that this section not be walked." So much for trails and trail guides in the immediate Milan area.

For the pre-Alps and Alps north of Milan, numerous maps and guidebooks are available. Specific recommendations are made in the trail descriptions that follow.

WEATHER AND CLIMATE

The southern slopes of the Alps are much warmer and wetter than their counterparts north of the mountains. Milan's yearly average temperature is about 13° C (55° F) compared with 7° C (45° F)for Munich. Humidity and rainfall are also somewhat higher in Milan, although summertime cloudiness is less. To the north in the pre-Alps, the climate is somewhat more continental in nature, reflecting the greater distance from the Mediterranean and the higher elevations. Thus Lugano is slightly cooler than Milan in the summer and the temperature range is greater. Winters are cool in Milan; only in January does the average minimum temperature dip below the freezing level. At higher elevations, snow and low temperatures are common in the winter.

Useful information

Tourist information

Ente Provinciale Turismo (Provincial Tourist Board). Via Marconi 1, I-30100 Milano. Tel. (02) 80 88 13; Central Station, Tel. (02) 20 60 30; Linate Airport, Tel. (02) 74 40 65.
City of Milan Information Office, Galleria Vittorio Emanuele, corner Piazza della Scala. Tel. (02) 87 05 45.

Maps, guidebooks, and trail information

Club Alpino Italiano, Via Silvio Pellico 6. Tel. (02) 80 84 21. Information on trails and huts maintained by the Italian Alpine Club.

Local transportation

Buses, trams, and subways run from 0600 to 0100. Honor system used, with tickets sold at newsstands with ATM logo. Subway tickets sold at station kiosks. Day tickets also available.

Accommodations and restaurants

According to the official list, there are 6 luxury hotels, 32 first-class hotels, 84 second-class hotels, 88 third-class hotels, 53 fourth-class hotels, and 141 pensions. Many of the *pensione* are quite comfortable and very reasonable. Try Pensione Soperga (Via Soperga 19, tel. 278-228) or Pensione Italia (Via Vitruvio 44, tel. 873-697). The tourist office at the Central Station will be helpful.
Youth Hostel Ostello Piero Rotta. Via Martino Bassi 2, 20148 Milano, near Viale Salmoiraghi. Tel. (02) 36 70 95. Away from the city center. Subway line 1 to QT8. Reasonable bed and breakfast. Four hundred beds.
Camping. Camping Chiesa Rossa, 5 kilometers south of the city center on Via Chiesa Rossa. Tel. (02) 8 49 77 94. Open May through September. Camping Milano-Idroscala, open year-round. Reputed to be noisy. Camping AGIP, 200 meters from the entrance to the Autostrada del Sole.
Restaurants. Hundreds of *trattorie* and *rosticcerie*. Many are closed in August. To fill that gap, the city sponsors an outdoor cafeteria in the Parco Sempione during that month.

Miscellaneous

American Consulate, Piazza della Repubblica 32, 20124 Milano. Tel. (02) 65
28 41.
Canadian Consulate, Via Vittor Pisani 19, 20124 Milano. Tel. (02) 65 26 00.

A high Alpine walk
in the "neglected" Ticino

DIFFICULTY	Grade 3–4, mostly below timberline
DISTANCE	10 km; 8 km if summit of Gaggio is omitted
WALKING TIME	5 hours; 4 hours without summit
MAPS	AK 1313, *Bellinzona,* 1:25,000
	AK 5007, *Locarno–Lugano*
	Bellinzona Tourist Office, *Hiking Map of Bellinzona*
	and Surroundings
GUIDEBOOK	K&F Wanderbuch 33, *Tessin*

The mountains around Bellinzona are not the highest in the southern
portions of Switzerland, but they have one major advantage for the
tourist who approaches from the south, from Italy. They lie along one
of the main rail and auto routes across the Alps, the St. Gotthard
route. Train service from Milan is good; the trip takes two hours by
express train. Although this is more than the one-hour limit we set
ourselves, the extra time is worth it if you want to take an easy walk
above timberline and return to Milan the same day. (Remember to
take your passport; Bellinzona is in Switzerland.)

The trip is really made possible by the existence of two cable cars
that eliminate climbing and descending through the less interesting
lower portions. One aspect of the cable cars that is different from
those in most of our trips is that they are *not* ski lifts. Both are operated
primarily for access to the village of Mornera high above Monte
Carasso and to the houses and farms above Carasso. The little cars
run in tandem: one for passengers in front, the other for freight
behind. They are off the tourist track; and on this walk, you are not
likely to be bothered by hordes of tourists. Indeed, you may find only
cows and sheep for companions. But it is a very pleasant walk that
leads to a mountaineers' hut at timberline and provides the oppor-

tunity for climbing to the summit of Gaggio, 2267 meters above sea level and nearly 2000 meters above Bellinzona. It provides a true Alpine experience.

The early morning train leaves the main station in Milan at 0710 and arrives in Bellinzona at 0916 (check current schedule!). The bus to the Funivia *Seilbahn* (cable car) in Monte Carasso leaves from the PTT (Postal Telephone and Telegraph) terminal, a few meters from the railroad station. To reach the terminal, go left from the railroad station down the main street to a set of steps on the right, near the Hotel Garni Moderno. From the steps, the yellow signs and buses of the PTT are visible to the left. The Cugnasco bus runs every half hour and reaches Monte Carasso in ten minutes. After leaving the bus, walk 100 meters in the same direction to a sign, "Funivia Mornera," pointing to the right, to the base station a few meters distant. Make sure that you do not get off at the midstation. There is a small restaurant at the top and you will usually find a group of the local farmers sitting around an outside table having their midmorning stein of beer.

At the elevation of Mornera, about 1400 meters, the vegetation is Alpine, predominantly Norway spruce, in sharp contrast to the Mediterranean vegetation in the valley. At the bottom, the forest is largely hardwood, with chestnut and olive trees. As the cable car ascends, it passes through a birch forest, finally reaching a Norway spruce forest. The views back toward the valley and the mountains on the other side are spectacular. Monte d'Arbino, directly across Bellinzona, rapidly changes from an imposing eminence towering above the town to a small peak dwarfed by the higher Alps behind. Indeed, when we reach Mornera, we are only 300 meters below its summit.

On the west side of the top end of the *Seilbahn*, there is a signpost with yellow trail markers. Three signs are on it; the one we are interested in indicates "Albagno capanna UTOE, 1 hour 30 minutes." (UTOE = Unione Ticinese Operai Escursionisti. It maintains the hut, or *capanna*.) Just up the hill from this sign, another signpost with "Capanna Albagno, 1 hour 30 minutes" is marked with white/red/white horizontal stripes. The well-marked and well-graded trail leads upward into the forest through a profusion of wildflowers, including wolfsbane, a snapdragon-like yellow flower that grows on a low bush, and the ground-hugging purple saxifrage. There are other paths in the area, so one must pay attention to the trail blazes and the occasional sign that says "Capanna UTOE."

In about fifteen minutes the trail comes to the top of a ridge and

Gaggio

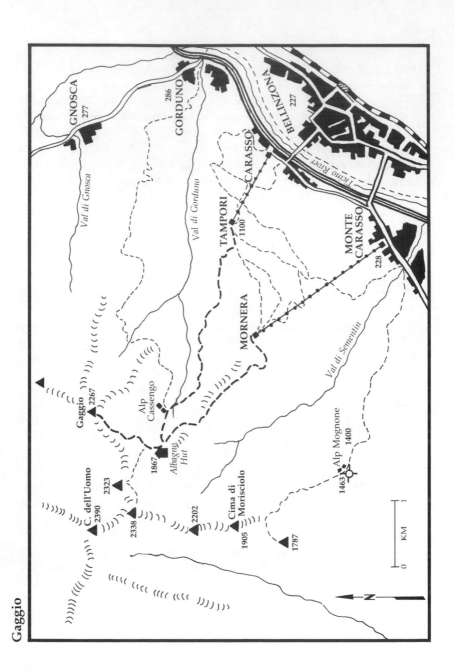

an opening at a spring and watering trough, a little pond, and a fine view of the ridge to the north and the peaks of Cima dell'Uomo and Gaggio. There are also good views of the mountains to the south and west. At about 1650 meters elevation the path comes out of the woods and climbs gently along a very steep, grassy slope. Just before reaching the ridge at 1720 meters, a marked trail diverges right. Our path crosses to the other side of the ridge at about 1780 meters and continues upward, soon reaching the hut at the saddle. The hut is not normally open, and no food is available.

The trail to Gaggio starts from the signpost near the hut and heads straight toward a small stone barn near a watering trough. Just behind the building, the path heads up a rather washed out and rocky way. In about 200 meters, you will come to a flat rock with a painted three-way sign, indicating the three-way junction that is marked on the map. The route to Gaggio is the right-hand route. The route starts up rather steeply, following a somewhat indistinct but well-paint-blazed pathway. It climbs diagonally up the slope, then switchbacks to the top of the ridge, which it follows to the summit. The view from the top is extensive in all directions. The top is unusual for an Alpine peak in that it is quite rounded. To return, retrace the route to the Capanna Albagno.

The route down to the Baltico *Seilbahn* starts at the signpost near the hut and heads straight down the valley, somewhat to the left of the path we took as we came up, on the opposite side of the ridge. The trail follows the north, or left, side of the creek. It stays a little bit above the creek and finally comes out into open pasture at three picturesque stone barns. This is Alp (pasture) Cassegno, at an elevation of 1620 meters. From this point (trail sign), a contour trail leads to the valley at the town of Gorduno. Our trail heads straight down toward the creek. Just below the stone huts the trail goes through a rather steep meadow that could be tricky in wet weather. At a flat stone with a paint blaze, the trail bends sharply to the right and heads for the creek, which it crosses in 50 meters, and promptly enters the woods.

The trail soon enters a larch forest with very large and tall larch trees, a really beautiful sight. The feathery needles—which are deciduous, unlike most conifers—are distinctive. The trail here is not as well worn and graded as the path coming up; nevertheless it is never difficult to follow. It has either a good visible footway or plenty of paint blazes.

Bellinzona

Maxell Cassette Tape Features

In the cassette Maxell adapts the unique 4-function leader to incorporate the cleaning properties of its original head cleaning tape. The special finish assures continuous cleaning without fear of head wear.

① Non-abrasive head cleaning leader tape.
② Indicates A or B side ready to play.
③ Arrows indicate direction of tape travel.
④ 5-second cueing line.

maxell
UR 90

Maxell Corporation of America
PROOF OF PURCHASE

Soon larches give way to an almost pure stand of Norway spruce, with an occasional understory of hardwoods. A lush growth of ferns carpets the forest floor. Fir trees are also found here, looking much like balsam fir with its flat, splayed leaves. This portion of the trail is not as well maintained as the other, and you may encounter blowdowns that have not been cleared. You must stay alert here; occasionally the trail zig-zags away from the obvious direction and you may find yourself bushwhacking. Special alertness is required after traversing blowdown areas. The trail stays on a contour of about 1290 meters for some time, just dipping up and down when it crosses brooks. At this elevation you will find that the vegetation is primarily beech.

The trail soon becomes a fine, easy path. The footing is mostly leaves, occasionally large boulders, but it is a beautiful woodland walk. The trail comes into open woods and a clearing past a spring and in 50 meters meets a path at a T and signpost. To the right is Mornera, where we started; to the left is Baltico. At this point the path becomes a forest road.

We now pass through a birch stand with white bark, a fine open, parklike stand, with fine views of Bellinzona and the valley towns far below. The trail briefly diverges right from the road, to a trail sign and another trail that comes in from the right, from the midstation of the Mornera *Seilbahn*. A sign here also points to the Baltico *Seilbahn*, which is reached in a few minutes.

There is no attendant at the top of the *Seilbahn*, only a telephone. You must telephone to the operator who is down below, a rather intimidating experience if you do not speak or understand Italian. Presumably he knows enough English, or something, to understand that you want to ride down. After you notify him (and the cable car arrives, if it was not at the top to begin with), wait until the attendant telephones back to verify that all is ready. Hop on the car and wait for it to start down.

To get to the bus stop from the base station of the *Seilbahn*, walk down the little street to the right, to the main highway, about 50 meters or so. Turn right and walk about 200 meters south to the post office, which also is the PTT bus stop. Buses run to Bellinzona, 2 kilometers away, about every forty minutes. From Bellinzona, express trains depart at 1745 and 1945 for the two-hour trip back to Milan.

A funicular ride
to the picturesque hill town of Brè

DIFFICULTY	Grade 1
DISTANCE	6 km
WALKING TIME	2 1/2 hours
MAP	*Lugano and Environs* (city map), 1:12,000
GUIDEBOOK	None

In the summer, the city of Lugano can be very warm indeed. Plantings of palm trees add to the illusion that we are in a tropical paradise. It seems to have more in common with Italian towns far to the south. Yet we are in Switzerland and in the southern foothills of the snowy Alps. St. Gotthard Pass is only 70 kilometers to the north. And the people are Swiss and love to walk and be in the mountains. The hills round Lugano provide many miles of walking trails, and a hot day finds many of the Luganans heading for the hills.

Monte Brè

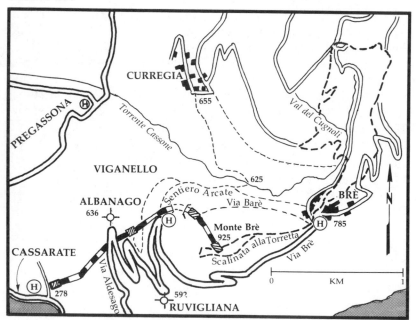

Brè

Lugano is an hour and a half from Milan by fast train. (Remember your passport, for you will cross from Italy into Switzerland.) The train that leaves Milan at 0710 reaches Lugano at 0840, in time for a good day's walk. Returning trains leave about every hour from 1600 on. Check the schedule for exact times.

Two funiculars provide rapid access to the hills: the one up Monte San Salvatore south of the city; and the Monte Brè funicular east of the city center. For a pleasant and breezy walk to the picturesque hill village of Brè, ride to the top of Monte Brè and walk from there. The base station of the funicular is reached via the number 2 trolley-bus from downtown. From the railroad station, take the number 6 bus and transfer to the number 2 at Piazza Manzoni, right on the lakeshore. (An alternative is to take the funicular from the station to the Piazza Cioccaro, then walk the 250 meters southeastward to Piazza Manzoni.) The number 2 bus will take you to the Funicolare Monte Brè stop in the Cassarate district. Walk a few meters to the base station.

The two-stage trip takes you 600 meters higher and six Celsius degrees (about eleven Fahrenheit degrees) cooler in just a few minutes. The breeze on top helps, too. Find an outdoor restaurant with a view of Lake Lugano. You may be tempted to spend the

afternoon over a cup of coffee or a glass of wine; but we want to visit
Brè and so must be off. Signposts indicate the walking path to the
village, the Scalinata alla Torretta, which starts at the very top of the
mountain and proceeds down a narrow ridge. It is soon joined by
the Sentiero della Battulle and together they proceed to Brè, a walk
of less than half an hour.

Brè is all cobbles and stone, a little church and shuttered windows, a restaurant or two, and lots of sunshine. Near the church, a
signpost announces the steep step-trail to Gandria on the lakefront

The bell tower at Brè

(from which a boat can be taken back to Lugano). We go up Via Brè on cobbles to Via Pineta, where we turn right at a signpost. Follow the narrow road along the east side of the ridge (good views of the lake far below), finally swinging around and crossing the ridge. Just after a watering trough, a path diverges right to Alpe Bolle and Monte Boglia. Our path contours around the head of the Cassone Creek to the waterworks at Carbonera and a trail junction. Here we follow the route south to Brè.

There are numerous roads and paths in this area, but intersections are well signed and you can always find your way back to Brè. From the village, it is possible to take a path, the Via Baré, that contours around the north side of Monte Brè, meeting the funicular at the first stop below the top. At the bottom station, follow the street left down to Viale Castagnola to the closest bus stop for the number 2 bus back to the Piazza Manzoni. From here, it is a short walk to the funicular that takes you back to the railroad station. Milan trains leave at 1613, 1729, 1813, and 2013.

A walk in the lake district
of southern Switzerland

DIFFICULTY	Grade 2
DISTANCE	9 km
WALKING TIME	3 1/2 hours
MAP	Lugano Tourist Office. Wanderkarte *Lugano e sottoceneri*. Accompanies guidebook listed below but may be purchased separately
GUIDEBOOK	Lugano Tourist Office. *Lugano und Sottoceneri. 100 Tourenvorschlage*. With trail map

Two mountains dominate the skyline around Lugano. Of these, the more impressive is Monte San Salvatore, which rises in the southern skyline. The mountain stands on a peninsula that divides Lake Lugano into two narrow arms forming a U open to the north. Thus the mountain and its long ridge to the south are almost completely surrounded by water; picturesque villages cling to the steep slopes that plunge precipitously into the azure blue lake. Several villages occupy portions of the ridgetop itself. Yet the ridge is largely

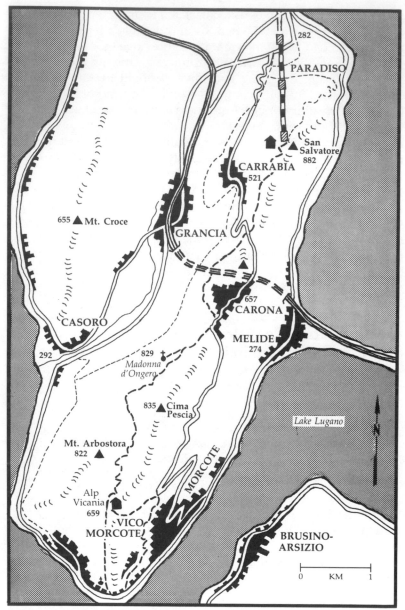

Morcote and San Salvatore

wooded and uninhabited, and a walk along the top passes through field and forest, through villages and past old ruins. It is an easy and delightful way to get away from the city on a warm day.

Because of its southerly location (Lugano is on the narrow point of Switzerland that juts into Italy; indeed, the town of Campione, directly across the lake from Lugano, occupies a tiny enclave of Italy along the shoreline), the climate is mild throughout the year. Although it does occasionally snow, the ground is rarely covered for any length of time and the walk along the ridge can be made almost any time of year. We have been told that April and May are the best times, for it is then that the wildflowers bloom in profusion.

The walk along the Monte San Salvatore Ridge can be made in one day from Milan if you get an early start. The 0710 train from Milan arrives in Lugano at 0840. (Remember your passport, for you will cross from Italy into Switzerland.) The mountaintop is made accessible by a funicular railway that climbs the northern flank from Paradiso just south of the city. The number 9 trolley-bus leads from the railroad station to Via Geretta near the base station of the Funicolare San Salvatore. The funicular leaves every half hour for the twenty-minute ride to the upper station. Take time to walk up to the lookout on the very top for fine views of Lugano and its lake.

From the top of the funicular, the path leads to the right past the hotel. It is well marked by *Wanderweg* signs indicating "Morcote, 2 hours 45 minutes." The path leads quickly downward along the spine of the mountain on a dirt path and numerous steps, zig-zagging down the rather sharp ridge. It is marked with occasional paint blazes, but the path is broad and easy to follow. We soon come to the little village of Ciona, where the path turns into a narrow paved street and then wanders through the village, following white/red/white paint blazes on the walls. The route meets and follows a paved street to a bus stop (possible transportation back to Lugano). The village is small, but very picturesque, with old stone houses and cobbled streets. Cross the main highway and pick up the dirt path to Carona at a trail sign.

From here the route follows a woods road, contouring the east side of the ridge, through a stately forest of beech and chestnut. We know we are on the south side of the Alps, for much of the vegetation here is typical of Mediterranean forests, especially the live oaks that can be seen along this stretch of trail. As we pass an old ruin just as we enter the village of Carona, a path branches right, down the hill, with a signpost marked Grancia. Avoid this branch and continue straight ahead to the paved road and follow it right toward the town.

At the main intersection 100 meters farther on, note the trail sign that indicates the trail to Morcote diverging right from the main road. Pass the Carona sport complex and follow the trail sign into a parking lot, past the swimming pool. At the end of the parking lot the trail begins as a gravel road leading into the forest.

At a small religious shrine, our path diverges left at a white/red paint blaze on an electric light pole. (The road straight ahead at this point leads to the shrine of the Madonna d'Ongero. It can be seen off to the right as we pass it. If you visit the shrine, you can rejoin the main path by heading uphill behind the building. There are fine views of the valley from the church.) Along here the path is a well-graded gravel track.

On a high point of the trail, just before it heads down, an outlook on the right overlooks the lake and towns surrounding it. Along this stretch, we find holly trees, another indication of our southerly location. The trail soon meets a road, which we follow right to Alp Vicania, a large alp or mountain meadow, occupying the southernmost tip of the ridge. After passing through a gate, the path leads along the right side of the meadow, along the edge of the forest. We stay more or less on a contour as we wind through the alp. Views to the south are extensive, but it must be admitted that smog frequently limits the scope of the view.

The path leads past the restaurant Alp Vicania, where you can obtain food and drink. About 100 meters south of the restaurant, a trail sign indicates an unpaved route to Morcote and Vico Morcote. A small path coming in from the right is marked as going to the Madonna d'Ongero and Carona. We follow the path straight down the mountain, first following a stone wall and wire fence. The path continues to follow the fence line on new steps that were being built in 1983. About halfway down the steps, just after leaving the stone wall and fence, a path comes in diagonally from the left from Vico Morcote. However, we continue down the steps to Morcote. Far below you can see the bell tower of the Chiesa Santa Maria del Sasso. We quickly reach the base of the tower and the church itself, which is supposed to contain some remarkable sixteenth-century frescoes, though we have not seen them. But the entire aspect of the church and its bell tower, the cypress trees, the cemetery, and the surrounding hillside houses forms a picture that you will not soon forget. Every new perspective seems worth a photograph.

Keep left to an outlook just below the church, to a platform, from which steps continue downward. The village is perched on the hillside, and streets and steps intertwine in a veritable maze. But you can't get lost—keep heading downward to the waterfront and the dock, marked with a Swiss flag. A ride on the boat back to Lugano makes a perfect ending to a fine mountain walk. The trip takes an hour; there are departures at 1600 and 1719. From the dock at Lugano, walk to the top of the funicular to the railroad station, at Piazza Cioccaro. Trains for Milan leave hourly until 1813; every two hours after that.

San Giorgio—
A walk in dinosaur land

DIFFICULTY	Grade 2
DISTANCE	8 km
WALKING TIME	2 1/2–3 hours
MAP	Lugano Tourist Office. Wanderkarte *Lugano e sottoceneri*. Accompanies guidebook listed below but may be purchased separately
GUIDEBOOK	Lugano Tourist Office. *Lugano und Sottoceneri. 100 Tourenvorschlage*. With trail map

Monte San Giorgio (1096 meters) is not the most imposing mountain in the southern Ticino. But it has the reputation of being the most scientifically interesting peak in the area, the one most worthy of a visit. Its slopes rise steeply from Lake Lugano, where it guards the two southern arms. The view from the summit of the Tessiner Voralpen, with the deep cut of the lake in the foreground, is certainly one of the most felicitous in the Ticino. It has a varied and beautiful vegetation. And most of all, the rocks of San Giorgio have yielded numerous fossils of the animal inhabitants of the Triassic period.

There is a small museum in the little village of Meride, high on the southern slopes of the mountain, that contains a small but excellent collection of fossils. And a circular nature path starting at Meride is punctuated with explanatory signposts. Although the text is in

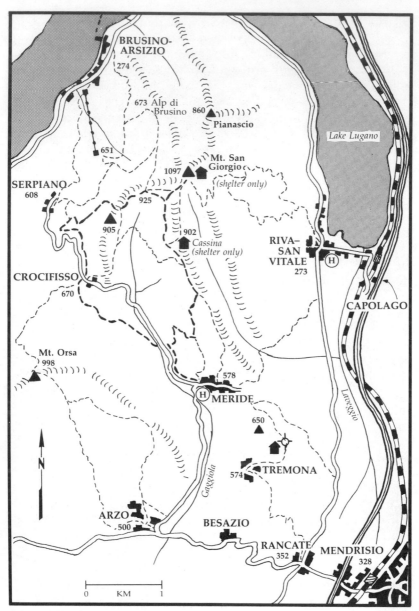

BRUSINO-
ARSIZIO

274

673 Alp di
Brusino 860
Pianascio

651

Lake Lugano

1097 Mt. San
Giorgio
(shelter only)

SERPIANO
608

925

905

902
Cassina
(shelter only)

RIVA–
SAN
VITALE
273

CROCIFISSO

670

CAPOLAGO

Mt. Orsa
998

578

Gaggiola

Laveggio

MERIDE

650

TREMONA
574

N

ARZO
500

BESAZIO

RANCATE
352

MENDRISIO
328

0   KM   1

Monte San Giorgio

Italian, the language of this part of Switzerland, the tablets contain many diagrams and scientific names. An explanatory brochure in German is available at the museum and local tourist offices. The best map is the one that accompanies the guide to the paths in the Lugano area, available locally.

As might be expected, the area around San Giorgio has numerous paths and is popular for day hikes. It is possible to take the boat from Lugano to Brusinó-Arsizio (departure at 0800) and take the cable car, eliminating about half the climb to the summit (see accompanying map). The shortest and steepest path starts at Riva-S. Vitale, reachable by train to Capolago. This is a two-and-a-half-hour climb. Our route starts at Meride, primarily because this take-off point permits a stop at the museum, and allows us to follow the nature trail its entire length.

From Milan, take the Gotthard line north to Chiasso. (Remember your passport, for you will cross from Italy into Switzerland.) The best train is the 0710, which reaches Chiasso at 0800. Transfer there to the local to Mendrisio, a ten-minute trip. If you are coming from Lugano, there are local trains that depart approximately hourly for the twenty-minute journey. Postal bus 835c runs from Mendrisio to Meride, a twenty-minute ride. The bus grinds its way up the narrow twisty road to Meride, stopping at several small towns on the way. It will drop you at the tiny post office. The museum is a five-minute walk from the bus stop, down the main street and to the left at the sign. (It is not too well marked, but Meride is a *very* small village.)

Monte San Giorgio and the village water supply

The nature trail starts at the village washhouse, a covered watering trough a short distance on the road to Serpiano. It heads north past a farmhouse and climbs on a moderate grade through woods, soon reaching a cobbled cart track, which it follows left, uphill. The limestone cobbles are well worn, indicating heavy use in an earlier era. The path climbs steadily, reaching the ridge, where it joins path 98, an alternative route from Meride. This junction is about an hour from the start.

Now the path northward along the ridge is nearly level. Although the way is heavily wooded, frequent views of the summit and the lake below are to be had. There are several nature-trail signs along this stretch. On the ridgetop path, some of the bedding planes of the Dolomites are exposed, showing their tilt toward the south. A little shrine, shelter hut, and picnic area are soon reached. The trail to the summit of San Giorgio continues straight ahead, whereas the nature trail diverges to the left. Follow the signs "Sentiero naturalis-

Church at Meride, Lake Lugano

tico." (Here also are garbage cans, filled to overflowing with picnic trash when we were there, one of the best arguments for "carry in, carry out" even in day-use areas.) This portion of the trail is also marked with yellow paint marks on the rocks. Continuing northward, we soon reach a junction where the trail to the summit diverges right and the nature trail bears left.

Shortly after station 5, trail 98 is rejoined. Signs here point back to Rifugio Santo Berto; the middle "Sentiero naturalistico" sign points in our direction. The path along here is graded gravel with a good footway. In 100 meters or so, we reach another trail junction. The nature trail (marked "Serpiano") diverges right. (The trail straight ahead also leads to Meride. Although shorter than the nature trail, it is rocky with rough footing.) The trail drops downhill, then comes close to the road to Serpiano, finally crossing the road where the rocky trail just referred to comes in from the left. This crossing is at Crocifisso, where there is a postal bus stop. (The one afternoon bus to Mendrisio from here leaves at 1840.) On the opposite side of the road there are two "Sentiero naturalistico" signs. Go straight ahead, avoiding the trail right to Serpiano.

About 100 meters in from the road, at an open place to which cars can be driven, the nature trail diverges left, and immediately comes upon sign 8. The trail follows the road, now just a track, a short way. It soon comes to a little picnic area with wood stove, fireplace, and picnic tables. The path now heads down gently through fields and past houses and barns. Finally it rejoins the main road, about 100 meters west of the Fontana watering trough.

It may be difficult to follow the described route because of the large number of paths in the area, some marked, others not. Nevertheless, there should be little chance of becoming lost since all of the trails heading eastward and southward eventually intersect the Serpiano–Meride road. At any rate, the area is most pleasant for walking, with much to interest the observant hiker. The large number of trails and convenient points of access permit the adventuresome to plan their own variant.

The bus from Meride runs at hourly intervals, but note that the last bus is at 1906, and then only on weekdays. The best one to take is the 1710, which connects with the 1745 train at Mendrisio. This will get you back to Milan at 1910, in time for a stylishly late dinner. The last bus from Meride, which runs only on weekdays and leaves at 1906, makes rather poor connections, bringing you back to Milan at 2140.

14. Ljubljana

Even with a map of Europe in front of us, it is difficult for most of us to realize that two of the major cities in Yugoslavia—Zagreb and Ljubljana—lie west of the longitude of Vienna. In fact, the southern border of Austria is nearly as much a border with Yugoslavia as it is with Italy. So it is perhaps not surprising that some of the most spectacular mountain scenery of the Alps lies in the northwest corner of Yugoslavia, hard up against its boundaries with Italy and Austria. The Karawanken, an eastward extension of the Dolomites, form the border between Austria and Yugoslavia. To the traveler from the north, they might appear to be the last range before reaching the lowlands bordering the Adriatic Sea. Though pleasant mountains, they are scarcely the towering giants of the Hohe Tauern to the north.

The true culmination of the eastern Alps lies farther south, in the Julian Alps, a southeastward-stretching finger of the Dolomites. The highest peak, Triglav, thrusting upward to a height of 2864 meters, actually lies on the divide between the Black Sea and the Mediterranean. It thus lays fair claim to being the eastern terminus of the Alpine chain. Triglav is also the highest peak in Yugoslavia and venerated in history and traditions. It has not escaped the notice of pioneering Alpinists, either. First climbed in 1778 by a German physician, L. Willonitzer, and three local guides, Kos, Korosec, and Rozic, it has become the traditional climb of the citizen of Slovenia.

Although Triglav was once considered to be a difficult climb, there are now numerous routes to the top, some suitable for an experienced walker. However, it is relatively inaccessible, and there are few if any routes suitable for a journey of a single day. This is especially true for the visitor to Ljubljana, the capital of Slovenia and the nearest large city. Although trains and buses provide access, the journey is too long for a single day.

Ljubljana lies some 60 kilometers southeast of Triglav, not a great distance, but the distance by road and trail is closer to 100 kilometers. Fortunately, there are interesting mountain walks that can be reached readily by train or bus and that afford fine views of this impressive mountain.

But first take time to see Ljubljana itself. This city of a third of a million inhabitants has a history stretching back to Roman times. Its Roman name was Aemona, and remnants of that earlier culture can be found in the Mirje district: walls, foundations, and mosaics. There are pleasant walks along the Ljubljanica River, which splits the city. From the castle tower, a steep walk up from the river, you can obtain fine views of the Alps to the north, as well as of the surrounding city.

TRANSPORTATION

Ljubljana is the westernmost major Yugoslavian city, both geographically and culturally, and is typically central European rather than Balkan in appearance. It is something of a transportation hub, being on the main railroad line from Salzburg to Belgrade. Two major superhighways intersect in Ljubljana. Air service connects the city to major European hubs.

MAPS AND GUIDEBOOKS

Perhaps surprisingly, there are good German-language maps and guidebooks available for the Julian Alps, that portion of the Alps in northern Italy and Yugoslavia that lies close to the Austrian border. Kümmerly and Frey publishes a hikers' map (Julische Alpen) at a scale of 1:100,000. The Slovenian Alpine Club (Planinska zveza Slovenije—PZS) publishes trail maps of the Yugoslavian portions at scales of 1:50,000 and 1:20,000. These may be obtained from the club office in Ljubljana or from newsstands and bookstores.

The only English-language guide to the area is *How to Climb Triglav: A Short Guide to Triglav*, published by Planinska zalozba, the publishing arm of the PZS, to commemorate the two hundredth anniversary of the first ascent of Triglav. It was published in 1979 and may still be available from the PZS. It contains a great deal of useful information, including a glossary of Slovenian words that you may run across on maps and on your travels in the mountains. Two German-language guides to the Julian Alps are published by Rudolf Rother in Munich.

WEATHER AND CLIMATE

The Julian Alps are south of the main Alpine divide and thus display a climatic regime similar to Bolzano and Lugano. That is, temperatures are higher than those of similar elevations on the north side of the Alps. An interesting and useful contrast is provided in the climatic data for Klagenfurt (Austria), just north of the border, and Zagreb, which is located in the Sava basin, as is Ljubljana. Both cities occupy valley bottoms and are within 300 meters elevation of each other. Nevertheless, the mean annual temperature at Zagreb is four Celsius degrees (seven Fahrenheit degrees) warmer than at Klagenfurt.

The Sava basin, in which both Ljubljana and Zagreb lie, is notorious for its fogs: an average of 150 foggy days per year. This is valley fog, however, and higher elevations will be relatively free of fog. The Julian Alps also have a rather high frequency of precipitation; Zagreb has an average of 156 days per year with measurable precipitation. The comparable value for Klagenfurt is 100 days per year. Despite this, the total annual precipitation for Zagreb (864 millimeters) is less than Klagenfurt's 926 millimeters.

The foehn, a warm, dry wind that blows off the mountains, is also common in the Julian Alps. Zagreb has an average of 70 days of foehn per year. In winter, days with foehn have temperatures about six Celsius degrees (approximately eleven Fahrenheit degrees) higher than non-foehn days; in the summer, the difference is less, about two Celsius degrees (four Fahrenheit degrees).

Thus the climate of the Julian Alps is somewhat warmer and wetter than comparable areas north of the main Alpine chains.

Useful information

Tourist information

Tourist Information Center, Titova Cesta 11, Ljubljana. Tel. 23-212.
Kompas Travel Agency, Prazakova 4, Ljubljana.
American Express (Atlas), Tomisceva 2, Ljubljana. Tel. 21-435.

Maps, guidebooks, and trail information

Planinska zveza Slovenije (Alpine Association of Slovenia), Dvoržakova 9, 61001 Ljubljana. Tel. 312-553.

Accommodations

Hotel Kompas, Miklošičeva 9. Nearest to railroad station. Moderate.
Hotel Union, Miklošičeva 1. Two hundred seventy rooms. Moderate.
Student hostels in Ljubljana: Dijaški dom Ivana Cankarja, Poljanska 26-28; Dom tehniskih sol, Vidovolanska 7; FSPN-Študenski dom, Dardeljeva pl. 5.
Youth hostels. Youth Hostel Bledec, Grajska 17, Bled. Tel. (064) 78-320 or 312-185. Fifty beds. Youth Hostel Bohinj, Mladinski Dom, Bohinj. Tel. (064) 76-469. Forty beds.
Camping. Autocamp Ježica, Titova 60, 4 kilometers north of Ljubljana center on the road to Maribor. Tel. 341-113. Camping Dragočajna, Zbiljsko jezero, 18 kilometers north of Ljubljana.

Views of Triglav, Yugoslavia's highest mountain

DIFFICULTY	Grade 2, good mountain paths
DISTANCE	12 km
WALKING TIME	4 hours
MAPS	F&B Wanderkarte 14, *Julische Alpen*, 1:100,000 *Julian Alps*—East Part. Ljubljana: Planinska Zveza Slovenije
GUIDEBOOK	Schöner, H. *Grosser Führer Julische Alpen*. München: Bergverlag Rudolf Rother. With trail map

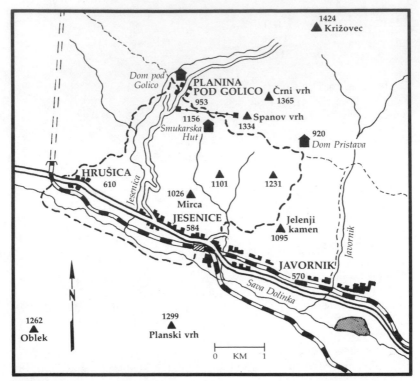

Jesenice

Sixty-three kilometers north of Ljubljana, in the beautiful Sava Valley, lies the little town of Jesenice. For the train traveler from Salzburg to Belgrade, this is the first town after the railroad tunnel that crosses beneath the Yugoslavian border. The valley deserves to be better known. The English inventor (and sometime Alpine explorer) Sir Humphrey Davy considered the Upper Sava Valley to be the most beautiful valley in the Alps. Our walk climbs 600 meters up the slopes of a minor Alpine summit, affording fine views of Triglav, Yugoslavia's highest peak, and of the main Alpine chain to the north.

Since Jesenice is on a main rail line, service is good. The fastest trains take just an hour for the trip from Ljubljana. There is a good train about 0930, but check train schedules for exact time and the possibility of earlier local trains that may take a few minutes longer.

From the station in Jesenice, walk eastward along the main street, picking up the trail on a side street just before the main street crosses the rail line. The trail heads northward up a small valley, soon switches back (right), and crosses the brook. It climbs through woods to a minor summit, then continues northward more or less on the contour.

At a major trail junction, we reach a main trail, the Slovene Alpine Transversal, which leads to Mount Triglav and eventually reaches the Adriatic Sea. It is marked with the numeral 1 on paint blazes. Dom Pristava, an Alpine hut, is close to this intersection. Now head west on trail 1 through woods and open fields, with fine views of Triglav and its neighbors, to Smukarska Dom, a mountain hut with overnight accommodations that is open year-round. The hut is close to a chair lift that serves a ski area.

From the hut, the trail heads northward, passing under the chair lift and angling down the slope to Planina pod Golico, a tiny settlement in the Jesenica Valley. The main trail crosses the road and reaches an intersection just before the stream. We follow the trail left down to the village of Hrušica. Trail 1 follows west along the highway a few hundred meters before turning south (left) and crossing the railroad and the Sava River. Just after the bridge, take the farm road left back to Jesenice.

If time is short, you can follow the road back to Jesenice from Planina pod Golico. There may be bus service along this road; make local inquiry. Trains to Ljubljana leave Jesenice at 1647 and 2008. The trip takes one hour.

Lake Bohinj—
The southern approach to Triglav

DIFFICULTY	Grade 2–3, depending on walk
DISTANCE	Various, see text
WALKING TIME	Various, see text
MAPS	F&B Wanderkarte 14, *Julische Alpen*, 1:100,000
	Julijske Alpe—Bohinj, 1:20,000. Ljubljana:
	Planinska Zveza Slovenije
GUIDEBOOK	*How to Climb Triglav*. Ljubljana: Planinska
	Založba, 1979

Lake Bled is reputed to be the most beautiful lake in Yugoslavia. An ancient Baroque church dominates a tiny island not far from the western shore. There are numerous hotels lining the shore and even an eighteen-hole golf course. And there are tourists and vacationers. Lake Bled is certainly worth visiting; but if you prefer wilder shores, try Lake Bohinj (Bohinjsko Jezero) a few miles farther up the Sava Bohinjka River. Here you will find a dark and peaceful lake, ringed about by steep, wooded slopes and towering cliffs. You will also find excellent hiking trails leading to a spectacular waterfall, the uninhabited shores of a brooding Alpine lake, and magnificent views of the Julian Alps.

Lake Bohinj is accessible by bus from Ljubljana, although the trip will take a bit more than the hour limit we set ourselves. Direct bus service connects Ljubljana with Bohinjska Bistrica (via Bled), a town about 5 kilometers from the lake itself. A local bus runs from there to Hotel Zlatorog, starting point for our walks. We have not taken these walks and have relied on a number of sources for the information. The trails are good, however, and there should be no trouble in following them.

The first walk is to Savica Falls, a few kilometers up the Savica, the main tributary to the lake. It is on one of the main trails to the summit of Mount Triglav through Triglav National Park. From the bus stop near the hotel, follow the road north across the inlet to the lake. You can follow this road to the Koca pri Savici and the nearby Dom Savica, mountain huts with food and overnight accommodations. Alternatively, you can take a path that parallels the road, a short distance to the north. From here, the path to the falls follows the main trail north to Komarca Crag, an imposing cliff guarding the southern approach to Triglav and the national park. It switchbacks up to the base of the cliffs, where a trail left leads to the fall. The waters of the Savica ("Little Sava") River spring in a nascent torrent from the mouth of a limestone cave high up the cliff and plunge 60 meters into a dark and narrow canyon. The waters come from the Seven Triglav Lakes through underground channels before reappearing at the falls.

If you have time, the climb up the Komarca cliffs to the upper valley is worthwhile. The climb is steep, but the route is well secured in exposed places. Three little lakes, reminiscent of the timberline lakes of California's Sierra Nevada, are at the center of the national park. One of the Triglav huts occupies the narrow spit of land be-

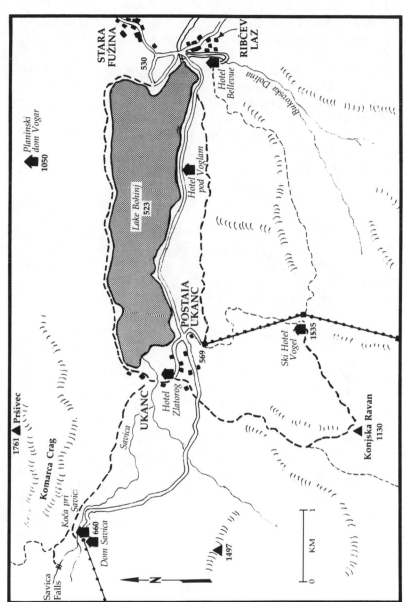

Lake Bohinj

tween two of the lakes. This point is about three hours from Savica Falls. The return journey from the falls to Hotel Zlatorog follows the route up.

The hotel is the starting point for another rewarding walk, completely around the lake. From the base station of the cable car a short distance south of the campground at the east end of the lake, a marked trail leads eastward. After climbing about 50 meters, it stays pretty much on the contour about 100 meters above the lake. The trail drops down to the road at the east end of the lake, crosses the outlet, and stays close to the uninhabited north shore. After swinging southward, it crosses the inlet and in a few meters reaches Hotel Zlatorog. The distance is about 12 kilometers and the walking time is about three to four hours.

A shorter trip affording fine views of Triglav and the Julian Alps starts from the Hotel Vogel at the top of the cable lift. From here, a trail leads southwestward, drops down to a plateau, then swings northward into Zagarjev Graben (valley). It skirts the bottom of the cliffs, then switchbacks down to the road just south of the Hotel Zlatorog. Walking distance is about 5 kilometers; walking time is about one and a half to two hours. Check at the hotel for times of operation of the cable car.

Conversion Tables

KILOMETER/MILE CONVERSION TABLE

mile	← km|mile →	km
0.6	1	1.6
1.2	2	3.3
1.9	3	4.8
2.5	4	6.4
3.1	5	8.0
3.7	6	9.6
4.3	7	11.3
5.0	8	12.9
5.6	9	14.5
6.2	10	16.1
12.4	20	32.2
18.7	30	48.3
24.9	40	64.4
31.1	50	80.4
62.2	100	160.9

TEMPERATURE CONVERSION TABLE

°F	← °C|°F →	°C
−40	−40	−40.0
−22	−30	−34.5
−4	−20	−28.9
+14	−10	−23.4
+32	0	−17.8
+50	+10	−12.2
+68	+20	−6.7
+86	+30	−1.1
+104	+40	+4.4
+122	+50	+10.0
+140	+60	+15.6
+158	+70	+21.1
+176	+80	+26.7
+194	+90	+32.2
+212	+100	+37.8

$1.8°F = 1°C$

$1 °F = 0.56°C$

Key to Map Symbols

Boundary	• • • • • • • •	Mountain Ridge with Pass	⟩⟩⟩⟩⟩⟩⟩] [⟨⟨⟨⟨
Highway (Autobahn)	═══════	Peak	▲
Road	═══════	Tunnel	⊣┈┈┈⊢
Described Trail	─ ─ ─ ─	Hut	🏠
Alternate Trail	┄┄┄┄┄	Buildings	▪ ▪
River	∼∼∼∼	Castle	⌂
Glacier	⟩⟩⟩⟩⟩⟩	Church	⚱
Railroad with Station	▬▬□▬▨	Place of Interest	∏
Gondola	▬•••••▬	Tower	⊤
Cableway	┼┼┼┼┼┼┼┼	View	⟡
Chair Lift	⟋⟋⟋⟋	Bus Stop	Ⓗ

Glossary

This glossary contains words that are likely to be found on maps or in foreign language guidebook descriptions of trail routes. It does not contain words that are used in common concourse; a small dictionary should be carried for that purpose. Nor does it contain words specifically related to technical rock-climbing. The words are arranged by the German inasmuch as most of the described routes are in German-speaking sections of the Alps.

German	English	French	Italian	Slovene
Abdachung	gentle slope	légère pente		
Abendessen	dinner (supper)	dîner	desinare	večérja
Abfahrt	departure	départ	partenza	
Abgrund	notch, cleft		forcella (forc.)	sedlo, škrbina
Abhang	slope	pente	declivio	pobóčje
Abkürzung	short cut	raccourci	scortiatoia	
Abort	toilet, WC	toilette, WC	gabinetto	
Absatz	platform	interruption	cengia	polica, gréda
Absturz	cliff, precipice	chute	precipizio	
abwärts	downward	vers la bas	in giù, in discesa	

German	English	French	Italian	Slovene
Alm, Alp	high pasture	haut pâturage	alpe, malga	planina
Almhütte, Alphütte	high hut or barn	chalet	baita, capanna	
Alpenblume	Alpine flower			
Alpenverein (AV)	Alpine club	club alpin (CAF)	Club Alpino Italiano (CAI)	Planinska založba
Ankunft	arrival	arrivée	arrivo	
Ansicht	view	vue	vista	
Ansichtkarte	picture postcard	carte postale		
aper	snow-free	dénudé		
Arve	stone pine	arolle		
aufwärts	upward	en haut	in alto	
Auskunft	information	renseignements	informazione	
Auslauf	outlet	issue		
Ausrüstung	outfit	équipment	equipaggiamento	opréma
Aussichtspunkt	viewpoint	endroit ayant une belle vue	vista	
Autobahn	expressway	autoroute	autostrada	
Bach	brook	ruisseau	sorgente, rio	réka, pótok
Band	ledge, bench	vire	cengia	polica, gréda
befahrbar	passable	practicable	passabile	
Berg	mountain	montagne	monte, montagna	góra
Bergföhre	mountain pine	pin mugho		
Bergführer	mountain guide	guide	guida alpina	
Berggasthaus, Berghotel	mountain inn	hotel en haute montagne		planinska kóča
Bergkrankheit	mountain sickness	mal de montagne	mal di montagna	

German	English	French	Italian	Slovene
Bergschrund	crevice between glacier and rock	rimaye		
Bergsteiger	mountain climber	alpiniste	alpinista	
Bergsturz	rockslide	éboulement		
Bergwander-er	mountain hiker	grimpeur	escursionista a piedi	
Bett	bed	lit	letto	póstelja
bewirt-schaftet	open for business	ouvert pour des achats		
bezeichnet (bez.)	marked	balisé	marcato	
Biwak	bivouac	bivouac	bivacco	
Blatt	sheet (map)	carte, feuille	carta	
Bogen	bend	courbure	svolta	
bratschig	broken up	cassé en petits morceaux	spezzato	
breit	broad	vaste, large	largo	
brüchig	broken, brittle	cassé	spezzato	
Brücke	bridge	pont	ponte	most
Bühel, Bühl	hill, hillock	colliné	col, colle	grebén
Decken	bedding, blankets	couvertures	coperta di lana	
Dom	dome, cathedral	dôme, cathédrale	duomo	
Dorf	village	village	villaggio	
Drahtseil	wire rope	câble		
draussen	outer (slope)	pente extérieure	esteriore	
Ebene	plain	plaine	piano, pian	
Ecke	corner, edge	carne, coin	angolo	
Einsenkung	saddle	selle	sella	
Eis	ice	glâce	ghiacciaio	
empfehlen	recommend	recomman-der		

German	English	French	Italian	Slovene
empor	up, upward	vers le haut	in alto	
eng	narrow	étroit	stretto	
erforderlich	required	demandé, nécessaire	richiedere	
Ersteigung	ascent	ascension	ascensione	
Fallinie	fall-line	pente directe		
Feldweg	meadow path			
Fels	rock slope	rocher		
Felsblock	boulder	bloc de rocher	roccia	skála
Felsig	rocky	rocheux	roccioso	
Felsnase	rock spur	becquet		
Felssporn	rock spur	becquet		
Felsstufe	rock ledge	saillie rocheuse		
Felsturm	rock tower	clocheton, clocher rocheux	torre	
Felswand	rock wall	paroi de rocher	croda	
Ferner	glacier	glacier	neve, ghiacciaio	ledenik
Fichte	Norway spruce	épicea commun		
Firnfeld	old-snow field	névé	neve	snežíšče
Firnschnee	old snow	neige de printemps		
First	ridge, crest	arête, crête	cresta	grebén
flach	flat	plat	pian	
Flanke	flank	flanc	fianco	
Fluh	steep rock slope	pente abrute		
Fluss	river	fleuve	fiume	réka, pótok
Föhn	warm, dry, down-slope wind	föhn		
Frühstück	breakfast	petit déjeuner	prima colazione	zájtrk

German	English	French	Italian	Slovene
Führe	route	itinéraire	via, sentiero	stezá, smer
Furka, Fürkele, Furgga, Fürggele	saddle or pass	col	passo, bocca	sédlo
Fussweg	footpath	sentier	sentiero	
Gasthaus, Gasthof, Gaststatte	inn	auberge	albergo	gostilna
Gaststube	common room	salon		
Gebiet	region	région	regione	
Gebirge	mountain range	chaîne de montagnes	catena montuosa	
Gebirgskette	mountain chain	chaîne de montagnes	catena montuosa	
Gefahr	danger	danger	pericolo	
gefährlich	dangerous	dangereux	pericoloso	
Gemse	chamois	chamois		
Geröll	scree, rubble	éboulis	breccia	melíšče
Gesims	overhang, projection	surplomb	sporgente	
Gestein	rock, stone	roche, roc	roccia	skála, kámen
Gipfel	peak, summit	sommet, cime	croz, cima, punta	vrh
Gipfelkreuz	cross erected on summit			
glatt	smooth	lisse		
Gletscher	glacier	glacier	vedretta, ghiacciaio	ledenik
Gletscher-spalte	crevasse	crevasse	crepaccio	
Gletscher-zunge	glacier tongue	langue glaciaire		
Gondelbahn	gondola lift	télécabine	funivia	
Graben	fault trench	ravin		
Granit	granite	granit		
Grat	ridge	arête	cresta	grebén

German	English	French	Italian	Slovene
Grube	barren cirque	cirque mon- tagneux	cadin	
Grübl	sink hole	trou	pozza	
Gruppe	(mountain) group	massif	catena montuosa	
Guter- seilbahn	supply cableway	funiculaire	funivia	
Halde	talus, rubble	talus de racaille	breccia	
Haltestelle	bus stop	halte de l'autobus	fermata	
Hang	slope	pente	declivio	pobóčje
Hänge- gletscher	hanging glacier	glacier suspendu		
Harsch	crusted snow	neige cassante		
Heilbad	hot springs	bains chauds		
Hilfe	help	secours	soccorso	
Hirsch	deer	cervides	cervo	
hoch	high	haut	alto	
Hochebene	tableland	haut-plateau		
Höhe	height, summit	altitude	altitudine	
Höhenlinien	contour	contour	contorno	
Höhen- messer	altimeter	altimètre		
Höhenpunkt	benchmark	point géo- désiques		
höher	higher	plus haut		
Höhle	cave	caverne	caverna	
Horn	horn, peak	pic	corno, sasso	
Hotel liste	hotel list	liste des hôtels		
Hügel	hill, hillock	colline	colle	grič
Hütte	hut, mountain inn	cabane, réfuge	rifugio	kóča
Hütten- gebühren	hut fees	honoraires		

German	English	French	Italian	Slovene
Hüttenruhe ab _____ Uhr	Quiet hours from _____ o'clock	Silence après _____ heures		
jenseits	beyond	au-delà		
Joch	pass	col	passo	sédlo
Jugend- herberge	youth hostel	auberge de jeunesse	ostello per la gioventù	dom
Kabinen- seilbahn	gondola lift	téléphérique	funivia	
Kalkstein	limestone	calcaire	calcina	
Kamin	chimney (rock)	cheminée	cammino	
Kamm	crest, ridge	crête, fil	cresta	grebén
Kante	edge, rim	arête, carne		rob
Kanzel	turret	tourelle	torre, campanile	
Kapelle	chapel	chapelle	cappella	cérkev
Kar	glacial de- pression, cirque	cirque de moraine, combe	cadìn	
Karboden	bottom of cirque			
Karrenfeld	eroded limestone	lapiaz		
Karrenweg	cart track	sentier étroit	mulattiera	
Karte	map, card	carte	carta	
Kehre	curve, turn	courbe		
Kessel	kettle, sinkhole	trou d'évier		
Kirche	church	église		cérkev
Klamm	ravine, gorge	gorge		soféska, korito
Kletterei	rock climb	ascension		
klettern	to climb, scramble	escalader	ascendere, scalare	
Kloster	monastery	monastère	monastero	
Kluft	crevice, gap, chasm	abîme		zleb, kuloár

German	English	French	Italian	Slovene
knapp	close, narrow	étroit		
Kogel	domed mountain			
Kompass	compass	boussole		kómpas
Kopf	head	tête		gláva
Krummholz	timberline vegetation	forêt de feuilles		
Kuppe	dome, rounded summit	dôme, calotte		
kurz	short	court	corto	
Kurzführer	condensed guidebook	guide condensé		
Landkarte	map	carte, plan	carta	
Landschaft	landscape	paysage	paesaggio	
Längsspalte	longitudinal crevasse	crevasse longitudi-nale		
Lärche	larch pine	mélèze d'Europe		
Lawine	avalanche	avalanche	valanga	plaz
Lebensmittel	food, grocery store	épicerie		
Legföhre	dwarf pine	pin mugho		
leicht	easy	facile	facile	
links	left	à gauche	a sinistra	
lohnend	rewarding	récompen-sant	di recom-pensa	
mächtig	mighty	puissant		
markiert	marked	repère	segnato	
Massenlager, Matratzen-lager	dormitory	dortoir	dormitorio	skúpno ležíšče
Materialbahn	supply cableway	funiculaire	funivia	
Mauer	wall, (moun-tain) face	mur, paroi moraine	croda	sténa
Mittagessen	lunch	déjeuner	merenda	kosilo

German	English	French	Italian	Slovene
Möglichkeit	possibility	possibilité	possibilità	
Moräne	moraine	moraine	morena	
morsch	rotten	pourri, cadue		
Mulde	depression	combe	pozza	
Murmeltier	marmot	marmotte	marmotta	
Nadel	needle	aiguille, pinacle		
nass	wet	mouillé		
Nebel	fog	brouillard	nebbia	meglá
Neben- strasse	secondary road	route secondaire		
Neigung	inclination	inclinaison, déclivité		
Neuschnee	new snow	neige fraîche		
nicht gestattet	not permitted	défense de _____	vietato	
nieder	lower, lesser	inférieur	di sotto	
Nische	niche	niche		
Nord	north	nord	nord	séver
Notlager	emergency accommo- dations			
Notsignal	distress signal	signale d'alarme		
nür für Geubte	only for experi- enced	grimpeurs experts	solo per esperti	
Ödland	barren land	pâturages		
Ost	east	est	oriente	vzhod
Pächter	lessee, hut warden	locatair, guardien	oste, ostessa	
Pass	pass	col	bocca, passo	sédlo
Pfad, Pfadspur	path	sentier, chemin	sentiero	
Pfeil	arrow	flèche		
Pfeiler	buttress	éperon, pilier		
Pickel	ice axe	piolet	piccozza	cepin

German	English	French	Italian	Slovene
Platte	plateau	plateau, plaque		
prächtig	splendid, magnificent	magnifique	splendido, magnificente	
Pulverschnee	powder snow	neige poudreuse		
Quelle	source, spring	source, fontaine		
Quellmulde	boggy hollow	creux marécageux		
Quergang	cross-over, traverse	traversée	traverso, obliquo	préčka
Querspalte	transverse crevasse	crevasse transversale		
Randkluft	crevasse between glacier and rock	rimaye		
rechts	right	à droite	a destra	
Reh	small species of deer			
Richtung	direction	direction	direzione	
Rille	furrow	cannelure	camino	
ringsum	surrounding			
Rinne	gulley, channel	couloir		
Rippe	rib	côte		
Riss	crack	feute		
Route	route	voie, route	via, strada, sentiero	
Rucksack	backpack	sac à dos	zaino	nahřbtnìk
Rüfe	rockslide	glissement de rochers		
Sattel	saddle, pass	selle		
Saumpfad	mule track	chemin muletier	mulattiera	

German	English	French	Italian	Slovene
Scharte	gap, col	brèche	colle	sédlo
Schichtung	layer	strate		
Schiefer	slate	schiste		
Schigebiet	ski area			
Schlafraum	sleeping room	dortoir		
schliesslich	eventually, finally	finalement	eventual-mente	
Schlucht	ravine, gorge	ravin, gorge	burrone	soféska, korito
schmal	narrow	étroit	stretto	
Schnee	snow	neige	neve	sneg
Schnee-brücke	snow bridge	pont de neige		
Schrofe, Schrofen	rocky mountain	rochers brisés		
schrofig	rocky, steep, and barren			
Schrund	crack, crevice	fente, fissure		
Schulter	shoulder	épaule	spallone	
Schutt	rubble, debris	blocaille		
Schutthalde	talus slope	talus		
Schutthang	talus fan			
Schuttkegel	debris cone	cône de déjections		
Schuttrinne	scree-filled gulley	pente d'éboulis		
Schutzhütte	shelter, hut	cabane, refuge	rifugio	kóča
Schwelle, Schwell-ung	mound, swell	tertre		
schwierig	difficult	difficile	difficile	
Schwierig-keit	difficulty	difficulté	difficoltà	
Schwierig-keitsgrad	degree of difficulty	degré de difficulté		

German	English	French	Italian	Slovene
Schwindel-frei	free from vertigo	sans avoir le vertige		
See	lake	lac	lago	jézero
Seil	rope	corde	corda	vrv
Seilbahn	cable car	téléphérique	funivia	
Senke	depression	dépression, croux	buso	
senkrecht	vertical	verticale	verticale	
Sennhütte	herder's cabin			
Sessellift	chair lift	tété-siège	seggiova	
Sicherheit	safety, security	sécurité		
Spalte	fissure, crevice	fissure, fente		
Speise-kammer	larder, storeroom	garde manger	dispensa	
Speisekarte	menu	menu	lista	
Sperrmauer	dam	barrage		
Spitze	peak, point	pointe	cima	vrh
Sporn	spur	éperon		
Spur	trail	trace		
Stafel	barn	grange		
Staudamm	dam	barrage		
Stausee	reservoir	réservoir		
Steg	narrow path, small bridge	chemin étroit		
Steig	mountain trail	sentier de montagne		
Steigeisen	crampons	crampons	rampone	deréze
Steigspur	spur trail			
steil	steep	raide		
Steilhang	steep descent	pente escarpée		
Stein	stone	pierre, caillou	roccia	

German	English	French	Italian	Slovene
Steinbock	mountain goat, Ibex			
Steinmann	cairn	cairn	mucchio di pietre	
Steinschlag	rock fall	chute de pierres		
Strohlager	hayloft for sleeping	fenil		
Stufe	step, notch	gradin		
Stunde (S. or St.)	hour	heure	ora	úra
Süd	south	sud	sud	jug
Sumpf	swamp	marécage	palude	
sumpfig	swampy	marécageux	paludoso	
Tal	valley	vallée	val, valle	dolina
Talstation	valley station			
Tanne	fir	sapin	abete	
Taschen-lampe	flashlight	lampe de poche	lampadina tascabile	svetilka
Tauern	pass	col	passo	sédlo
Teich	pool, pond	étang	vivaio	
Terrasse	terrace	terrasse	terrazzo	gredina
Tobel, Tobl	wooded ravine	ravin boisé		
Törl	narrow pass, cleft	fente étroite		
Touristen-lager	tourist accommo-dations, dormitory			
Trittsicher-heit	sure-footedness		di piede fermo	
Trockenraum	drying room	pièce pour l'étandage		
Turm	tower	tour	torre	
über	via, over	via, par-dessus	sopra	
Übergang	crossing, bridge	passage		

German	English	French	Italian	Slovene
Überhang	overhang	surplomb	sporgente	
Über-schreitung	crossing	traversée		
Ufer	river bank	rive		
ü.M. or ü.d.M.	above sea level	sur la mer		
Umgebung	vicinity	proximité		
und so weiter (usw)	and so forth (etc.)	et cetera		
unerlässlich	indispen-sable	indispen-sable		
Unfall	accident, tragedy	accident	accidente	nesréča
Unterkunft	accommo-dations	logement		
Unterkunfts-haus	inn, guest-house	auberge	albergo, taverna	dom, kóča
Verbandzeug	first aid kit	trousse de secours		
vereist	glaciated	verglacé		
Verkehrs-verein	tourist office	bureau de tourisme	Azienda auto-noma di soggiorno e turismo	
Verschneid-ung	corner	dièdre		
Vieh	cattle, stock	bétail		
Vierzacker	4-point crampons	crampons à-pointe		
Vorgipfel	secondary summit	antécime		
Vorsprung	rock ledge	promontoir		
waagerecht	horizontal	horizontal	orizzontale	
Wächte	cornice	corniche		
Wald	forest, woods	forêt, bois	bosco	gozd
Waldföhre	Scotch pine	pin commun		
Waldstreif	forest strip	mur, paroi		

German	English	French	Italian	Slovene
Wand	wall, (mountain) face		croda	sténa
Wanderweg	footpath	sentier	sentiero	
Wanne	cirque, depression	cirque		
Wasser	water	eau	acqua	vóda
"Wasser sparen"	"save water"	"conserver l'eau"		
Wasserfall	waterfall	cascade	cascata	
Wasser- scheide	divide			
WC	water closet, toilet	toilette, WC	gabinetto	
Weg	path, way	chemin	sentiero	steza, pot
Weggabel- ung	fork in trail	bifurcation	bivio	
weglos	trailless	sans chemin		
Wegtafel	trail sign	poteau indicateur	segno	
Wegteilung	trail fork	bifurcation	bivio	
Wegweiser	signpost	poteau indicateur	segno	
Weide	pasture	pâturage	campo	
Weisstanne	silver fir	sapin pectiné		
weiter	farther	plus loin	avanti	
West	west	ouest	occidente	zahód
Wetter	weather	temps	tempo	vréme
wichtig	important	important	importante	
Wiese	meadow	pré	prato	trávnik
Wildbach	torrent	torrent	torrente	pótok, hudoúrnik
Wirt, Wirt- schafter	hut manager	guardien	oste, ostessa	
Wirtshaus	inn, tavern	auberge, taverne	albergo	dom, kóča
Zahn	tooth	dent		

German	English	French	Italian	Slovene
Zahnrad-bahn	cog railway	train à crémaillère		
Zelt	tent	tente	tenda	
Zeltplatz	campground	camping	campeggio	
Zickzack	zig-zag, switchback	montagnes russes	serpentino	
Zimmer-nachweis	tourist-room list	tableau des chambres		
	secured path		via ferrata	zavárovana pot

Bibliography

Since publication in the early 1970s of the first English-language books specifically oriented to hikers rather than mountain climbers, Ruth Rudner's *Wandering* and the Sierra Club totebook *Hut Hopping in the Austrian Alps*, there has been a minor deluge. We present here an annotated list of hikers' books on the Alps.

Hiking guides

Evans, Craig. *On Foot through Europe*. New York: Quill, 1982. There are seven titles in this series, four of which cover portions of the Alps: (1) West Germany; (2) Austria, Switzerland, and Liechtenstein; (3) France and the Benelux Nations; and (4) Europe's long-distance footpaths. They are compendia of information useful to the Alpine hiker: hiking regions, weather, equipment, Alpine safety, sources of books and maps, information on the huts, and much, much more. Although many hikes are suggested, Evans makes no attempt to provide detailed trail descriptions. Extremely useful for anyone serious about European hiking.

Jones, J. Sydney. *Tramping in Europe: A Walking Guide*. Englewood Cliffs, N.J.: Prentice-Hall, 1984. The most recent hikers' guide. Highly personal descriptions of walks of various lengths and difficulties in eleven European countries. Also see his *Viennawalks* for detailed descriptions of several walking tours in historic Vienna.

Merrick, Hugh. *Companion to the Alps*. New York: Hastings House, 1974. The "multifarious aspects and activities of the Alpine world." Lots of background information by an Alpine mountaineer to make your walks more meaningful and enjoyable.

Reifsnyder, William E. *Hut Hopping in the Austrian Alps*. San Francisco: Sierra Club Books, 1973. Everything you need to know about backpacking in three popular hiking regions.

Reifsnyder, William E. *Footloose in the Swiss Alps*. San Francisco: Sierra Club Books, 1974. A sequel to the above, covering seven regions in Switzerland.

Rudner, Ruth. *Wandering: A Walker's Guide to the Mountain Trails of Europe*. New York: Dial Press, 1972. "Pages from a wanderer's diary" accurately describes this memoir of rambles through the mountains of Europe. It will give you the flavor of Alpine hiking as well as lots of solid information on trails to take and huts to visit.

Rudner, Ruth. *Huts and Hikes in the Dolomites*. San Francisco: Sierra Club Books, 1974. Detailed descriptions of hikes in the Dolomites of northern Italy.

Spring, Ira, and Harvey Edwards. *100 Hikes in the Alps*. Seattle: The Mountaineers, 1979. Brief descriptions and beautiful pictures of Alpine hikes lasting from a half day to two weeks.

Natural history

Grey-Wilson, Christopher, and Marjorie Blamey. *The Alpine Flowers of Britain and Europe*. London: Collins, 1979. A comprehensive guide to the native flowering plants occurring above 1000 meters elevation. Good keys, good color illustrations. Includes trees and shrubs, but not the grasses, sedges, and rushes. A standard guide.

Kwiatkowski, Gerhard, ed. *Schlag nach! für Wanderer und Bergsteiger*. Mannheim: Bibliographisches Institut, 1976. In German. A comprehensive encyclopedic lexicon of Alpine words and facts. Contains short articles on Alpine geology, glaciers, weather, and other natural phenomena.

Paulcke, Wilhelm, and Helmut Dumler. *Hazards in Mountaineering*. New York: Oxford University Press, 1973. Although primarily for the rock-climber and mountaineer, this book contains a wealth of information on above-timberline hazards of weather, snow, and rock. Should be read by anyone venturing above timberline on an extensive trip.

Reifsnyder, William E. *Weathering the Wilderness: The Sierra Club Guide to Practical Meteorology*. San Francisco: Sierra Club Books, 1980. The first half deals with weather and climate for outdoor recreationists, applicable to the Alps or any other mountain region.

Schneider, Adolf. *Wetter und Bergsteigen*. München: Bergverlag Rudolf Rother, 1977. If you can read German, this little pocketbook will provide you with an excellent introduction to Alpine weather. Excellent color photographs of clouds and other atmospheric phenomena.

Wendelberger, Elfrune. *Alpenblumen*. München: BLV Verlagsgesellschaft, 1982. This little book is half beautiful color photographs, most of them full page. Although the text is in German, most of it is easy to translate. Covers the common Alpine flowers.

Tourist guidebooks

Harvard Student Agencies. *Let's Go: Europe*. A no-nonsense guide packed with information, especially inexpensive accommodations such as student hostels, good but inexpensive restaurants, and the like.

Manston, Peter B. *Travel Key Europe*. Sacramento, Calif.: Travel Keys (P.O. Box 160691, Sacramento, CA 95816), 1985. A mine of information on telephones, transportation, and toilets in Europe. Pocket-size paperback. Essential information that doesn't show up in most travel guides.

Michelin Tourist Guides ("Green Guides"). Our choice for general background information, city information, brief histories, and main sights to see. Geared to the auto traveler, but really useful for any European tourist. Pick up the guides for the countries you plan to visit.

Index

A Note to the Reader

Readers are invited to send updated information and corrections for any title in the Sierra Club Adventure Travel Guide series to the author, c/o Travel Editor, Sierra Club Books, 730 Polk Street, San Francisco CA 94109.